Python Machine Learning Blueprints

Intuitive data projects you can relate to

An approachable guide to applying advanced machine learning methods to everyday problems

Alexander T. Combs

[PACKT] open source✶
PUBLISHING community experience distilled

BIRMINGHAM - MUMBAI

Python Machine Learning Blueprints

First published: July 2016

Production reference: 1270716

Published by Packt Publishing Ltd.

Livery Place

35 Livery Street

Birmingham B3 2PB, UK.

ISBN 978-1-78439-475-2

www.packtpub.com

Credits

Author

Alexander T. Combs

Reviewer

Kushal Khandelwal

Commissioning Editor

Kartikey Pandey

Acquisition Editor

Vivek Anantharaman
Manish Nainani

Content Development Editor

Merint Thomas Mathew

Technical Editor

Abhishek R. Kotian

Copy Editor

Priyanka Ravi

Project Coordinator

Suzanne Coutinho

Proofreader

Safis Editing

Indexer

Rekha Nair

Production Coordinator

Melwyn Dsa

Cover Work

Melwyn Dsa

About the Author

Alexander T. Combs is an experienced data scientist, strategist, and developer with a background in financial data extraction, natural language processing and generation, and quantitative and statistical modeling. He is currently a full-time lead instructor for a data science immersive program in New York City.

Writing a book is truly a massive undertaking that would not be possible without the support of others. I would like to thank my family for their love and encouragement and Jocelyn for her patience and understanding. I owe all of you tremendously.

About the Reviewer

Kushal Khandelwal is a data scientist and a full-stack developer. His interests include building scalable machine learning and image processing software applications. He is adept at coding in Python and contributes actively to various open source projects. He is currently serving as the Head of technology at Truce.in, a farmer-centric start-up where he is building scalable web applications to assist farmers.

www.PacktPub.com

For support files and downloads related to your book, please visit www.PacktPub.com.

eBooks, discount offers, and more

Did you know that Packt offers eBook versions of every book published, with PDF and ePub files available? You can upgrade to the eBook version at www.PacktPub.com and as a print book customer, you are entitled to a discount on the eBook copy. Get in touch with us at customercare@packtpub.com for more details.

At www.PacktPub.com, you can also read a collection of free technical articles, sign up for a range of free newsletters and receive exclusive discounts and offers on Packt books and eBooks.

https://www2.packtpub.com/books/subscription/packtlib

Do you need instant solutions to your IT questions? PacktLib is Packt's online digital book library. Here, you can search, access, and read Packt's entire library of books.

Why subscribe?

- Fully searchable across every book published by Packt
- Copy and paste, print, and bookmark content
- On demand and accessible via a web browser

Free access for Packt account holders

Get notified! Find out when new books are published by following @PacktEnterprise on Twitter or the Packt Enterprise Facebook page.

Table of Contents

Preface

Machine learning is rapidly becoming a fixture in our data-driven world. It is relied upon in fields as diverse as robotics and medicine to retail and publishing. In this book, you will learn how to build real-world machine learning applications step by step.

Working through easy-to-understand projects, you will learn how to process various types of data and how and when to apply different machine learning techniques such as supervised or unsupervised learning.

Each of the projects in this book provides educational as well as practical value. For example, you'll learn how to use clustering techniques to find bargain airfares and how to use linear regression to find a cheap apartment. This book will teach you how to use machine learning to collect, analyze, and act on massive quantities of data in an approachable, no-nonsense manner.

What this book covers

Chapter 1, *The Python Machine Learning Ecosystem*, delves into Python, which has a deep and active developer community, and many of these developers come from the scientific community as well. This has provided Python with a rich array of libraries for scientific computing. In this chapter, we will discuss the features of these key libraries and how to prepare your environment to best utilize them.

Chapter 2, *Build an App to Find Underpriced Apartments*, guides us to build our first machine learning application, and we begin with a minimal but practical example: building an application to identify underpriced apartments. By the end of this chapter, we will create an application that will make finding the right apartment a bit easier.

Chapter 3, *Build an App to Find Cheap Airfares*, demonstrates how to build an application that continually monitors fare pricing. Once an anomalous price appears, our app will generate an alert that we can quickly act on.

Chapter 4, *Forecast the IPO Market using Logistic Regression*, shows how we can use machine learning to decide which IPOs are worth a closer look and which ones we may want to skip.

Chapter 5, *Create a Custom Newsfeed*, covers how to build a system that understands your taste in news and will send you a personally tailored newsletter each day.

Chapter 6, *Predict whether Your Content Will Go Viral*, examines some of the most shared content and attempts to find the common elements that differentiate it from the content that people are less willing to share.

Chapter 7, *Forecast the Stock Market with Machine Learning*, discusses how to build and test a trading strategy. There are countless pitfalls to avoid when trying to devise your own system, and it is quite nearly an impossible task. However, it can be a lot of fun, and sometimes, it can even be profitable.

Chapter 8, *Build an Image Similarity Engine*, helps you construct an advanced, image-based, deep learning application. We will also cover deep learning algorithms to understand why they are so important and why there is such a hype surrounding them.

Chapter 9, *Build a Chatbot*, demonstrates how to construct a chatbot from scratch. Along the way, you'll learn more about the history of the field and its future prospects.

Chapter 10, *Build a Recommendation Engine*, explores the different varieties of recommendation systems. We'll see how they're implemented commercially and how they work. We will also implement our own recommendation engine to find GitHub repos.

What you need for this book

All you need is Python 3.x and a desire to build real-world machine learning projects. You can refer to the detailed software list provided along with the code files of this book.

Who this book is for

This book targets Python programmers, data scientists, and architects with a good knowledge of data science and all those who want to build complete Python-based machine learning systems.

Conventions

In this book, you will find a number of text styles that distinguish between different kinds of information. Here are some examples of these styles and an explanation of their meaning.

Code words in text, database table names, folder names, filenames, file extensions, pathnames, dummy URLs, user input, and Twitter handles are shown as follows: "This can be done by calling .corr() on our DataFrame."

A block of code is set as follows:

```
<category>
  <pattern>I LIKE TURTLES</pattern>
  <template>I feel like this whole <set name="topic">turle</set>
  thing could be a problem. What do you like about them?</template>
</category>
```

Any command-line input or output is written as follows:

```
sp = pd.read_csv(r'/Users/alexcombs/Downloads/spy.csv')
sp.sort_values('Date', inplace=True)
```

New terms and **important words** are shown in bold. Words that you see on the screen, for example, in menus or dialog boxes, appear in the text like this: "Right-click on the page and click on **Inspect element**."

Warnings or important notes appear in a box like this.

Tips and tricks appear like this.

Reader feedback

Feedback from our readers is always welcome. Let us know what you think about this book-what you liked or disliked. Reader feedback is important for us as it helps us develop titles that you will really get the most out of.

To send us general feedback, simply e-mail feedback@packtpub.com, and mention the book's title in the subject of your message.

If there is a topic that you have expertise in and you are interested in either writing or contributing to a book, see our author guide at www.packtpub.com/authors.

Customer support

Now that you are the proud owner of a Packt book, we have a number of things to help you to get the most from your purchase.

Downloading the example code

You can download the example code files for this book from your account at http://www.packtpub.com. If you purchased this book elsewhere, you can visit http://www.packtpub.com/support and register to have the files e-mailed directly to you.

You can download the code files by following these steps:

1. Log in or register to our website using your e-mail address and password.
2. Hover the mouse pointer on the **SUPPORT** tab at the top.
3. Click on **Code Downloads & Errata**.
4. Enter the name of the book in the **Search** box.
5. Select the book for which you're looking to download the code files.
6. Choose from the drop-down menu where you purchased this book from.
7. Click on **Code Download**.

You can also download the code files by clicking on the **Code Files** button on the book's webpage at the Packt Publishing website. This page can be accessed by entering the book's name in the Search box. Please note that you need to be logged in to your Packt account.

Once the file is downloaded, please make sure that you unzip or extract the folder using the latest version of:

- WinRAR / 7-Zip for Windows
- Zipeg / iZip / UnRarX for Mac
- 7-Zip / PeaZip for Linux

The code bundle for the book is also hosted on GitHub at https://github.com/packtpublishing/pythonmachinelearningblueprints. We also have other code bundles from our rich catalog of books and videos available at https://github.com/PacktPublishing/. Check them out!

Errata

Although we have taken every care to ensure the accuracy of our content, mistakes do happen. If you find a mistake in one of our books-maybe a mistake in the text or the code-we would be grateful if you could report this to us. By doing so, you can save other readers from frustration and help us improve subsequent versions of this book. If you find any errata, please report them by visiting `http://www.packtpub.com/submit-errata`, selecting your book, clicking on the **Errata Submission Form** link, and entering the details of your errata. Once your errata are verified, your submission will be accepted and the errata will be uploaded to our website or added to any list of existing errata under the Errata section of that title.

To view the previously submitted errata, go to `https://www.packtpub.com/books/content/support` and enter the name of the book in the search field. The required information will appear under the **Errata** section.

Piracy

Piracy of copyrighted material on the Internet is an ongoing problem across all media. At Packt, we take the protection of our copyright and licenses very seriously. If you come across any illegal copies of our works in any form on the Internet, please provide us with the location address or website name immediately so that we can pursue a remedy.

Please contact us at `copyright@packtpub.com` with a link to the suspected pirated material.

We appreciate your help in protecting our authors and our ability to bring you valuable content.

Questions

If you have a problem with any aspect of this book, you can contact us at `questions@packtpub.com`, and we will do our best to address the problem.

1

The Python Machine Learning Ecosystem

Machine learning is rapidly changing our world. As the centerpiece of artificial intelligence, it is difficult to go a day without reading how it will transform our lives. Some argue it will lead us into a Singularity-style techno-utopia. Others suggest we are headed towards a techno-pocalypse marked by constant battles with job-stealing robots and drone death squads. But while the pundits may enjoy discussing these hyperbolic futures, the more mundane reality is that machine learning is rapidly becoming a fixture of our daily lives. Through subtle but progressive improvements in how we interact with computers and the world around us, machine learning is quietly improving our lives.

If you shop at online retailers such as Amazon.com, use streaming music or movie services such as Spotify or Netflix, or even just perform a Google search, you have encountered a machine learning application. The data generated by the users of these services is collected, aggregated, and fed into models that improve the services by creating tailored experiences for each user.

Now is an ideal time to dive into developing machine learning applications, and as you will discover, Python is an ideal choice with which to develop these applications. Python has a deep and active developer community, and many of these developers come from the scientific community as well. This has provided Python with a rich array of libraries for scientific computing. In this book, we will discuss and use a number of these libraries from this Python scientific stack.

In the chapters that follow, we'll learn step by step how to build a wide variety of machine learning applications. But before we begin in earnest, we'll spend the remainder of this chapter discussing the features of these key libraries and how to prepare your environment to best utilize them.

We'll cover the following topics in this chapter:

- The data science/machine learning workflow
- Libraries for each stage of the workflow
- Setting up your environment

The data science/machine learning workflow

Building machine learning applications, while similar in many respects to the standard engineering paradigm, differs in one crucial way: the need to work with data as a raw material. The success of a data project will, in large part, depend on the quality of the data that you acquired as well as how it's handled. And because working with data falls into the domain of data science, it is helpful to understand the data science workflow:

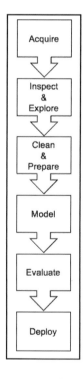

The process proceeds through these six steps in the following order: acquisition, inspection and exploration, cleaning and preparation, modeling, evaluation, and finally deployment. There is often the need to circle back to prior steps, such as when inspecting and preparing the data or when evaluating and modeling, but the process at a high level can be described as shown in the preceding diagram.

Let's now discuss each step in detail.

Acquisition

Data for machine learning applications can come from any number of sources; it may be e-mailed as a CSV file, it may come from pulling down server logs, or it may require building a custom web scraper. The data may also come in any number of formats. In most cases, it will be text-based data, but as we'll see, machine learning applications may just as easily be built utilizing images or even video files. Regardless of the format, once the data is secured, it is crucial to understand what's in the data—as well as what isn't.

Inspection and exploration

Once the data has been acquired, the next step is to inspect and explore it. At this stage, the primary goal is to sanity-check the data, and the best way to accomplish this is to look for things that are either impossible or highly unlikely. As an example, if the data has a unique identifier, check to see that there is indeed only one; if the data is price-based, check whether it is always positive; and whatever the data type, check the most extreme cases. Do they make sense? A good practice is to run some simple statistical tests on the data and visualize it. Additionally, it is likely that some data is missing or incomplete. It is critical to take note of this during this stage as it will need to be addressed it later during the cleaning and preparation stage. Models are only as good as the data that goes into them, so it is crucial to get this step right.

Cleaning and preparation

When all the data is in order, the next step is to place it in a format that is amenable to modeling. This stage encompasses a number of processes such as filtering, aggregating, imputing, and transforming. The type of actions that are necessary will be highly dependent on the type of data as well as the type of library and algorithm utilized. For example, with natural-language-based text, the transformations required will be very different from those required for time series data. We'll see a number of examples of these types of transformations throughout the book.

Modeling

Once the data preparation is complete, the next phase is modeling. In this phase, an appropriate algorithm is selected and a model is trained on the data. There are a number of best practices to adhere to during this stage, and we will discuss them in detail, but the basic steps involve splitting the data into training, testing, and validation sets. This splitting up of the data may seem illogical—especially when more data typically yields better models—but as we'll see, doing this allows us to get better feedback on how the model will perform in the real world, and prevents us from the cardinal sin of modeling: overfitting.

Evaluation

Once the model is built and making predictions, the next step is to understand how well the model does that. This is the question that evaluation seeks to answer. There are a number of ways to measure the performance of a model, and again it is largely dependent on the type of data and the model used, but on the whole, we are seeking to answer the question of how close are the model's predictions to the actual value. There are arrays of confusing-sounding terms such as root mean-square error, Euclidean distance, and F1 score, but in the end, they are all just a measure of distance between the actual value and the estimated prediction.

Deployment

Once the model's performance is satisfactory, the next step is deployment. This can take a number of forms depending on the use case, but common scenarios include utilization as a feature within another larger application, a bespoke web application, or even just a simple cron job.

Python libraries and functions

Now that we have an understanding of each step in the data science workflow, we'll take a look at a selection of useful Python libraries and functions within these libraries for each step.

Acquisition

Because one of the more common ways of accessing data is through a RESTful API, one library that to be aware of is the Python Requests library (http://www.python-requests.org/en/latest/). Dubbed *HTTP for humans*, it provides a clean and simple way to interact with APIs.

Let's take a look at a sample interaction using Requests to pull down data from GitHub's API. Here we will make a call to the API and request a list of starred repositories for a user:

```
import requests
r = requests.get(r"https://api.github.com/users/acombs/starred")
r.json()
```

This will return a JSON document of all the repositories that the user has starred along with their attributes. Here is a snippet of the output for the preceding call:

```
[{'archive_url': 'https://api.github.com/repos/matryer/bitbar/{archive_format}{/ref}',
 'assignees_url': 'https://api.github.com/repos/matryer/bitbar/assignees{/user}',
 'blobs_url': 'https://api.github.com/repos/matryer/bitbar/git/blobs{/sha}',
 'branches_url': 'https://api.github.com/repos/matryer/bitbar/branches{/branch}',
 'clone_url': 'https://github.com/matryer/bitbar.git',
 'collaborators_url': 'https://api.github.com/repos/matryer/bitbar/collaborators{/collaborator}',
 'comments_url': 'https://api.github.com/repos/matryer/bitbar/comments{/number}',
 'commits_url': 'https://api.github.com/repos/matryer/bitbar/commits{/sha}',
 'compare_url': 'https://api.github.com/repos/matryer/bitbar/compare/{base}...{head}',
 'contents_url': 'https://api.github.com/repos/matryer/bitbar/contents/{+path}',
 'contributors_url': 'https://api.github.com/repos/matryer/bitbar/contributors',
 'created_at': '2013-11-13T21:00:12Z',
 'default_branch': 'master',
 'deployments_url': 'https://api.github.com/repos/matryer/bitbar/deployments',
 'description': 'Put the output from any script or program in your Mac OS X Menu Bar',
 'downloads_url': 'https://api.github.com/repos/matryer/bitbar/downloads',
 'events_url': 'https://api.github.com/repos/matryer/bitbar/events',
 'fork': False,
 'forks': 174,
 'forks_count': 174,
```

The `requests` library has an amazing number of features—far too many to cover here, but I do suggest that you check out the documentation in the link provided above.

Inspection

Because inspecting data is a critical step in the development of machine learning applications, we'll now have an in-depth look at several libraries that will serve us well in this task.

The Jupyter notebook

There are a number of libraries that will help ease the data inspection process. The first is the Jupyter notebook with IPython (http://ipython.org/). This is a full-fledged, interactive computing environment that's ideal for data exploration. Unlike most development environments, the Jupyter notebook is a web-based frontend (to the IPython kernel) that is divided into individual code blocks or cells. Cells can be run individually or all at once, depending on the need. This allows the developer to run a scenario, see the output, then step back through the code, make adjustments, and see the resulting changes—all without leaving the notebook. Here is a sample interaction in the Jupyter notebook:

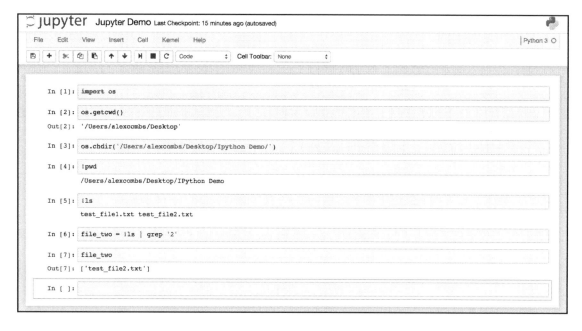

Notice that we have done a number of things here and interacted with not only the IPython backend, but the terminal shell as well. This particular instance is running a Python 3.5 kernel, but you can just as easily run a Python 2.X kernel if you prefer. Here, we have imported the Python os library and made a call to find the current working directory (cell #2), which you can see is the output below the input code cell. We then changed directories using the os library in cell #3, but then stopped utilizing the os library and began using Linux-based commands in cell #4. This is done by adding the ! prepend to the cell. In cell #6, you can see that we were even able to save the shell output to a Python variable (file_two). This is a great feature that makes file operations a simple task.

Now let's take a look at some simple data operations using the notebook. This will also be our first introduction to another indispensable library, `pandas`.

Pandas

Pandas is a remarkable tool for data analysis. According to the pandas documentation (`htt p://pandas.pydata.org/pandas-docs/version/0.17.1/`):

> *It has the broader goal of becoming the most powerful and flexible open source data analysis/manipulation tool available in any language.*

If it doesn't already live up to this claim, it can't be too far off. Let's now take a look:

```
import os
import pandas as pd
import requests

PATH = r'/Users/alexcombs/Desktop/iris/'

r =
requests.get('https://archive.ics.uci.edu/ml/machine-learning-databases/iri
s/iris.data')

with open(PATH + 'iris.data', 'w') as f:
    f.write(r.text)

os.chdir(PATH)

df = pd.read_csv(PATH + 'iris.data', names=['sepal length', 'sepal width',
'petal length', 'petal width', 'class'])

df.head()
```

	sepal length	sepal width	petal length	petal width	class
0	5.1	3.5	1.4	0.2	Iris-setosa
1	4.9	3.0	1.4	0.2	Iris-setosa
2	4.7	3.2	1.3	0.2	Iris-setosa
3	4.6	3.1	1.5	0.2	Iris-setosa
4	5.0	3.6	1.4	0.2	Iris-setosa

As seen in the preceding code and screenshot we have downloaded a classic machine learning dataset, `iris.data`, from `https://archive.ics.uci.edu/ml/datasets/Iris` and written it into the `iris` directory. This is actually a CSV file, and using Pandas, we made a call to read in the file. We also added column names, as this particular file lacked a header row. If the file did contain a header row, pandas would have automatically parsed and reflected this. Compared to other CSV libraries, pandas makes this a simple operation.

Parsing files is just one small feature of this library. To work with datasets that will fit on a single machine, pandas is the ultimate tool; it is a bit like Excel on steroids. Like the popular spreadsheet program, the basic units of operation are columns and rows of data in the form of tables. In the terminology of pandas, columns of data are Series and the table is a DataFrame.

Using the same `iris` DataFrame as shown in the preceding screenshot, let's have a look at a few common operations:

```
df['sepal length']
```

```
0     5.1
1     4.9
2     4.7
3     4.6
4     5.0
5     5.4
6     4.6
7     5.0
8     4.4
9     4.9
10    5.4
11    4.8
12    4.8
```

The first action was just to select a single column from the DataFrame by referencing it by its column name. Another way that we can perform this **data slicing** is to use the `.ix[row, column]` notation. Let's select the first two columns and first four rows using this notation:

```
df.ix[:3,:2]
```

The preceding code generates the following output:

	sepal length	sepal width
0	5.1	3.5
1	4.9	3.0
2	4.7	3.2
3	4.6	3.1

Using the `.ix` notation and Python list slicing syntax, we were able to select a slice of this DataFrame. Now let's take it up a notch and use a list iterator to select just the width columns:

```
df.ix[:3, [x for x in df.columns if 'width' in x]]
```

The preceding code generates the following output:

	sepal width	petal width
0	3.5	0.2
1	3.0	0.2
2	3.2	0.2
3	3.1	0.2

What we have done here is create a list that is a subset of all the columns. The preceding df.columns returns a list of all the columns and our iteration uses a conditional statement to select only those with width in the title. Obviously, in this situation, we could have just as easily typed out the columns that we wanted in a list, but this illustrates the power available when dealing with much larger datasets.

We've seen how to select slices based on their position in the DataFrame, but let's now look at another method to select data. This time we will select a subset of the data based on some specific conditions. We start by listing all the available unique classes and then selecting one of these:

```
df['class'].unique()
```

The preceding code generates the following output:

```
array(['Iris-setosa', 'Iris-versicolor', 'Iris-virginica'], dtype=object)
```

```
df[df['class']=='Iris-virginica']
```

	sepal length	sepal width	petal length	petal width	class
100	6.3	3.3	6.0	2.5	Iris-virginica
101	5.8	2.7	5.1	1.9	Iris-virginica
102	7.1	3.0	5.9	2.1	Iris-virginica
103	6.3	2.9	5.6	1.8	Iris-virginica
104	6.5	3.0	5.8	2.2	Iris-virginica
105	7.6	3.0	6.6	2.1	Iris-virginica
106	4.9	2.5	4.5	1.7	Iris-virginica
107	7.3	2.9	6.3	1.8	Iris-virginica
108	6.7	2.5	5.8	1.8	Iris-virginica
109	7.2	3.6	6.1	2.5	Iris-virginica
110	6.5	3.2	5.1	2.0	Iris-virginica

In the far right-hand column, we can see that our DataFrame only contains data for the Iris-virginica class. In fact, the size of the DataFrame is now 50 rows, down from the original 150 rows:

```
df.count()
```

```
sepal length    150
sepal width     150
petal length    150
petal width     150
class           150
dtype: int64
```

```
df[df['class']=='Iris-virginica'].count()
```

```
sepal length    50
sepal width     50
petal length    50
petal width     50
class           50
dtype: int64
```

We can also see that the index on the left retains the original row numbers. We can now save this data as a new DataFrame and reset the index, as shown in the following code and screenshot:

```
virginica = df[df['class']=='Iris-virginica'].reset_index(drop=True)
virginica
```

	sepal length	sepal width	petal length	petal width	class
0	6.3	3.3	6.0	2.5	Iris-virginica
1	5.8	2.7	5.1	1.9	Iris-virginica
2	7.1	3.0	5.9	2.1	Iris-virginica
3	6.3	2.9	5.6	1.8	Iris-virginica
4	6.5	3.0	5.8	2.2	Iris-virginica
5	7.6	3.0	6.6	2.1	Iris-virginica
6	4.9	2.5	4.5	1.7	Iris-virginica
7	7.3	2.9	6.3	1.8	Iris-virginica
8	6.7	2.5	5.8	1.8	Iris-virginica
9	7.2	3.6	6.1	2.5	Iris-virginica
10	6.5	3.2	5.1	2.0	Iris-virginica

We have selected data by placing a condition on one column; let's now add more conditions. We'll go back to our original DataFrame and select data using two conditions:

```
df[(df['class']=='Iris-virginica')&(df['petal width']>2.2)]
```

	sepal length	sepal width	petal length	petal width	class
100	6.3	3.3	6.0	2.5	Iris-virginica
109	7.2	3.6	6.1	2.5	Iris-virginica
114	5.8	2.8	5.1	2.4	Iris-virginica
115	6.4	3.2	5.3	2.3	Iris-virginica
118	7.7	2.6	6.9	2.3	Iris-virginica
120	6.9	3.2	5.7	2.3	Iris-virginica
135	7.7	3.0	6.1	2.3	Iris-virginica
136	6.3	3.4	5.6	2.4	Iris-virginica
140	6.7	3.1	5.6	2.4	Iris-virginica
141	6.9	3.1	5.1	2.3	Iris-virginica
143	6.8	3.2	5.9	2.3	Iris-virginica
144	6.7	3.3	5.7	2.5	Iris-virginica
145	6.7	3.0	5.2	2.3	Iris-virginica
148	6.2	3.4	5.4	2.3	Iris-virginica

The DataFrame now includes data only from the `Iris-virginica` class with a petal width greater than 2.2.

Let's now use pandas to get some quick descriptive statistics from our Iris dataset:

```
df.describe()
```

	sepal length	sepal width	petal length	petal width
count	150.000000	150.000000	150.000000	150.000000
mean	5.843333	3.054000	3.758667	1.198667
std	0.828066	0.433594	1.764420	0.763161
min	4.300000	2.000000	1.000000	0.100000
25%	5.100000	2.800000	1.600000	0.300000
50%	5.800000	3.000000	4.350000	1.300000
75%	6.400000	3.300000	5.100000	1.800000
max	7.900000	4.400000	6.900000	2.500000

With a call to the DataFrame `.describe()` method, we received a breakdown of the descriptive statistics for each of the relevant columns. (Notice that class was automatically removed as it is not relevant for this.)

We could also pass in custom percentiles if we wanted more granular information:

```
df.describe(percentiles=[.20,.40,.80,.90,.95])
```

	sepal length	sepal width	petal length	petal width
count	150.000000	150.000000	150.000000	150.000000
mean	5.843333	3.054000	3.758667	1.198667
std	0.828066	0.433594	1.764420	0.763161
min	4.300000	2.000000	1.000000	0.100000
20%	5.000000	2.700000	1.500000	0.200000
40%	5.600000	3.000000	3.900000	1.160000
50%	5.800000	3.000000	4.350000	1.300000
80%	6.520000	3.400000	5.320000	1.900000
90%	6.900000	3.610000	5.800000	2.200000
95%	7.255000	3.800000	6.100000	2.300000
max	7.900000	4.400000	6.900000	2.500000

Next, let's check whether there is any correlation between these features. This can be done by calling `.corr()` on our DataFrame:

```
df.corr()
```

	sepal length	sepal width	petal length	petal width
sepal length	1.000000	-0.109369	0.871754	0.817954
sepal width	-0.109369	1.000000	-0.420516	-0.356544
petal length	0.871754	-0.420516	1.000000	0.962757
petal width	0.817954	-0.356544	0.962757	1.000000

The default returns the Pearson correlation coefficient for each row-column pair. This can be switched to Kendall's tau or Spearman's rank correlation coefficient by passing in a method argument (for instance, `.corr(method="spearman")` or `.corr(method="kendall")`).

Visualization

So far, we have seen how to select portions of a DataFrame and get summary statistics from our data, but let's now move on to learning how to visually inspect the data. But first, why even bother with visual inspection? Let's see an example to understand why.

The following table illustrates the summary statistics for four distinct series of x and y values:

Series of x and y	Values
Mean of x	9
Mean of y	7.5
Sample variance of x	11
Sample variance of y	4.1
Correlation between x and y	0.816
Regression line	$y=3.00+0.500x$

Based on the series having identical summary statistics, we might assume that these series would appear visually similar. We would, of course, be wrong. Very wrong. The four series are part of Anscombe's quartet, and they were deliberately created to illustrate the importance of visual data inspection. Each series is plotted in the following image:

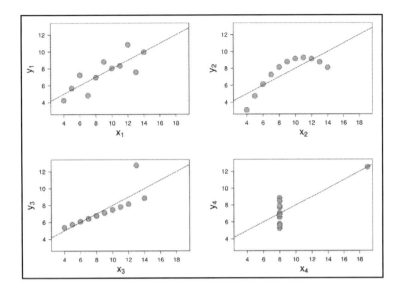

The Anscombe's quartet taken from `https://en.wikipedia.org/wiki/Anscombe%27s_quartet`.

Clearly, we would not treat these datasets as identical after having visualized them. So now that we understand the importance of visualization, let's take a look at a pair of useful Python libraries for this.

The matplotlib library

The first library that we'll take a look at is `matplotlib`. It is the great grandfather of Python plotting libraries. Originally created to emulate the plotting functionality of MATLAB, it grew into a fully-featured library in its own right with an enormous range of functionality. For those that have not come from a MATLAB background, it can be hard to understand how all the pieces work together to create the graphs.

We'll break down the pieces into logical components to make sense of what's going on. Before diving into `matplotlib` in full, let's set up our Jupyter notebook to allow us to see our graphs in line. To do this, we'll need to add the following lines to our `import` statements:

```
import matplotlib.pyplot as plt
plt.style.use('ggplot')
%matplotlib inline
import numpy as np
```

The first line imports `matplotlib`, the second line sets the styling to approximate R's `ggplot` library (this requires matplotlib 1.41), the third line sets the plots so that they are visible in the notebook, and the final line imports `numpy`. We'll use `numpy` for a number of operations later in the chapter.

Now, let's generate our first graph on the Iris dataset using the following code:

```
fig, ax = plt.subplots(figsize=(6,4))
ax.hist(df['petal width'], color='black');
ax.set_ylabel('Count', fontsize=12)
ax.set_xlabel('Width', fontsize=12)
plt.title('Iris Petal Width', fontsize=14, y=1.01)
```

The preceding code generates the following output:

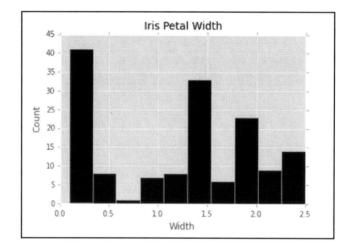

There is a lot going on even in this simple example, but we'll break it down line by line. The first line creates a single subplot with a width of 6" and height of 4". We then plot a histogram of the petal width from our `iris` DataFrame by calling `.hist()` and passing in our data. We also set the bar color to `black` here. The next two lines place labels on our *y* and *x* axes, respectively, and the final line sets the title for our graph. We tweak the title's y position relative to the top of the graph with the `y` parameter and increase the font size slightly over the default. This gives us a nice histogram of our petal width data. Let's now expand on this and generate histograms for each column of our `iris` dataset:

```
fig, ax = plt.subplots(2,2, figsize=(6,4))

ax[0][0].hist(df['petal width'], color='black');
ax[0][0].set_ylabel('Count', fontsize=12)
```

```
ax[0][0].set_xlabel('Width', fontsize=12)
ax[0][0].set_title('Iris Petal Width', fontsize=14, y=1.01)

ax[0][1].hist(df['petal length'], color='black');
ax[0][1].set_ylabel('Count', fontsize=12)
ax[0][1].set_xlabel('Lenth', fontsize=12)
ax[0][1].set_title('Iris Petal Lenth', fontsize=14, y=1.01)

ax[1][0].hist(df['sepal width'], color='black');
ax[1][0].set_ylabel('Count', fontsize=12)
ax[1][0].set_xlabel('Width', fontsize=12)
ax[1][0].set_title('Iris Sepal Width', fontsize=14, y=1.01)

ax[1][1].hist(df['sepal length'], color='black');
ax[1][1].set_ylabel('Count', fontsize=12)
ax[1][1].set_xlabel('Length', fontsize=12)
ax[1][1].set_title('Iris Sepal Length', fontsize=14, y=1.01)

plt.tight_layout()
```

The output for the preceding code is shown in the following screenshot:

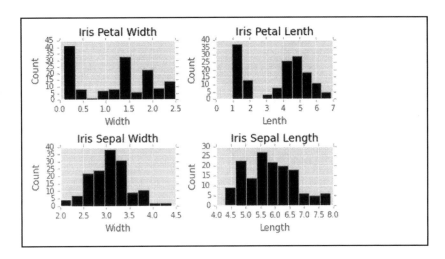

Obviously, this is not the most efficient way to code this, but it is useful to demonstrate how `matplotlib` works. Notice that instead of the single subplot object, `ax`, that we had in the first example, we now have four subplots, which are accessed through what is now the `ax` array. A new addition to the code is the call to `plt.tight_layout()`; this method will nicely adjust the subplots automatically to avoid crowding.

Let's now take a look at a few other types of plots available in `matplotlib`. One useful plot is a **scatterplot**. Here, we will plot the petal width against the petal length:

```
fig, ax = plt.subplots(figsize=(6,6))
ax.scatter(df['petal width'],df['petal length'], color='green')
ax.set_xlabel('Petal Width')
ax.set_ylabel('Petal Length')
ax.set_title('Petal Scatterplot')
```

The preceding code generates the following output:

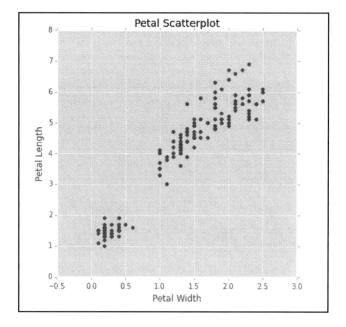

As explained earlier, we could add multiple subplots to examine each facet.

Another plot we could examine is a simple line plot. Here we look at a plot of the petal length:

```
fig, ax = plt.subplots(figsize=(6,6))
ax.plot(df['petal length'], color='blue')
ax.set_xlabel('Specimen Number')
ax.set_ylabel('Petal Length')
ax.set_title('Petal Length Plot')
```

The preceding code generates the following output:

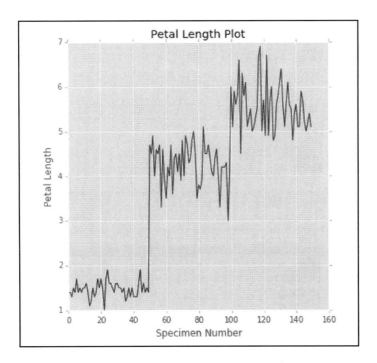

Based on this simple line plot, we can already see that there are distinctive clusters of lengths for each class—remember that our sample dataset had 50 ordered examples of each class. This tells us that the petal length is likely to be a useful feature to discriminate between classes.

Let's look at one final type of chart from the `matplotlib` library, the bar chart. This is perhaps one of the more common charts that you'll see. Here, we'll plot a bar chart for the mean of each feature for the three classes of irises, and to make it more interesting, we'll make it a stacked bar chart with a number of additional `matplotlib` features:

```
fig, ax = plt.subplots(figsize=(6,6))
bar_width = .8
labels = [x for x in df.columns if 'length' in x or 'width' in x]
ver_y = [df[df['class']=='Iris-versicolor'][x].mean() for x in
labels]
vir_y = [df[df['class']=='Iris-virginica'][x].mean() for x in
labels]
set_y = [df[df['class']=='Iris-setosa'][x].mean() for x in labels]
x = np.arange(len(labels))
ax.bar(x, vir_y, bar_width, bottom=set_y, color='darkgrey')
```

```
ax.bar(x, set_y, bar_width, bottom=ver_y, color='white')
ax.bar(x, ver_y, bar_width, color='black')
ax.set_xticks(x + (bar_width/2))
ax.set_xticklabels(labels, rotation=-70, fontsize=12);
ax.set_title('Mean Feature Measurement By Class', y=1.01)
ax.legend(['Virginica','Setosa','Versicolor'])
```

The preceding code generates the following output:

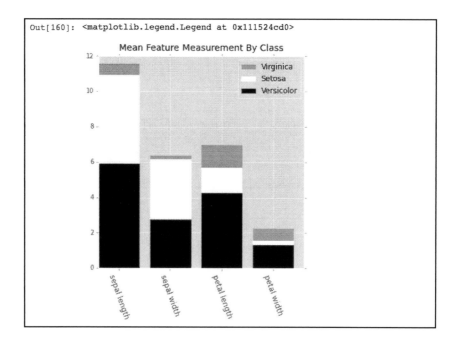

To generate the bar chart, we need to pass the x and y values to the `.bar()` method. In this case, the x values will just be an array of the length of the features that we are interested in—four here, or one for each column in our DataFrame. The `np.arange()` function is an easy way to generate this, but we could nearly as easily input this array manually. As we don't want the x axis to display this 1 through 4, we call the `.set_xticklabels()` method and pass in the column names that we want to display. To line up the x labels properly, we also need to adjust the spacing of the labels; this is why we set `xticks` to x plus half the size of `bar_width`, which we also set earlier at `0.8`. The y values come from taking the mean of each feature for each class. We then plot each by calling `.bar()`. It is important to note that we pass in a `bottom` parameter for each series that sets its minimum y point equal to the maximum y point of the series below it. This creates the stacked bars. Finally, we add a legend that describes each series. The names are inserted into the legend list in order of the placement of the bars from top to bottom.

The seaborn library

The next visualization library that we'll look at is called `seaborn` (`http://stanford.edu/~mwaskom/software/seaborn/index.html`). It is a library that was created specifically for statistical visualizations. In fact, it is perfect for use with `pandas` DataFrames where the columns are features and rows are observations. This style of DataFrame is called **tidy** data, and it is the most common form for machine learning applications.

Let's now take a look at the power of `seaborn`:

```
import seaborn as sns
sns.pairplot(df, hue="class")
```

With just these two lines of code, we get the following output:

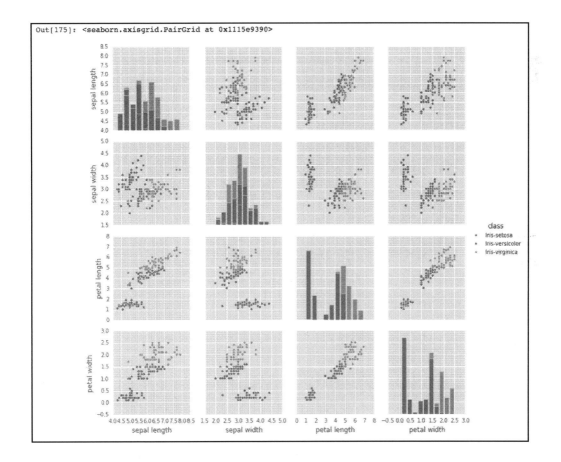

Having just detailed the intricate nuances of `matplotlib`, the simplicity with which we generated this plot is notable. All of our features have been plotted against each other and properly labeled with just two lines of code. Was learning pages of `matplotlib` a waste, when `seaborn` makes these types of visualizations so simple? Fortunately, that isn't the case as `seaborn` is built on top of `matplotlib`. In fact, we can use all of what we learned about `matplotlib` to modify and work with `seaborn`. Let's take a look at another visualization:

```
fig, ax = plt.subplots(2, 2, figsize=(7, 7))
sns.set(style='white', palette='muted')
sns.violinplot(x=df['class'], y=df['sepal length'], ax=ax[0,0])
sns.violinplot(x=df['class'], y=df['sepal width'], ax=ax[0,1])
sns.violinplot(x=df['class'], y=df['petal length'], ax=ax[1,0])
sns.violinplot(x=df['class'], y=df['petal width'], ax=ax[1,1])
fig.suptitle('Violin Plots', fontsize=16, y=1.03)
for i in ax.flat:
    plt.setp(i.get_xticklabels(), rotation=-90)
fig.tight_layout()
```

The preceding lines of code generate the following output:

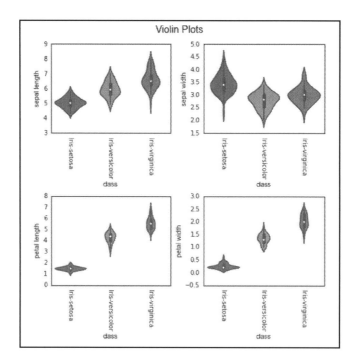

Here, we generated a violin plot for each of the four features. A violin plot displays the distribution of the features. For example, we can easily see that the petal length of `iris-setosa` is highly clustered between 1 and 2 cm, while `iris-virginica` is much more dispersed from near 4 to over 7 cm. We can also notice that we have used much of the same code that we used when constructing the `matplotlib` graphs. The main difference is the addition of the `sns.plot()` calls in place of the `ax.plot()` calls previously. We have also added a title above all of the subplots rather than over each individually with the `fig.suptitle()` method. One other notable addition is the iteration over each of the subplots to change the rotation of `xticklabels`. We call `ax.flat()` and then iterate over each subplot axis to set a particular property using `.setp()`. This prevents us from having to individually type out `ax[0][0]...ax[1][1]` and set the properties as we did in the earlier matplotlib subplot code.

The graphs we've used here are a great start, but there are hundreds of styles of graphs that you can generate using `matplotlib` and `seaborn`. I highly recommend that you dig into the documentation for these two libraries-it will be time well spent.

Preparation

We've learned a great deal about inspecting the data that we have, but now let's move on to learning how to process and manipulate our data. Here we will learn about the `Series.map()`, `Series.apply()`, `DataFrame.apply()`, `DataFrame.applymap()`, and `DataFrame.groupby()` methods of `pandas`. These are invaluable for working with data and are especially useful in the context of machine learning for feature engineering, a concept that we will discuss in detail in later chapters.

Map

The `map` method works on series, so in our case, we will use it to transform a column of our DataFrame, which remember is just a `pandas` Series. Suppose that we decide that the class names are a bit long for our taste and we would like to code them using our special three-letter coding system. We'll use the `map` method with a Python dictionary as the argument to accomplish this. We'll pass in a replacement for each of the unique iris types:

```
df['class'] = df['class'].map({'Iris-setosa': 'SET', 'Iris-virginica':
'VIR', 'Iris-versicolor': 'VER'})
df
```

	sepal length	sepal width	petal length	petal width	class
0	5.1	3.5	1.4	0.2	SET
1	4.9	3.0	1.4	0.2	SET
2	4.7	3.2	1.3	0.2	SET
3	4.6	3.1	1.5	0.2	SET
4	5.0	3.6	1.4	0.2	SET
5	5.4	3.9	1.7	0.4	SET
6	4.6	3.4	1.4	0.3	SET
7	5.0	3.4	1.5	0.2	SET
8	4.4	2.9	1.4	0.2	SET
9	4.9	3.1	1.5	0.1	SET

Let's look at what we have done here. We ran the `map` method over each of the values of the existing `class` column. As each value was found in the Python dictionary, it was added to the return series. We assigned this return series to the same `class` name, so it replaced our original `class` column. Had we chosen a different name, say `short class`, this column would have been appended to the DataFrame and we would then have the original `class` column plus the new `short class` column.

We could have instead passed another Series or function to the `map` method to perform this transformation on a column, but this is functionality that is also available through the apply method, which we'll take a look at next. The dictionary functionality is unique to the `map` method, and the most common reason to choose `map` over apply for a single column transformation. Let's now take a look at the `apply` method.

Apply

The `apply` method allows us to work with both DataFrames and Series. We'll start with an example that would work equally well with `map`, then we'll move on to examples that would work only with `apply`.

Using the `iris` DataFrame, let's make a new column based on the petal width. We previously saw that the mean for the petal width was 1.3. Let's now create a new column in our DataFrame, wide petal, that contains binary values based on the value in the `petal` width column. If the petal width is equal to or wider than the median, we will code it with a 1, and if it is less than the median, we will code it 0. We'll do this using the apply method on the petal width column:

```
df['wide petal'] = df['petal width'].apply(lambda v: 1 if v >= 1.3 else 0)
df
```

The preceding code generates the following output:

	sepal length	sepal width	petal length	petal width	class	wide petal
0	5.1	3.5	1.4	0.2	Iris-setosa	0
1	4.9	3.0	1.4	0.2	Iris-setosa	0
2	4.7	3.2	1.3	0.2	Iris-setosa	0
3	4.6	3.1	1.5	0.2	Iris-setosa	0
4	5.0	3.6	1.4	0.2	Iris-setosa	0
5	5.4	3.9	1.7	0.4	Iris-setosa	0
6	4.6	3.4	1.4	0.3	Iris-setosa	0
7	5.0	3.4	1.5	0.2	Iris-setosa	0
8	4.4	2.9	1.4	0.2	Iris-setosa	0
9	4.9	3.1	1.5	0.1	Iris-setosa	0

A few things happened here; let's walk through them step by step. First, we were able to append a new column to the DataFrame simply using the column selection syntax for a column name that we want to create, in this case, wide petal. We set this new column equal to the output of the apply method. Here, we ran apply on the petal width column, which returned the corresponding values in the wide petal column. The apply method works by running through each value of the petal width column. If the value is greater or equal to 1.3, the function returns 1; otherwise, it returns . This type of transformation is a fairly common feature-engineering transformation in machine learning, so it is good to be familiar with how to perform it.

Let's now take a look at using apply on a DataFrame rather than a single Series. We'll now create a feature based on petal area:

```
df['petal area'] = df.apply(lambda r: r['petal length'] * r['petal width'],
axis=1)
df
```

	sepal length	sepal width	petal length	petal width	class	wide petal	petal area
0	5.1	3.5	1.4	0.2	Iris-setosa	0	0.28
1	4.9	3.0	1.4	0.2	Iris-setosa	0	0.28
2	4.7	3.2	1.3	0.2	Iris-setosa	0	0.26
3	4.6	3.1	1.5	0.2	Iris-setosa	0	0.30
4	5.0	3.6	1.4	0.2	Iris-setosa	0	0.28
5	5.4	3.9	1.7	0.4	Iris-setosa	0	0.68
6	4.6	3.4	1.4	0.3	Iris-setosa	0	0.42
7	5.0	3.4	1.5	0.2	Iris-setosa	0	0.30
8	4.4	2.9	1.4	0.2	Iris-setosa	0	0.28
9	4.9	3.1	1.5	0.1	Iris-setosa	0	0.15
10	5.4	3.7	1.5	0.2	Iris-setosa	0	0.30

Notice that we called `apply`, not on a Series here, but on the entire DataFrame, and because `apply` was called on the entire DataFrame, we passed in `axis=1` in order to tell `pandas` that we want to apply the function row-wise. If we passed in `axis=0`, then the function would operate column-wise. Here, each column is processed sequentially, and we choose to multiply the values from the `petal length` and `petal width` columns. The resultant series then becomes the `petal area` column in our DataFrame. This type of power and flexibility is what makes `pandas` an indispensable tool for data manipulation.

Applymap

We've looked at manipulating columns and explained how to work with rows, but suppose that you'd like to perform a function across all data cells in your DataFrame; this is where `applymap` is the right tool. Let's take a look at an example:

```
df.applymap(lambda v: np.log(v) if isinstance(v, float) else v)
```

	sepal length	sepal width	petal length	petal width	class	wide petal	petal area
0	1.629241	1.252763	0.336472	-1.609438	Iris-setosa	0	-1.272966
1	1.589235	1.098612	0.336472	-1.609438	Iris-setosa	0	-1.272966
2	1.547563	1.163151	0.262364	-1.609438	Iris-setosa	0	-1.347074
3	1.526056	1.131402	0.405465	-1.609438	Iris-setosa	0	-1.203973
4	1.609438	1.280934	0.336472	-1.609438	Iris-setosa	0	-1.272966
5	1.686399	1.360977	0.530628	-0.916291	Iris-setosa	0	-0.385662
6	1.526056	1.223775	0.336472	-1.203973	Iris-setosa	0	-0.867501
7	1.609438	1.223775	0.405465	-1.609438	Iris-setosa	0	-1.203973
8	1.481605	1.064711	0.336472	-1.609438	Iris-setosa	0	-1.272966

Here, we called `applymap` on our DataFrame in order to get the log of every value (`np.log()` utilizes the `numpy` library to return this value) if that value is an instance of the type float. This type checking prevents returning an error or a float for the `class` or `wide petal` columns, which are string and integer values respectively. Common uses for `applymap` are to transform or format each cell based on meeting some conditional criteria.

Groupby

Let's now look at an operation that is highly useful but often difficult for new pandas users to get their heads around—the DataFrame `.groupby()` method. We'll walk through a number of examples step by step in order to illustrate the most important functionality.

The `groupby` operation does exactly what it says—it groups data based on some class or classes that you choose. Let's take a look at a simple example using our `iris` dataset. We'll go back and reimport our original `iris` dataset and run our first `groupby` operation:

```
df.groupby('class').mean()
```

class	sepal length	sepal width	petal length	petal width	wide petal	petal area
Iris-setosa	5.006	3.418	1.464	0.244	0.0	0.3628
Iris-versicolor	5.936	2.770	4.260	1.326	0.7	5.7204
Iris-virginica	6.588	2.974	5.552	2.026	1.0	11.2962

Data for each class is partitioned and the mean for each feature is provided. Let's take it a step further now and get full descriptive statistics for each class:

```
df.groupby('class').describe()
```

class		petal area	petal length	petal width	sepal length	sepal width	wide petal
	count	50.000000	50.000000	50.000000	50.000000	50.000000	50.00000
	mean	0.362800	1.464000	0.244000	5.006000	3.418000	0.00000
	std	0.183248	0.173511	0.107210	0.352490	0.381024	0.00000
	min	0.110000	1.000000	0.100000	4.300000	2.300000	0.00000
Iris-setosa	25%	0.265000	1.400000	0.200000	4.800000	3.125000	0.00000
	50%	0.300000	1.500000	0.200000	5.000000	3.400000	0.00000
	75%	0.420000	1.575000	0.300000	5.200000	3.675000	0.00000
	max	0.960000	1.900000	0.600000	5.800000	4.400000	0.00000
	count	50.000000	50.000000	50.000000	50.000000	50.000000	50.00000
	mean	5.720400	4.260000	1.326000	5.936000	2.770000	0.70000
	std	1.368403	0.469911	0.197753	0.516171	0.313798	0.46291
	min	3.300000	3.000000	1.000000	4.900000	2.000000	0.00000
Iris-versicolor	25%	4.860000	4.000000	1.200000	5.600000	2.525000	0.00000
	50%	5.615000	4.350000	1.300000	5.900000	2.800000	1.00000
	75%	6.750000	4.600000	1.500000	6.300000	3.000000	1.00000
	max	8.640000	5.100000	1.800000	7.000000	3.400000	1.00000
	count	50.000000	50.000000	50.000000	50.000000	50.000000	50.00000
	mean	11.296200	5.552000	2.026000	6.588000	2.974000	1.00000
	std	2.157412	0.551895	0.274650	0.635880	0.322497	0.00000
	min	7.500000	4.500000	1.400000	4.900000	2.200000	1.00000
Iris-virginica	25%	9.717500	5.100000	1.800000	6.225000	2.800000	1.00000
	50%	11.445000	5.550000	2.000000	6.500000	3.000000	1.00000
	75%	12.790000	5.875000	2.300000	6.900000	3.175000	1.00000
	max	15.870000	6.900000	2.500000	7.900000	3.800000	1.00000

Now we can see the full breakdown bucketed by `class`. Let's now look at some other `groupby` operations that we can perform. We saw previously that the petal length and width had some relatively clear boundaries between classes; let's see how we might use `groupby` to see this:

```
df.groupby('petal width')['class'].unique().to_frame()
```

	class
petal width	
0.1	[Iris-setosa]
0.2	[Iris-setosa]
0.3	[Iris-setosa]
0.4	[Iris-setosa]
0.5	[Iris-setosa]
0.6	[Iris-setosa]
1.0	[Iris-versicolor]
1.1	[Iris-versicolor]
1.2	[Iris-versicolor]
1.3	[Iris-versicolor]
1.4	[Iris-versicolor, Iris-virginica]
1.5	[Iris-versicolor, Iris-virginica]
1.6	[Iris-versicolor, Iris-virginica]
1.7	[Iris-versicolor, Iris-virginica]
1.8	[Iris-versicolor, Iris-virginica]
1.9	[Iris-virginica]
2.0	[Iris-virginica]
2.1	[Iris-virginica]
2.2	[Iris-virginica]
2.3	[Iris-virginica]
2.4	[Iris-virginica]
2.5	[Iris-virginica]

In this case, we grouped each unique class by the petal width that they were associated with. This is a manageable number of measurements to group by, but if it were to become much larger, we would likely need to partition the measurements into brackets. As we saw previously, this can be accomplished with the `apply` method.

Let's now take a look at a custom aggregation function:

```
df.groupby('class')['petal width']\
.agg({'delta': lambda x: x.max() - x.min(), 'max': np.max, 'min': np.min})
```

	min	max	delta
class			
Iris-setosa	0.1	0.6	0.5
Iris-versicolor	1.0	1.8	0.8
Iris-virginica	1.4	2.5	1.1

In this code, we grouped the petal width by class using the functions: `np.max` and `np.min`, and a `lambda` function that returns the maximum petal width minus the minimum petal width. (The two `np` functions are from the `numpy` library.) These were passed to the `.agg()` method in the form of a dictionary in order to return a DataFrame with the keys as column names. A single function can be run or the functions can be passed as a list, but the column names are less informative.

 We've only just touched on the functionality of the `groupby` method; there is a lot more to learn, so I encourage you to read the documentation at `http://pandas.pydata.org/pandas-docs/stable/`.

We now have a solid base-level understanding of how to manipulate and prepare data in preparation for our next step, which is modeling. We will now move on to discuss the primary libraries in the Python machine learning ecosystem.

Modeling and evaluation

Python has an excellent selection of well-documented libraries for statistical modeling and machine learning. We'll touch on just a few of the most popular libraries below.

Statsmodels

The first library that we'll cover is the `statsmodels` library (`http://statsmodels.sourceforge.net/`). Statsmodels is a Python package that was developed to explore data, estimate models, and run statistical tests. Let's use it here to build a simple linear regression model of the relationship between the sepal length and sepal width for the `setosa` class.

First, let's visually inspect the relationship with a scatterplot:

```
fig, ax = plt.subplots(figsize=(7,7))
ax.scatter(df['sepal width'][:50], df['sepal length'][:50])
```

```
ax.set_ylabel('Sepal Length')
ax.set_xlabel('Sepal Width')
ax.set_title('Setosa Sepal Width vs. Sepal Length', fontsize=14,
y=1.02)
```

The preceding code generates the following output:

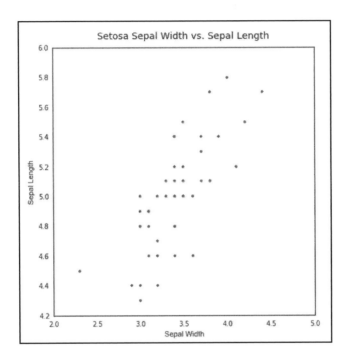

We can see that there appears to be a positive linear relationship, that is, as the sepal width increases, sepal length does as well. We next run a linear regression model on the data using statsmodels to estimate the strength of this relationship:

```
import statsmodels.api as sm

y = df['sepal length'][:50]
x = df['sepal width'][:50]
X = sm.add_constant(x)

results = sm.OLS(y, X).fit()
print(results.summary())
```

The preceding code generates the following output:

```
                        OLS Regression Results
================================================================================
Dep. Variable:          sepal length   R-squared:                      0.558
Model:                           OLS   Adj. R-squared:                 0.548
Method:                Least Squares   F-statistic:                    60.52
Date:               Sun, 11 Oct 2015   Prob (F-statistic):          4.75e-10
Time:                       18:14:39   Log-Likelihood:                2.0879
No. Observations:                 50   AIC:                          -0.1759
Df Residuals:                     48   BIC:                            3.648
Df Model:                          1
================================================================================
                 coef    std err          t      P>|t|      [95.0% Conf. Int.]
--------------------------------------------------------------------------------
const          2.6447      0.305      8.660      0.000       2.031      3.259
sepal width    0.6909      0.089      7.779      0.000       0.512      0.869
================================================================================
Omnibus:                       0.252   Durbin-Watson:                  2.517
Prob(Omnibus):                 0.882   Jarque-Bera (JB):               0.436
Skew:                         -0.110   Prob(JB):                       0.804
Kurtosis:                      2.599   Cond. No.                        34.0
================================================================================
```

The preceding screenshot shows the results of our simple regression model. As this is a linear regression, the model takes the format of $Y = B0+B1X$, where $B0$ is the intercept and $B1$ is the regression coefficient. Here, the formula would be *Sepal Length = 2.6447 + 0.6909 * Sepal Width*. We can also see that $R2$ for the model is a respectable 0.558, and the *p*-value (Prob) is highly significant—at least for this class.

Let's now use the results object to plot our regression line:

```
fig, ax = plt.subplots(figsize=(7,7))
ax.plot(x, results.fittedvalues, label='regression line')
ax.scatter(x, y, label='data point', color='r')
ax.set_ylabel('Sepal Length')
ax.set_xlabel('Sepal Width')
ax.set_title('Setosa Sepal Width vs. Sepal Length', fontsize=14,
y=1.02)
ax.legend(loc=2)
```

The preceding code generates the following output:

By plotting `results.fittedvalues`, we can get the resulting regression line from our model.

There are a number of other statistical functions and tests in the `statsmodels` package, and I invite you to explore them. It is an exceptionally useful package for standard statistical modeling in Python. Let's now move on to the king of Python machine learning packages, `scikit-learn`.

Scikit-learn

Scikit-learn is an amazing Python library with unrivaled documentation designed to provide a consistent API to dozens of algorithms. It is built on—and is itself—a core component of the Python scientific stack, namely, NumPy, SciPy, pandas, and matplotlib. Here are some of the areas that scikit-learn covers: classification, regression, clustering, dimensionality reduction, model selection, and preprocessing.

We'll look at a few examples. First, we will build a classifier using our `iris` data, and then we'll look at how we can evaluate our model using the tools of scikit-learn.

The first step to building a machine learning model in scikit-learn is understanding how the data must be structured. The independent variables should be a numeric *n* x *m* matrix, X; a dependent variable, y; and an *n* x *1* vector. The *y* vector may be either numeric continuous or categorical or string categorical. These are then passed into the `.fit()` method on the chosen classifier. This is the great benefit of using scikit-learn; each classifier utilizes the same methods to the extent that's possible. This makes swapping them in and out a breeze. Let's see this in action in our first example:

```
from sklearn.ensemble import RandomForestClassifier
from sklearn.cross_validation import train_test_split

clf = RandomForestClassifier(max_depth=5, n_estimators=10)

X = df.ix[:,:4]
y = df.ix[:,4]

X_train, X_test, y_train, y_test = train_test_split(X, y,
test_size=.3)

clf.fit(X_train,y_train)

y_pred = clf.predict(X_test)

rf = pd.DataFrame(list(zip(y_pred, y_test)), columns=['predicted',
'actual'])
rf['correct'] = rf.apply(lambda r: 1 if r['predicted'] ==
r['actual'] else 0, axis=1)
rf
```

The preceding code generates the following output:

	predicted	actual	correct
0	Iris-virginica	Iris-virginica	1
1	Iris-versicolor	Iris-versicolor	1
2	Iris-virginica	Iris-virginica	1
3	Iris-virginica	Iris-virginica	1
4	Iris-setosa	Iris-setosa	1
5	Iris-virginica	Iris-virginica	1
6	Iris-virginica	Iris-virginica	1
7	Iris-versicolor	Iris-versicolor	1
8	Iris-versicolor	Iris-versicolor	1
9	Iris-setosa	Iris-setosa	1
10	Iris-versicolor	Iris-versicolor	1
11	Iris-versicolor	Iris-versicolor	1
12	Iris-versicolor	Iris-virginica	0
13	Iris-versicolor	Iris-versicolor	1
14	Iris-setosa	Iris-setosa	1
15	Iris-setosa	Iris-setosa	1

Now, let's take a look at the following line of code:

```
rf['correct'].sum()/rf['correct'].count()
```

This will generate the following output:

```
0.9555555555555556
```

In the preceding few lines of code, we built, trained, and tested a classifier that has a 95% accuracy level on our Iris dataset. Let's unpack each of the steps. In the first two lines of code, we made a couple of imports; the first two are from scikit-learn, which, thankfully, is shortened to `sklearn` in import statements. The first import is a random forest classifier, and the second is a module to split our data into training and testing cohorts. This data partitioning is critical in building machine learning applications for a number of reasons. We'll get into this in later chapters, but suffice it to say for now that it is a must. This `train_test_split` module also shuffles our data, which again is important as the order can contain information that would bias your actual predictions

In this book we'll be using the latest Python version, as of the time of writing, which is version 3.5. If you are on Python version 2.X, you will need to add an additional import statement for integer division to work as it does in Python 3.X. Without this line, your accuracy will be reported as 0 rather than 95%. That line is as follows:

from __future__ import division

The first curious-looking line after the imports instantiates our classifier, in this case, a random forest classifier. We select a forest that uses 10 decision trees, and each tree is allowed a maximum split depth of five. This is put in place to avoid *overfitting*, something that we will discuss in depth in later chapters.

The next two lines create our X matrix and y vector. Our original iris DataFrame contained four features: the petal width and length and the sepal width and length. These features are selected and become our independent feature matrix, X. The last column, the iris class names, then become our dependent y vector.

These are then passed into the train_test_split method, which shuffles and partitions our data into four subsets, X_train, X_test, y_train, and y_test. The test_size parameter is set to .3, which means that 30% of our dataset will be allocated to the X_test and y_test partitions, while the rest will be allocated to the training partitions, X_train and y_train.

Next, our model is fit using the training data. Having trained the model, we then call the predict method on our classifier using our test data. Remember that the test data is data that the classifier has not seen. The return of this prediction is a list of prediction labels. We then create a DataFrame of the actual labels versus the predicted labels. We finally sum the correct predictions and divide by the total number of instances, which we can see gave us a very accurate prediction. Let's now see which features gave us the most discriminative or predictive power:

```
f_importances = clf.feature_importances_f_names = df.columns[:4]
f_std = np.std([tree.feature_importances_ for tree in
clf.estimators_], axis=0)

zz = zip(f_importances, f_names, f_std)
zzs = sorted(zz, key=lambda x: x[0], reverse=True)

imps = [x[0] for x in zzs]
labels = [x[1] for x in zzs]
errs = [x[2] for x in zzs]
```

```
plt.bar(range(len(f_importances)), imps, color="r", yerr=errs,
align="center")
plt.xticks(range(len(f_importances)), labels);
```

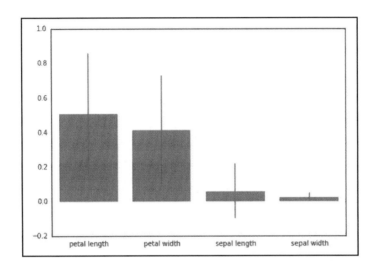

As we expected, based upon our earlier visual analysis, the petal length and width have more discriminative power when differentiating between the `iris` classes. Where exactly did these numbers come from though? The random forest has a method called `.feature_importances_` that returns the relative power of the feature to split at the leaves. If a feature is able to consistently and cleanly split a group into distinct classes, it will have a high feature importance. This number will always sum to one. As you will notice here, we have included the standard deviation, which helps to illustrate how consistent each feature is. This is generated by taking the feature importance for each of the features for each ten trees and calculating the standard deviation.

Let's now take a look at one more example using scikit-learn. We will now switch our classifier and use a **support vector machine (SVM)**:

```
from sklearn.multiclass import OneVsRestClassifier
from sklearn.svm import SVC
from sklearn.cross_validation import train_test_split

clf = OneVsRestClassifier(SVC(kernel='linear'))

X = df.ix[:,:4]
y = np.array(df.ix[:,4]).astype(str)

X_train, X_test, y_train, y_test = train_test_split(X, y,
test_size=.3)
```

```
clf.fit(X_train,y_train)

y_pred = clf.predict(X_test)

rf = pd.DataFrame(list(zip(y_pred, y_test)), columns=['predicted',
'actual'])
rf['correct'] = rf.apply(lambda r: 1 if r['predicted'] ==
r['actual'] else 0, axis=1)
rf
```

The preceding code generates the following output:

	predicted	actual	correct
0	Iris-setosa	Iris-setosa	1
1	Iris-setosa	Iris-setosa	1
2	Iris-setosa	Iris-setosa	1
3	Iris-versicolor	Iris-versicolor	1
4	Iris-virginica	Iris-virginica	1
5	Iris-versicolor	Iris-versicolor	1
6	Iris-versicolor	Iris-virginica	0
7	Iris-virginica	Iris-virginica	1
8	Iris-setosa	Iris-setosa	1
9	Iris-versicolor	Iris-versicolor	1
10	Iris-setosa	Iris-setosa	1
11	Iris-versicolor	Iris-versicolor	1
12	Iris-virginica	Iris-virginica	1
13	Iris-versicolor	Iris-versicolor	1
14	Iris-versicolor	Iris-versicolor	1
15	Iris-virginica	Iris-virginica	1

Now, let's execute the following line of code:

```
rf['correct'].sum()/rf['correct'].count()
```

The preceding code generates the following output:

```
0.9777777777777775
```

Here, we have swapped in a support vector machine without changing virtually any of our code. The only changes were the ones related to the importing of the SVM instead of the random forest, and the line that instantiates the classifier. (One small change to the format of the y labels was required, as the SVM wasn't able to interpret them as NumPy strings like the random forest classifier was).

This is just a fraction of the capability of scikit-learn, but it should serve to illustrate the functionality and power of this magnificent tool for machine learning applications. There are a number of additional machine learning libraries that we won't have a chance to discuss here but will explore in later chapters, but I strongly suggest that if this is your first time utilizing a machine learning library and you want a strong general purpose tool, scikit-learn is your go-to choice.

Deployment

There are a number of options available when putting a machine learning model into production. It depends substantially on the nature of the application. Deployment could include anything from a cron job run on your local machine to a full-scale implementation deployed on an Amazon EC2 instance.

We won't go into detail about specific implementations here, but we will have a chance to delve into different deployment examples throughout the book.

Setting up your machine learning environment

We've covered a number of libraries throughout this chapter that can be installed individually with pip, Python's package manager. I would strongly urge you, however, to go with a prepacked solution such as Continuum's Anaconda Python distribution. This is a a single executable that contains nearly all the packages and dependencies needed. And because the distribution is targeted to Python scientific stack users, it is essentially a one-and-done solution.

Anaconda also includes a package manager that makes updating packages a simple task. Simply type `conda update <package_name>`, and the library will be updated to the most recent stable release.

Summary

In this chapter, we introduced the data science/machine learning workflow. We saw how to take our data step by step through each stage of the pipeline, going from acquisition all the way through to deployment. We also covered key features of each of the most important libraries in the Python scientific stack.

We will now take this knowledge and these lessons and begin to apply them to create unique and useful machine learning applications. In the next chapter, we'll see how we can apply regression modeling to find a cheap apartment. Let's get started!

2

Build an App to Find Underpriced Apartments

In the previous chapter, we learned the essentials for working with data. We'll now apply this knowledge to build our first machine learning application. We'll begin with a minimal but practical example: building an application to identify underpriced apartments.

If you've ever searched for an apartment, you will appreciate how frustrating the process can be. Not only is it time-consuming, but even when you do find an apartment that you like, how do you know if it's the *right* apartment?

You likely have a target budget and location in mind. However, if you are anything like me, you are also willing to make a few trade-offs. For example, I live in New York City, and being near an amenity like the subway is a big plus. But how much is that *really* worth? Should I trade being in a building with an elevator for being closer to the train? How many minutes of walking to the train is worth walking up a flight up stairs? When renting, there are dozens of questions like this to consider. So how might we use machine learning to help us make these decisions?

We'll spend the remainder of this chapter exploring just that. We won't be able to get answers to all the questions that we have (for reasons that will become clear later), but by the end of the chapter, we'll have created an application that will make finding the right apartment just a little bit easier.

We'll cover the following topics in this chapter:

- Sourcing the apartment listing data
- Inspecting and preparing the data
- Visualizing the data

- Building a regression model
- Forecasting

Sourcing the apartment listing data

In the early 1970s, if you wanted to purchase a stock, you would need to engage a broker who would charge you a fixed commission of nearly 1%. If you wanted to purchase an airline ticket, you would need to contact a travel agent who would earn a commission of around 7%. If you wanted to sell a home, you would contact a real estate agent who would earn a commission of 6%. In 2016, you can do the first two essentially for free. The last one remains as it was in the 1970s.

Why is this the case, and more importantly, what does any of this have to do with machine learning? The reality is, it all comes down to data and who has access to it.

You might assume that you can access troves of real estate listing data quite easily through APIs or by **web-scraping** real estate websites. You would be wrong. Well, wrong if you intend to follow the terms and conditions of these sites. Real estate data is tightly controlled by the **National Association of Realtors** (**NAR**) who run **Multiple Listing Service** (**MLS**). This is a service that aggregates the listing data and is available to brokers and agents only at great expense. So, as you might imagine, they aren't too keen on letting just anyone download it, *en masse*.

This is unfortunate, as opening up this data would undoubtedly lead to useful consumer applications. This seems especially important for a purchase decision that represents the largest portion of a family's budget.

With this said, not all hope is lost. Although getting data directly from MLS providers is forbidden by the terms of service, we can utilize third-party tools to pull down the data.

We'll now take a look at one useful tool for getting the data we need.

Pulling listing data using import.io

There are a number of excellent Python–based libraries for scraping web pages including **requests**, **Beautiful Soup**, and **Scrapy**. We'll explore some of these and more in the chapters that follow, but for our purposes here, we're going to utilize a code-free alternative.

Import.io (`http://www.import.io`) is a free, web-based service that automates web scraping. This is a great option that will allow us to avoid having to create a web scraper from scratch. And fortunately for us, they provide a sample API with real estate listing data from Zillow.com.

The following image is from `http://www.import.io/examples`. Type Zillow.com into the import.io search box to retrieve the sample Zillow data.

Image from https://www.import.io/examples/

The data that they provide is for San Francisco, but we'll be using New York in our example. To change the city, we'll need to replace the URL that they provide in the demo for the URL that lists the data we're interested in.

We can do this by opening a separate browser tab and navigating over to Zillow.com. We need to perform an apartment search there. Let's limit the search to apartments priced between $1,500 and $3,000 in Manhattan.

Once the results are returned, we'll need to copy the Zillow.com URL from browser bar, and paste it in the import.io extraction box in the other tab as shown in the following screenshots.

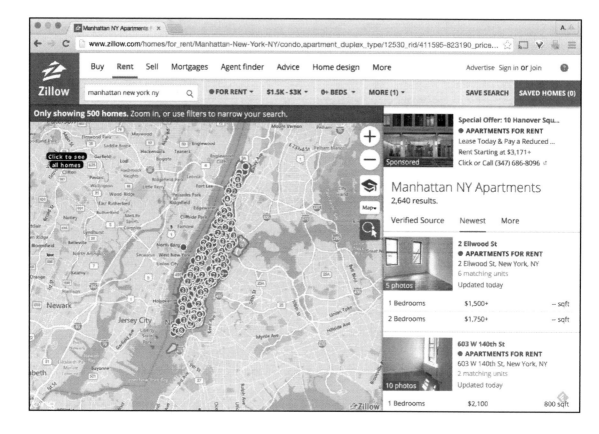

Image from https://www.zillow.com

Copy the URL from the Zillow.com search bar as seen in the preceding image. Paste that in the import.io search bar as seen in the following image.

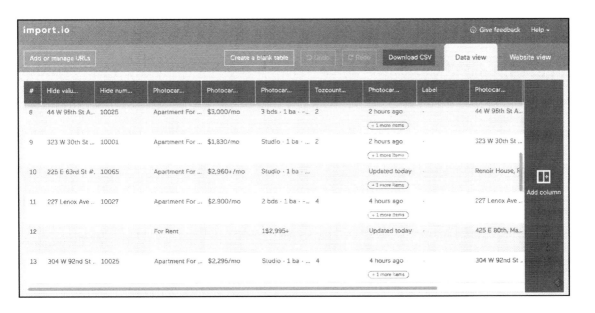

Image from https://www.import.io/

Click on the **Extract data** button in the upper left-hand corner, and you will be presented with a table of results with just the data you want.

We can now easily download our data just by clicking on **Download CSV**. The pop-up dialog box will ask us how many pages we want to download, and as we can see, our search on Zillow returned 2,640 results; we'd need to download 106 pages to get the entire dataset. Import.io will allow us to download only 20, so we'll have to make do with that for now.

Inspecting and preparing the data

We now have a dataset of 500 apartment listings. Let's take a look at what's in our data. We'll begin by importing the data with `pandas` in a Jupyter Notebook:

```
import pandas as pd
import re
import numpy as np
import matplotlib.pyplot as plt

plt.style.use('ggplot')
%matplotlib inline

pd.set_option("display.max_columns", 30)
pd.set_option("display.max_colwidth", 100)
pd.set_option("display.precision", 3)

# Use the file location of your Import.io csv
CSV_PATH = r"/Users/alexcombs/Downloads/magic.csv"

df = pd.read_csv(CSV_PATH)
df.columns
```

The preceding code generates the following output:

```
Index([u'routablemask_link', u'routablemask_link/_text',
       u'routablemask_link/_title', u'routablemask_link_numbers',
       u'routablemask_content', u'imagebadge_value',
       u'imagebadge_value_numbers', u'routable_link', u'routable_link/_text',
       u'routable_link/_title', u'routable_link_numbers', u'listingtype_value',
       u'pricelarge_value', u'pricelarge_value_prices', u'propertyinfo_value',
       u'propertyinfo_value_numbers', u'fineprint_value',
       u'fineprint_value_numbers', u'tozcount_number', u'tozfresh_value',
       u'tablegrouped_values', u'tablegrouped_values_prices', u'_PAGE_NUMBER'],
      dtype='object')
```

The last line, `df.columns`, gives us the column header output for our data. Let's also use `df.head().T` to see a sample of the data. The `.T` syntax at the end of the line transposes our DataFrame to display it vertically:

	0	1	2	3
routablemask_link	http://www.zillow.com/b/2-Ellwood-St-New-York-...	http://www.zillow.com/b/603-W-140th-St-New-Yor...	http://www.zillow.com/homedetails/9-E-129th-St...	http://www.zillow.com/hoi Riversid...
routablemask_link/_text	5 photos	10 photos	NaN	9 photos
routablemask_link/_title	NaN	NaN	NaN	NaN
routablemask_link_numbers	5	10	NaN	9
routablemask_content	NaN	NaN	NaN	NaN
imagebadge_value	5 photos	10 photos	NaN	9 photos
imagebadge_value_numbers	5	10	NaN	9
routable_link	http://www.zillow.com/b/2-Ellwood-St-New-York-...	http://www.zillow.com/b/603-W-140th-St-New-Yor...	http://www.zillow.com/homedetails/9-E-129th-St...	http://www.zillow.com/hoi Riversid...
routable_link/_text	2 Ellwood St	603 W 140th St	9 E 129th St # 1, New York, NY10035	710 Riverside Dr APT 2C, NY10031
routable_link/_title	2 Ellwood St APT 5H, New York, NY Real Estate	603 W 140th St APT 44, New York, NY Real Estate	9 E 129th St # 1, New York, NY Real Estate	710 Riverside Dr APT 2C, Real Estate
routable_link_numbers	2	603; 140	9; 129; 1	710; 2
listingtype_value	Apartments For Rent	Apartments For Rent	Apartment For Rent	Apartment For Rent
pricelarge_value	NaN	NaN	$1,750/mo	$3,000/mo
pricelarge_value_prices	NaN	NaN	1750	3000
propertyinfo_value	2 Ellwood St, New York, NY	603 W 140th St, New York, NY	1 bd • 1 ba	2 bds • 2 ba • 1,016 sqft
propertyinfo_value_numbers	2	603; 140	1; 1	2; 2; 1016
fineprint_value	6 matching units	2 matching units	NaN	NaN
fineprint_value_numbers	6	2	NaN	NaN
tozcount_number	NaN	NaN	48	1
tozfresh_value	Updated today	Updated today	minutes ago	hour ago
tablegrouped_values	1 Bedrooms $1,500+ 1.0 ba -- sqft; 2 Bedrooms ...	1 Bedrooms $2,100 1.0 ba 800 sqft; 2 Bedrooms ...	NaN	NaN
tablegrouped_values_prices	1500; 1750	2100; 2595	NaN	NaN
_PAGE_NUMBER	1	1	1	1

Already, we can see that our data has a number of missing values (**NaN**). It's also going to require a number of operations to normalize this data. The columns in our dataset (or rows in the image above since they are transposed) appear to represent the individual lines of data for each listing on Zillow. It also appears that there are two types of listings—one type is for an individual unit, and the other type is for multiple units.

The two types can be seen in the following image.

routable_link/_text	203 Rivington St	280 E 2nd St # 604, New York, NY10009
routable_link/_title	203 Rivington St APT 5B, New York, NY Real Estate	280 E 2nd St # 604, New York, NY Real Estate
routable_link_numbers	203	280; 2; 604
listingtype_value	Apartments For Rent	Apartment For Rent
pricelarge_value	NaN	$2,850/mo
pricelarge_value_prices	NaN	2850
propertyinfo_value	203 Rivington St, New York, NY	1 bd • 1 ba
propertyinfo_value_numbers	203	1; 1
fineprint_value	2 matching units	NaN
fineprint_value_numbers	2	NaN
tozcount_number	NaN	NaN
tozfresh_value	NaN	NaN
tablegrouped_values	1 Bedrooms $3,0001.0ba750sqft; 2Bedrooms$3,000 1.0 ba -- sqft	NaN
tablegrouped_values_prices	3000; 3000	NaN

The two listings correspond to the images seen on Zillow.com.

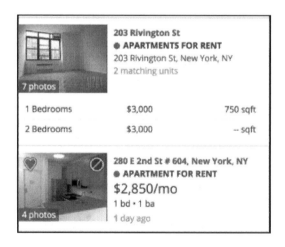

Image from https://www.zillow.com/

The key to splitting these up is the `listingtype_value` header. We'll split up our data into those that are single units, **Apartment for Rent**, versus those that are multiple units, **Apartments for Rent:**

```
# multiple units
mu = df[df['listingtype_value'].str.contains('Apartments For')]

# single units
su = df[df['listingtype_value'].str.contains('Apartment For')]
```

Now let's see the number of listings in each:

```
len(mu)
```

The preceding code generates the following output:

```
161
```

```
len(su)
```

The preceding code generates the following output:

```
339
```

As most of the listings fall in the single unit group, we'll work with this for now.

Next, we need to format the data in a standard structure. For example, at a minimum, we'll need a column for the number of bedrooms, number of bathrooms, square footage, and address.

On examination, we already have a clean price column, `pricelarge_value_prices`. Fortunately, there are no missing values in the column, so we won't lose any listings for lack of data.

The number of bedrooms and bathrooms and the square footage will require some parsing as they are all clumped together into a single column. Let's fix that.

Let's take a look at the column first:

```
su['propertyinfo_value']
```

The preceding code generates the following output:

```
451                                                   2 bds • 1 ba
452                                                    1 bd • 1 ba
453                                                    1 bd • 1 ba
454                                                    1 bd • 1 ba
457    Studio • 1 ba • 540 sqft • 2.00 ac lot • Built 1961
458                                                   2 bds • 1 ba
459                                                Studio • 1 ba
460                                                    1 bd • 1 ba
461                                                Studio • 1 ba
462                                    Studio • 1 ba • Built 1993
464                    Studio • 1 ba • 485 sqft • Built 1962
466                                        2 bds • 1 ba • 600 sqft
467                    Studio • 1 ba • 522 sqft • Built 2013
468                    Studio • 1 ba • 480 sqft • Built 1998
470                                                Studio • 1 ba
471                                                Studio • 1 ba
475                        1 bd • 1 ba • 475 sqft • Built 1900
```

The data seems to always include the number of bedrooms and bathrooms and will occasionally include additional information such as the year. Let's check this assumption before we proceed with parsing:

```
# check the number of rows that do not contain 'bd' or 'Studio'
len(su[~(su['propertyinfo_value'].str.contains('Studio')\
|su['propertyinfo_value'].str.contains('bd'))])
```

The preceding code generates the following output:

```
0
```

Now let's take a look at the following lines of code:

```
# check the number of rows that do not contain 'ba'
len(su[~(su['propertyinfo_value'].str.contains('ba'))])
```

The preceding code generates the following output:

```
6
```

It appears that several rows are missing data for the number of bathrooms. There are a number of reasons why this might be the case, and there are a number of methods we could use to address this. One example would be to fill in, or impute, these missing data points.

The subject of missing data could fill an entire chapter quite easily, if not an entire book, and I do suggest investing the time to understand the topic; it is a critical component of the modeling process. For our purposes here, however, we will assume that the data is randomly missing and will not unduly bias our sample if we drop the listings with missing bathrooms:

```
# select those listings with a bath
no_baths = su[~(su['propertyinfo_value'].str.contains('ba'))]

# exclude those missing bathroom info
sucln = su[~su.index.isin(no_baths.index)]
```

Now we can move on to parse out the bedroom and bathroom information:

```
# split using the bullet
def parse_info(row):
        if not 'sqft' in row:
            br, ba = row.split('')[:2]
            sqft = np.nan
        else:
            br, ba, sqft = row.split('.')[:3]
        return pd.Series({'Beds': br, 'Baths': ba, 'Sqft': sqft})

attr = sucln['propertyinfo_value'].apply(parse_info)

attr
```

The preceding code generates the following output:

	Baths	Beds	Sqft
2	1 ba	1 bd	NaN
3	2 ba	2 bds	1,016 sqft
4	1 ba	Studio	NaN
5	1 ba	2 bds	NaN
7	1 ba	2 bds	NaN
10	1 ba	1 bd	NaN
11	1 ba	1 bd	496 sqft
12	1 ba	Studio	NaN
13	1 ba	1 bd	NaN
17	1 ba	1 bd	NaN
18	1 ba	Studio	NaN

What did we do here? We ran the `apply` function on our **propertyinfo_value** column. This then returned a DataFrame with columns for each of the individual apartment attributes. We have a couple of additional steps to go before we're finished. We need to remove the strings (`bd`, `ba`, and `sqft`) from the values, and we need to join this new DataFrame back to our original data. Let's do this now:

```
#remove the strings from our values
attr_cln = attr.applymap(lambda x: x.strip().split(' ')[0] if
isinstance(x,str) else np.nan)

attr_cln
```

The preceding code generates the following output:

	Baths	Beds	Sqft
2	1	1	NaN
3	2	2	1,016
4	1	Studio	NaN
5	1	2	NaN
7	1	2	NaN
10	1	1	NaN
11	1	1	496
12	1	Studio	NaN
13	1	1	NaN
17	1	1	NaN
18	1	Studio	NaN

Let's take a look at the following code:

```
sujnd = sucln.join(attr_cln)

sujnd.T
```

The preceding code generates the following output:

	2	3	4
routablemask_link	http://www.zillow.com/homedetails/9-E-129th-St-1-New-York-NY-10035/2100761096_zpid/	http://www.zillow.com/homedetails/710-Riverside-Dr-APT-2C-New-York-NY-10031/124451755_zpid/	http://www.zillow.com/homedetails/413-E-84th-St-APT-8-New-York-NY-10028/2100761260_zpid/
routablemask_link/_text	NaN	9 photos	5 photos
routablemask_link/_title	NaN	NaN	NaN
routablemask_link_numbers	NaN	9	5
routablemask_content	NaN	NaN	NaN
imagebadge_value	NaN	9 photos	5 photos
imagebadge_value_numbers	NaN	9	5
routable_link	http://www.zillow.com/homedetails/9-E-129th-St-1-New-York-NY-10035/2100761096_zpid/	http://www.zillow.com/homedetails/710-Riverside-Dr-APT-2C-New-York-NY-10031/124451755_zpid/	http://www.zillow.com/homedetails/413-E-84th-St-APT-8-New-York-NY-10028/2100761260_zpid/
routable_link/_text	9 E 129th St # 1, New York, NY 10035	710 Riverside Dr APT 2C, New York, NY 10031	413 E 84th St APT 8, New York, NY 10028
routable_link/_title	9 E 129th St # 1, New York, NY Real Estate	710 Riverside Dr APT 2C, New York, NY Real Estate	413 E 84th St APT 8, New York, NY Real Estate
routable_link_numbers	9; 129; 1	710; 2	413; 84; 8
listingtype_value	Apartment For Rent	Apartment For Rent	Apartment For Rent
pricelarge_value	$1,750/mo	$3,000/mo	$2,300/mo
pricelarge_value_prices	1750	3000	2300
propertyinfo_value	1 bd • 1 ba	2 bds • 2 ba • 1,016 sqft	Studio • 1 ba
propertyinfo_value_numbers	1; 1	2; 2; 1016	1
fineprint_value	NaN	NaN	NaN
fineprint_value_numbers	NaN	NaN	NaN
tozcount_number	48	1	2
tozfresh_value	minutes ago	hour ago	hours ago
tablegrouped_values	NaN	NaN	NaN
tablegrouped_values_prices	NaN	NaN	NaN
_PAGE_NUMBER	1	1	1
Baths	1	2	1
Beds	1	2	Studio
Sqft	NaN	1,016	NaN

At this point, our dataset is starting to come together. We'll be able to test assumptions about the value of the apartments based on the number of bedrooms, bathrooms and square footage. But as they say, real estate is all about location. Let's take the same approach that we used before to parse out the apartments' attributes and apply this to the address.

We'll also try to extract the floor information where we can. We assume that in a pattern where a letter follows a number, the number represents the floor of the building:

```
# parse out zip, floor
def parse_addy(r):
    so_zip = re.search(', NY (\d+)', r)
    so_flr = re.search('(?:APT|#)\s+(\d+)[A-Z]+,', r)
    if so_zip:
        zipc = so_zip.group(1)
    else:
        zipc = np.nan
    if so_flr:
        flr = so_flr.group(1)
    else:
        flr = np.nan
    return pd.Series({'Zip':zipc, 'Floor': flr})

flrzip = sujnd['routable_link/_text'].apply(parse_addy)

suf = sujnd.join(flrzip)

suf.T
```

The preceding code generates the following output:

	2	3	4
routablemask_link	http://www.zillow.com/homedetails/9-E-129th-St-1-New-York-NY-10035/2100761096_zpid/	http://www.zillow.com/homedetails/710-Riverside-Dr-APT-2C-New-York-NY-10031/124451755_zpid/	http://www.zillow.com/homedetails/413-E-84th-St-APT-8-New-York-NY-10028/2100761260_zpid/
routablemask_link/_text	NaN	9 photos	5 photos
routablemask_link/_title	NaN	NaN	NaN
routablemask_link_numbers	NaN	9	5
routablemask_content	NaN	NaN	NaN
imagebadge_value	NaN	9 photos	5 photos
imagebadge_value_numbers	NaN	9	5
routable_link	http://www.zillow.com/homedetails/9-E-129th-St-1-New-York-NY-10035/2100761096_zpid/	http://www.zillow.com/homedetails/710-Riverside-Dr-APT-2C-New-York-NY-10031/124451755_zpid/	http://www.zillow.com/homedetails/413-E-84th-St-APT-8-New-York-NY-10028/2100761260_zpid/
routable_link/_text	9 E 129th St # 1, New York, NY10035	710 Riverside Dr APT 2C, New York, NY10031	413 E 84th St APT 8, New York, NY10028
routable_link/_title	9 E 129th St # 1, New York, NY Real Estate	710 Riverside Dr APT 2C, New York, NY Real Estate	413 E 84th St APT 8, New York, NY Real Estate
routable_link_numbers	9; 129; 1	710; 2	413; 84; 8
listingtype_value	Apartment For Rent	Apartment For Rent	Apartment For Rent
pricelarge_value	$1,750/mo	$3,000/mo	$2,300/mo
pricelarge_value_prices	1750	3000	2300
propertyinfo_value	1 bd · 1 ba	2 bds · 2 ba · 1,016 sqft	Studio · 1 ba
propertyinfo_value_numbers	1; 1	2; 2; 1016	1
fineprint_value	NaN	NaN	NaN
fineprint_value_numbers	NaN	NaN	NaN
tozcount_number	48	1	2
tozfresh_value	minutes ago	hour ago	hours ago
tablegrouped_values	NaN	NaN	NaN
tablegrouped_values_prices	NaN	NaN	NaN
_PAGE_NUMBER	1	1	1
Baths	1	2	1
Beds	1	2	Studio
Sqft	NaN	1,016	NaN
Floor	NaN	2	NaN
Zip	10035	10031	10028

As you can see, we were able to successfully parse out the floor and ZIP information where present. This gave us 320 ZIP codes of the 333 listings and 164 floors.

One last bit of clean up, and we'll be ready to begin examining our dataset.

```
# we'll reduce the data down to the columns of interest
sudf = suf[['pricelarge_value_prices', 'Beds', 'Baths', 'Sqft', 'Floor',
'Zip']]

# we'll also clean up the weird column name and reset our index
sudf.rename(columns={'pricelarge_value_prices':'Rent'}, inplace=True)

sudf.reset_index(drop=True, inplace=True)

sudf
```

The preceding code generates the following output:

	Rent	Beds	Baths	Sqft	Floor	Zip
0	1750	1	1	NaN	NaN	10035
1	3000	2	2	1,016	2	10031
2	2300	Studio	1	NaN	NaN	10028
3	2500	2	1	NaN	6	10035
4	2800	2	1	NaN	NaN	10012
5	2490	1	1	NaN	4	10036
6	2750	1	1	496	5	10021
7	2150	Studio	1	NaN	3	10024
8	2875	1	1	NaN	2	10023
9	2225	1	1	NaN	4	10036
10	2450	Studio	1	NaN	4	10014

Analyzing the data

At this point, our data is in the format that we need in order to begin our analysis. We'll begin by looking at some summary statistics:

```
sudf.describe()
```

The preceding code generates the following output:

	Rent
count	333.000000
mean	2492.627628
std	366.882478
min	1500.000000
25%	2200.000000
50%	2525.000000
75%	2800.000000
max	3000.000000

Here we see the statistical breakdown of the rent. Don't forget that we selected only the apartments priced between $1,500 and $3,000 a month in our original data pull from Zillow. One thing that we can't see here is the average number of bedrooms and bathrooms or the average floor. We have two problems causing this. The first relates to the bedrooms. We need all numerical data to get the stats. We can fix this by calling a studio apartment what it really is, a zero-bedroom apartment:

```
# we'll replace 'Studio' with 0 where present
sudf.loc[:,'Beds'] = sudf['Beds'].map(lambda x: 0 if 'Studio' in x else x)

sudf
```

The preceding code generates the following output:

	Rent	Beds	Baths	Sqft	Floor	Zip
0	1750	1	1	NaN	NaN	10035
1	3000	2	2	1,016	2	10031
2	2300	0	1	NaN	NaN	10028
3	2500	2	1	NaN	6	10035
4	2800	2	1	NaN	NaN	10012
5	2490	1	1	NaN	4	10036
6	2750	1	1	496	5	10021
7	2150	0	1	NaN	3	10024
8	2875	1	1	NaN	2	10023
9	2225	1	1	NaN	4	10036
10	2450	0	1	NaN	4	10014

This fixes our first problem, but we still have another problem. Any columns that we want statistical data for have to have a numeric datatype. As you can see in the following screenshot, this isn't the case:

```
sudf.info()
```

The preceding code generates the following output:

```
<class 'pandas.core.frame.DataFrame'>
Int64Index: 333 entries, 0 to 332
Data columns (total 6 columns):
Rent      333 non-null float64
Beds      333 non-null object
Baths     333 non-null object
Sqft      108 non-null object
Floor     164 non-null object
Zip       320 non-null object
dtypes: float64(1), object(5)
memory usage: 18.2+ KB
```

We can fix this by changing the datatype as shown in the following code:

```
# let's fix the datatype for the columns
sudf.loc[:,'Rent'] = sudf['Rent'].astype(int)
sudf.loc[:,'Beds'] = sudf['Beds'].astype(int)

# half baths require a float
sudf.loc[:,'Baths'] = sudf['Baths'].astype(float)

# with NaNs we need float, but we have to replace commas first
sudf.loc[:,'Sqft'] = sudf['Sqft'].str.replace(',','')

sudf.loc[:,'Sqft'] = sudf['Sqft'].astype(float)
sudf.loc[:,'Floor'] = sudf['Floor'].astype(float)
```

Let's execute the following line of code and look at the results:

```
sudf.info()
```

The preceding code generates the following output:

```
<class 'pandas.core.frame.DataFrame'>
Int64Index: 333 entries, 0 to 332
Data columns (total 6 columns):
Rent       333 non-null int64
Beds       333 non-null int64
Baths      333 non-null float64
Sqft       108 non-null float64
Floor      164 non-null float64
Zip        320 non-null object
dtypes: float64(3), int64(2), object(1)
memory usage: 18.2+ KB
```

Let's execute the following line of code so that we finally get our statistics:

```
sudf.describe()
```

The preceding code generates the following output:

	Rent	Beds	Baths	Sqft	Floor
count	333.00	333.00	333.00	108.00	164.00
mean	2492.63	0.82	1.01	528.98	11.20
std	366.88	0.72	0.08	133.05	86.18
min	1500.00	0.00	1.00	280.00	1.00
25%	2200.00	0.00	1.00	447.50	2.00
50%	2525.00	1.00	1.00	512.00	4.00
75%	2800.00	1.00	1.00	600.00	5.00
max	3000.00	3.00	2.00	1090.00	1107.00

Our numbers for rent, bedroom, bathrooms, and square footage all look good, but there seems to be a problem with the `Floor` column. There are a number of very tall buildings in New York, but none I imagine are over 1,000 floors.

A quick look reveals that *APT 1107A* gave us this result. Most likely, this is an 11th floor apartment, but just to be safe and consistent, we'll drop the listing. Fortunately, this was the only listing above the 30th floor, so we appear to be in good shape:

```
# index 318 was the problem listing, so we'll drop it
sudf = sudf.drop([318])

sudf.describe()
```

The preceding code generates the following output:

	Rent	Beds	Baths	Sqft	Floor
count	332.00	332.00	332.00	108.00	163.00
mean	2493.51	0.82	1.01	528.98	4.48
std	367.08	0.72	0.08	133.05	3.86
min	1500.00	0.00	1.00	280.00	1.00
25%	2200.00	0.00	1.00	447.50	2.00
50%	2527.50	1.00	1.00	512.00	4.00
75%	2800.00	1.00	1.00	600.00	5.00
max	3000.00	3.00	2.00	1090.00	32.00

Our data looks good now, so let's continue with the analysis. Let's pivot the data to first examine the price by the ZIP code and number of bedrooms. Pandas has a `.pivot_table()` function that makes this easy:

```
sudf.pivot_table('Rent', 'Zip', 'Beds', aggfunc='mean')
```

The preceding code generates the following output:

Beds	0.0	1.0	2.0	3.0
Zip				
10001	2737.50	NaN	NaN	NaN
10002	2283.44	2422.51	2792.65	NaN
10003	2109.89	2487.81	2525.00	NaN
10004	2798.75	2850.00	NaN	NaN
10005	2516.00	NaN	NaN	NaN
10006	2611.00	2788.00	NaN	NaN
10009	2200.91	2568.44	2530.00	NaN
10010	NaN	2299.00	2940.00	NaN
10011	2774.67	2852.00	2595.00	NaN
10012	2547.00	2744.91	2581.67	NaN
10013	2709.29	2584.44	2650.00	NaN
10014	2450.00	NaN	NaN	NaN
10016	2615.00	2450.00	NaN	NaN
10017	NaN	2733.33	NaN	NaN
10019	2195.00	2661.67	2925.00	NaN
10021	1900.00	2388.33	2500.00	NaN
10022	2170.00	NaN	NaN	NaN
10023	2165.00	2773.33	NaN	NaN
10024	2322.50	2621.50	NaN	NaN
10025	2500.00	NaN	NaN	NaN
10026	NaN	2800.00	NaN	NaN
10027	NaN	1850.00	NaN	NaN
10028	2100.00	2333.33	NaN	NaN
10029	1597.50	2097.50	2650.00	NaN
10031	NaN	NaN	2531.25	2700

This operation lets us view the mean price by the ZIP code. As you can see, as we add to the number of bedrooms, we see fewer listings—as evidenced by the NaN values. To explore this further, we can pivot on the count of listings:

```
sudf.pivot_table('Rent', 'Zip', 'Beds', aggfunc='count')
```

The preceding code generates the following output:

Beds	0.0	1.0	2.0	3.0
Zip				
10001	2	NaN	NaN	NaN
10002	16	39	17	NaN
10003	9	16	2	NaN
10004	4	1	NaN	NaN
10005	4	NaN	NaN	NaN
10006	4	1	NaN	NaN
10009	11	34	8	NaN
10010	NaN	1	1	NaN
10011	3	1	1	NaN
10012	5	11	3	NaN
10013	7	9	2	NaN
10014	1	NaN	NaN	NaN
10016	3	1	NaN	NaN
10017	NaN	3	NaN	NaN
10019	1	3	1	NaN
10021	1	3	1	NaN
10022	1	NaN	NaN	NaN
10023	3	3	NaN	NaN
10024	6	2	NaN	NaN
10025	1	NaN	NaN	NaN
10026	NaN	2	NaN	NaN
10027	NaN	2	NaN	NaN
10028	2	3	NaN	NaN
10029	2	4	1	NaN
10031	NaN	NaN	4	1

As we can see, our data is sparse when viewed at the level of ZIP codes and bedrooms. This is unfortunate; ideally, we would have more data. Despite this, we can still work with what we have.

Let's now move on to examining at our data visually.

Visualizing the data

As the data is based on ZIP codes, the best way to visualize it is with a heat map. If you're unfamiliar with a heat map, it is simply a visualization that represents the data according to a color spectrum. Let's do this now using a Python mapping library called `folium` (`https://github.com/python-visualization/folium`).

Based upon the lack of availability of apartments in the two- and three-bedroom range, let's pare down our dataset to include only studios and one bedrooms:

```
su_lt_two = sudf[sudf['Beds']<2]
```

Now we'll go ahead and create our visualization:

```
import folium

map = folium.Map(location=[40.748817, -73.985428], zoom_start=13)
map.geo_json(geo_path=r'/Users/alexcombs/Downloads/nyc.json',
data=su_lt_two,
            columns=['Zip', 'Rent'],
            key_on='feature.properties.postalCode',
            threshold_scale=[1700.00, 1900.00, 2100.00, 2300.00, 2500.00,
2750.00],
            fill_color='YlOrRd', fill_opacity=0.7, line_opacity=0.2,
            legend_name='Rent (%)',
             reset=True)
map.create_map(path='nyc.html')
```

The preceding code generates the following output:

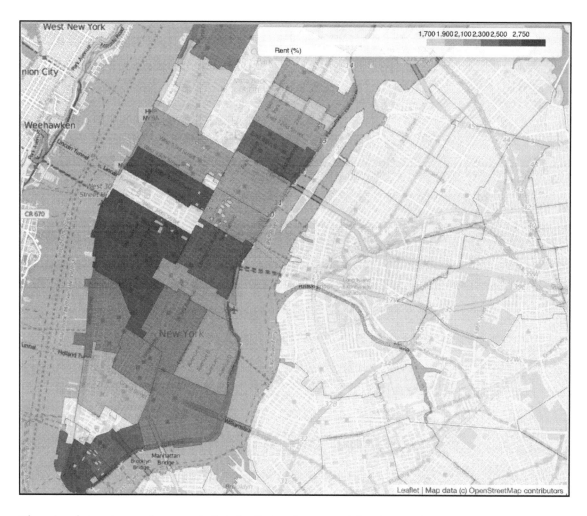

There's a lot going on here, so let's take it step by step. After importing `folium`, we create a `.Map()` object. We need to pass in coordinates and a zoom level to center the map. I did a Google search for the coordinates of the Empire State Building (you'll need to flip the sign on the longitude) and adjusted the zoom to get it centered where I wanted it.

The next line requires something called a GeoJSON file. This is an open format to represent geographic attributes. I found one by searching for NYC GeoJSON files—specifically ones with ZIP code mappings. Once you have the GeoJSON file passed in with the ZIP codes, you need to pass in your DataFrame.

Then you'll need to reference the key column (`Zip` in this case) as well as the column that you wish to use for the heat map. In our case, we'll use median rent. The other options determine the color pallette, values where the colors change, and certain other parameters to adjust the legend and coloring. Finally, the last line determines the name of the output file.

 If you are using this on your local machine, you may run into a problem using Chrome. The shading will appear not to work. Chrome rejects it as a cross-origin request, and because of this, you won't be able to see the heat map overlay. Internet Explorer and Safari should work.

With the heat map completed, we can begin to get a sense of which areas have higher or lower rents. This can help when targeting a particular area to rent, but let's take our analysis deeper using regression modeling.

Modeling the data

Let's begin using our one- and two-bedroom dataset. We're going to examine the effect that the ZIP code and number of bedrooms have on the rental price. We'll use two packages here: the first, `statsmodels`, we discussed briefly in the previous chapter, but the second package, `patsy` (`https://patsy.readthedocs.org/en/latest/index.html`), makes working with `statsmodels` easier. Patsy allows the use of R-style formulas when running a regression.

Let's do this now:

```
import patsy
import statsmodels.api as sm

f = 'Rent ~ Zip + Beds'
y, X = patsy.dmatrices(f, su_lt_two, return_type='dataframe')

results = sm.OLS(y, X).fit()
print(results.summary())
```

The preceding code generates the following output:

```
                          OLS Regression Results
==============================================================================
Dep. Variable:                   Rent   R-squared:                       0.377
Model:                            OLS   Adj. R-squared:                  0.283
Method:                 Least Squares   F-statistic:                     4.034
Date:                Sat, 31 Oct 2015   Prob (F-statistic):           1.21e-10
Time:                        13:44:15   Log-Likelihood:                -1856.8
No. Observations:                 262   AIC:                             3784.
Df Residuals:                     227   BIC:                             3908.
Df Model:                          34
==============================================================================
                 coef    std err          t      P>|t|      [95.0% Conf. Int.]
------------------------------------------------------------------------------
Intercept     2737.5000    219.893     12.449      0.000     2304.207  3170.793
Zip[T.10002]  -503.2729    226.072     -2.226      0.027     -948.740   -57.806
Zip[T.10003]  -519.1638    230.290     -2.254      0.025     -972.943   -65.384
Zip[T.10004]    29.8051    260.334      0.114      0.909     -483.175   542.785
Zip[T.10005]  -221.5000    269.313     -0.822      0.412     -752.174   309.174
Zip[T.10006]  -132.7949    260.334     -0.510      0.610     -645.775   380.185
Zip[T.10009]  -416.4142    227.231     -1.833      0.068     -864.166    31.338
Zip[T.10010]  -646.9746    383.461     -1.687      0.093    -1402.572   108.623
Zip[T.10011]     4.3813    269.543      0.016      0.987     -526.746   535.508
Zip[T.10012]  -197.7638    235.233     -0.841      0.401     -661.283   265.755
Zip[T.10013]  -215.7045    234.573     -0.920      0.359     -677.924   246.515
Zip[T.10014]  -287.5000    380.867     -0.755      0.451    -1037.986   462.986
Zip[T.10016]  -215.8687    269.543     -0.801      0.424     -746.996   315.258
Zip[T.10017]  -212.6413    287.352     -0.740      0.460     -778.860   353.577
Zip[T.10019]  -348.8560    271.376     -1.286      0.200     -883.594   185.882
Zip[T.10021]  -627.6060    271.376     -2.313      0.022    -1162.344   -92.868
Zip[T.10022]  -567.5000    380.867     -1.490      0.138    -1317.986   182.986
Zip[T.10023]  -372.5707    254.885     -1.462      0.145     -874.814   129.673
Zip[T.10024]  -392.3687    246.100     -1.594      0.112     -877.302    92.564
Zip[T.10025]  -237.5000    380.867     -0.624      0.534     -987.986   512.986
Zip[T.10026]  -145.9746    314.148     -0.465      0.643     -764.994   473.045
Zip[T.10027] -1095.9746    314.148     -3.489      0.001    -1714.994  -476.955
Zip[T.10028]  -622.5848    261.550     -2.380      0.018    -1137.960  -107.209
Zip[T.10029]  -945.6498    255.640     -3.699      0.000    -1449.382  -441.918
Zip[T.10033] -1120.9746    383.461     -2.923      0.004    -1876.572  -365.377
Zip[T.10035]  -983.8560    271.376     -3.625      0.000    -1518.594  -449.118
Zip[T.10036]  -321.4831    285.429     -1.126      0.261     -883.912   240.946
Zip[T.10037] -1130.9746    314.148     -3.600      0.000    -1749.994  -511.955
Zip[T.10038]  -176.8475    240.922     -0.734      0.464     -651.578   297.883
Zip[T.10040] -1395.9746    383.461     -3.640      0.000    -2151.572  -640.377
Zip[T.10065]  -564.5848    261.550     -2.159      0.032    -1079.960   -49.209
Zip[T.10075]  -529.2373    270.232     -1.958      0.051    -1061.721     3.247
Zip[T.10280]   -19.4915    254.345     -0.077      0.939     -520.670   481.687
Zip[T.11229]  -350.9746    383.461     -0.915      0.361    -1106.572   404.623
Beds           208.4746     44.528      4.682      0.000      120.734   296.215
==============================================================================
Omnibus:                        3.745   Durbin-Watson:                   2.039
Prob(Omnibus):                  0.154   Jarque-Bera (JB):                2.546
Skew:                          -0.012   Prob(JB):                        0.280
Kurtosis:                       2.518   Cond. No.                         84.2
==============================================================================
```

With these few lines of code, we have just run our first machine learning algorithm.

 While most people don't tend to think of linear regression as machine learning, that's exactly what it is. Linear regression is a type of supervised machine learning. Supervised, in this context, simply means that we provide the output values for our training set.

Let's now unpack what happened here. After our imports, we have two lines that relate to the `patsy` module. The first line is the formula that we will be using. On the left-hand side (before the tilde) is our response or dependent variable, `Rent`. On the right-hand side, we have our independent or predictor variables, `Zip` and `Beds`. This formula simply means that we want to know how the ZIP code and number of bedrooms will affect the rental price.

Our formula is then passed to `patsy.dmatrices()` along with our DataFrame containing the corresponding column names. Patsy is then set to return a DataFrame with our X matrix of predictor variables and a y vector with our response variable. These are then passed to `sm.OLS()`, which we also call `.fit()` on to run our model. Finally, we print out the results of the model.

As you can see, there is a lot of information provided in the result output. Let's begin by looking at the topmost section. We can see that the model included 262 observations, it has an adjusted $R2$ of .283, and it is significant with an `F-statistic` probability of 1.21e-10. What is the significance of this? It means that we have created a model that is able to explain about a third of the variance in price just using bedrooms and the ZIP code. Is this a good result? In order to better answer this, let's now look at the center section of the output.

The center section provides us with information on each of the independent variables in our model. From left to right, we can see the following information: the variable, variable's coefficient in the model, standard error, *t*-statistic, *p*-value for the *t*-statistic, and 95% confidence interval.

What does all of this tell us? If we look at the *p*-value column, we can determine if our individual variables are statistically significant. Statistically significant in a regression model means that the relationship between an independent variable and response variable is unlikely to have occurred by chance. Typically, statisticians use a *p*-value of .05 when determining this. A .05 p-value means that the results that we see would occur by chance only 5% of the time. In terms of our output here, the number of bedrooms are clearly significant. What about the ZIP codes?

The first thing to notice here is that our intercept represents the 10001 ZIP code. When modeling a linear regression, an intercept is needed. The intercept is simply where the regression line meets the *y* axis. Statsmodels will automatically select one of the predictor variables to use as the intercept. Here, it decided on Chelsea (10001).

Like the number of bedrooms, the intercept is statistically significant. However, what about the other ZIP codes?

For the most part, they are not significant. However, let's take a look at a few that are. The ZIP codes—10027, 10029, and 10035—are all highly significant and all have highly negative confidence intervals. This tells us that they will tend to have a lower rental price than a similarly equipped apartment in Chelsea.

As Chelsea is considered a *posh* area in New York, and these three neighborhoods are in or around the Harlem area – which certainly would not be considered posh – the model fits with our real-world intuitions.

Let's now use our model to make a number of forecasts.

Forecasting

Let's say that we've decided, from our prior analysis, that we are interested in three particular ZIP codes: `10002`, `10003`, and `10009`. How can we use our model to determine what we should pay for a given apartment? Let's now take a look.

First, we need to know what the inputs to the model looked like so that we can know how to enter a new set of values. Let's take a look at our X matrix:

```
X.head()
```

The preceding code generates the following output:

	intercept	Zip[T.10002]	Zip[T.10003]	Zip[T.10004]	Zip[T.10005]	Zip[T.10006]	Zip[T.10009]	Zip[T.10010]	Zip[T.10011]	Zip[T.10012]
0	1	0	0	0	0	0	0	0	0	0
2	1	0	0	0	0	0	0	0	0	0
5	1	0	0	0	0	0	0	0	0	0
6	1	0	0	0	0	0	0	0	0	0
7	1	0	0	0	0	0	0	0	0	0

What we can see is that our input is coded with what is called a **dummy variable**. To represent a ZIP code feature, as it is not numerical, dummy coding is used. If the apartment is in `10003`, then this column will be coded as `1` while all the other ZIP codes are coded as zero. Beds will be coded according to the actual number as they are numerical. So, lets' now create our own input row to predict:

```
to_pred_idx = X.iloc[0].index
to_pred_zeros = np.zeros(len(to_pred_idx))
tpdf = pd.DataFrame(to_pred_zeros, index=to_pred_idx, columns=['value'])

tpdf
```

The preceding code generates the following output:

	value
Intercept	0
Zip[T.10002]	0
Zip[T.10003]	0
Zip[T.10004]	0
Zip[T.10005]	0
Zip[T.10006]	0
Zip[T.10009]	0
Zip[T.10010]	0
Zip[T.10011]	0
Zip[T.10012]	0
Zip[T.10013]	0
Zip[T.10014]	0
Zip[T.10016]	0
Zip[T.10017]	0

We have just used the index from the X matrix and filled in the data all with zeros. Let's now fill in our values. We going to price a one-bedroom apartment in the 10009 area code:

```
tpdf.loc['Intercept'] = 1
tpdf.loc['Beds'] = 1
tpdf.loc['Zip[T.10009]'] = 1

tpdf
```

The intercept value for a linear regression must always be set to 1 for the model to return accurate statistical values.

The preceding code generates the following output:

	value
Intercept	1
Zip[T.10002]	0
Zip[T.10003]	0
Zip[T.10004]	0
Zip[T.10005]	0
Zip[T.10006]	0
Zip[T.10009]	1
Zip[T.10010]	0
Zip[T.10011]	0
Zip[T.10012]	0

Here we can see the intercept and the 10009 zip code has been set to 1.

And here, we can see the number of bedrooms has been set to 1 as well.

Zip[T.10029]	0
Zip[T.10033]	0
Zip[T.10035]	0
Zip[T.10036]	0
Zip[T.10037]	0
Zip[T.10038]	0
Zip[T.10040]	0
Zip[T.10065]	0
Zip[T.10075]	0
Zip[T.10280]	0
Zip[T.11229]	0
Beds	1

We set our features to the appropriate values, so let's now use our model to return a prediction:

```
results.predict(tpdf['value'])
```

The preceding code generates the following output:

```
2529.5604669841355
```

Remember that `results` was the variable name we saved our model to. This model object has a `.predict()` method, which we call with our input values. As you can see, the model returns a predicted value.

What if we want to add another bedroom?

Let's change our inputs and see:

```
tpdf['value'] = 0
tpdf.loc['Intercept'] = 1
tpdf.loc['Beds'] = 2
tpdf.loc['Zip[T.10009]'] = 1

tpdf
```

The preceding code generates the following output:

Zip[T.10035]	0
Zip[T.10036]	0
Zip[T.10037]	0
Zip[T.10038]	0
Zip[T.10040]	0
Zip[T.10065]	0
Zip[T.10075]	0
Zip[T.10280]	0
Zip[T.11229]	0
Beds	2

We can see that bedrooms has been updated to 2.

Now we'll run the prediction again:

```
results.predict(tpdf['value'])
```

The preceding code generates the following output:

```
2738.035104645339
```

Looks like that extra bedroom will cost us about $200 more a month. What if we choose 10002 instead? Let's implement this in our code:

```
tpdf['value'] = 0
tpdf.loc['Intercept'] = 1
tpdf.loc['Beds'] = 2
```

```
tpdf.loc['Zip[T.10002]'] = 1

results.predict(tpdf['value'])
```

The preceding code generates the following output:

```
2651.1763504369078
```

According to our model, it appears that we could save some money if we choose the `10002` area over the `10009` area for our two-bedroom apartment.

Extending the model

At this point, we have only examined the relationship between the ZIP code, bedrooms, and rental price. While our model had some explanatory power, we had a minimal dataset and far too few features to adequately examine the complex world of real estate valuation.

Fortunately, however, if we were to add more data and features to the model, we could use the exact same framework to expand our analysis.

Some possible future extensions to explore would be utilizing data for restaurants and bars available from APIs such as Foursquare or Yelp, or walkability and transportation proximity measures from providers such as Walk Score.

There are a number of ways to extend the model, and I suggest that you pursue working on a project, such as by exploring a variety of measures. With more data being released every day, the chance to improve your model can only increase.

Summary

In this chapter, you learned how to acquire data on real estate listings, utilize the functionality of pandas to manipulate and sanitize this data, inspect the data visually with heat maps, and finally, build and use regression modeling to price out an apartment.

At this point, we have just scratched the surface of machine learning. We'll continue to explore different algorithms and applications in the chapters that follow.

In the next chapter, we'll explore how we can use clustering algorithms to find ultra-rare, heavily-discounted airfares.

3

Build an App to Find Cheap Airfares

Let's talk about mistakes. They're a part of life; everyone makes them – even airlines.

In 2014, I happened to be reading my Twitter feed one afternoon when one of the accounts I follow tweeted that a major U.S. airline had fares to Europe that were significantly below what would be expected. At that time, the cheapest fare from New York to Vienna was around $800. However, the advertised fares for a select number of dates were between $350 and $450. This seemed too good to be true, but it wasn't. I had chanced upon what's known in the industry as a *mistake fare*.

In the super-secretive society of travel hackers and mileage junkies, it's well-known that airlines occasionally – and accidentally – post fares that exclude fuel surcharges. Remarkably, this isn't the only type of mistake that they make. You might expect that advanced algorithms would be updating fares for each flight, taking into account an enormous number of factors. For the most part, you'd be right. However, due to legacy systems and the complexity of dealing with multiple carriers and multiple jurisdictions, mistakes do occur.

Now that you know these fares exist, how can you get in on them? Machine learning, of course! As they typically last just a few hours before they disappear, we're going to build an application that continually monitors fare pricing. Once an anomalous price appears, our app will generate an alert that we can quickly act on.

We'll cover the following topics in this chapter:

- Sourcing airfare pricing on the Web
- Retrieving fare data with advanced web scraping techniques
- Parsing the Document Object Model to extract prices

- Identifying outlier fares with clustering techniques
- Sending real-time text alerts with IFTTT

Sourcing airfare pricing data

Fortunately, airfare pricing data is easier to obtain than real estate data, so it isn't hard to find. There are both free and paid API sources as well as numerous websites that provide the data. I tested a number of these services, but in the end, there was only one that provided the data in a workable format. This format made it super simple to find the lowest-priced flights months in advance.

Before I tell you which service it is, let me show you the typical flight search interface:

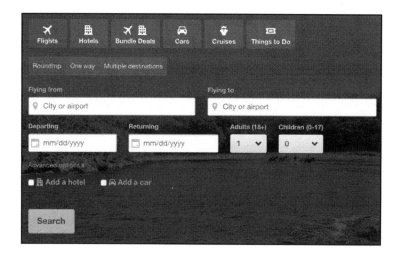

Image from https://www.expedia.com/

The problem with this type of interface for our purposes – and all the APIs have the same fields – is that we would need to run queries for all the dates that we are interested in for every possible trip length for each airport. While possible, it is ugly and would take far too much effort.

Fortunately, there is a better way. There is a little-known tool that Google provides called the **Flight Explorer**. This tool lets you view the lowest cost fares from one region to another over a period of months.

Here is an example of a search for 8-12 day trips from New York to Europe. The cities are returned sorted in order of price, from the lowest cost to highest:

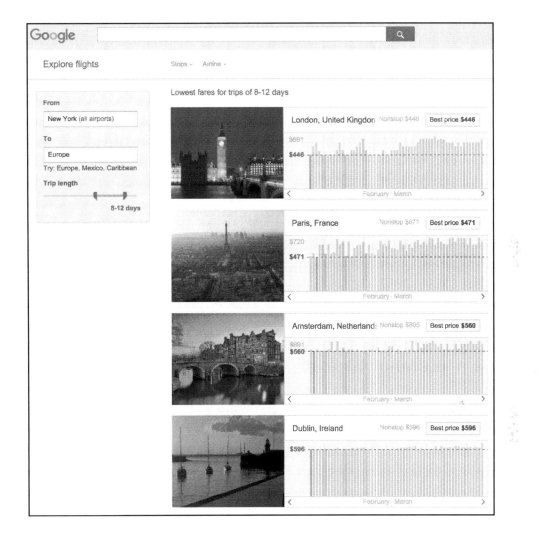

Image from https://www.google.com/flights/explore/

This format is ideal to find mistake fares as the results are returned sorted by price for an entire region over a 60-day period. This ensures that outlier fares surface to the top when they occur.

That's the good news. The bad news is that Google has made pulling down this data programmatically quite challenging. Fortunately, with a bit of clever coding, we can still get the data that we need.

Retrieving the fare data with advanced web scraping techniques

We've seen in the previous chapters how to use the `requests` library to retrieve web pages. As I've said before, it is a fantastic tool, but, unfortunately, won't work for us here. The page that we want to scrape is entirely AJAX-based. Asynchronous JavaScript (AJAX) is a method to retrieve data from a server without having to reload the page. What this means for us is that we'll need to use a browser to retrieve the data. While this might sound like it would require an enormous amount of overhead, there are two libraries that when used together make it a lightweight task.

The two libraries are **Selenium** and PhantomJS. Selenium is a powerful tool to automate web browsers, and PhantomJS is a browser. Why use PhantomJS rather than Firefox or Chrome? PhantomJS is what's known as a **headless browser**. This means that it has no UI. This keeps it lean, making it ideal for what we're trying to do.

 To install PhantomJS, you can download the binaries or source from `http://phantomjs.org/download.html`. As for Selenium, it can be pip-installed.

We'll also need another library called **BeautifulSoup4** to parse the data from the page. If you don't have this installed, you should pip-install this as well.

With this done, let's get started. We'll start out working the Jupyter notebook. Jupyter works best for exploratory analysis. Later, when we've completed our exploration, we'll move on to working in a text editor. Text editors are better for writing code that we want to deploy as an app.

First, we will import the libraries:

```
import pandas as pd
import numpy as np

from selenium import webdriver
from selenium.webdriver.common.desired_capabilities import
DesiredCapabilities
```

```
from bs4 import BeautifulSoup

import matplotlib.pyplot as plt
%matplotlib inline
```

Next, we'll set up the code to instantiate the browser object. It is this object that will pull down the page for us. You can select the airports or regions that you'd like by running a search in your browser and copying the URL. Here, I'm searching for trips between New York airports and several cities in Asia:

```
url =
"https://www.google.com/flights/explore/#explore;f=JFK,EWR,LGA;t=
HND,NRT,TPE,HKG,KIX;s=1;li=8;lx=12;d=2016-04-01"

driver = webdriver.PhantomJS()

dcap = dict(DesiredCapabilities.PHANTOMJS)
dcap["phantomjs.page.settings.userAgent"] = ("Mozilla/5.0
(Macintosh; Intel Mac OS X 10_10_5) AppleWebKit/537.36 (KHTML, like
Gecko) Chrome/46.0.2490.80 Safari/537.36")

driver = webdriver.PhantomJS(desired_capabilities=dcap,
service_args=['--ignore-ssl-errors=true'])

driver.implicitly_wait(20)
driver.get(url)
```

We need to send the receiving server a user agent. You can use the agent I listed here, or you can swap this out for your own agent if you prefer. It becomes important when we get to the parsing stage. If you are using one agent to select **Document Object Model (DOM)** elements in your normal browser and then passing a different agent in your code, you may end up with problems parsing the page as the DOM can be user agent-dependent.

You can find your user agent just by running a Google search for `what is my user agent?`. Copy this information and then use it in the preceding code if you plan on using this for other scrapers.

Once the preceding code has been run, you can use the following line to save a screenshot of the page. Check it to make sure that everything looks good:

```
driver.save_screenshot(r'flight_explorer.png')
```

If all goes as planned, you should see `True` as the output and have a file with the image of the page that you scraped. It should look just like the page in your normal web browser.

Next, we'll move on to parsing the page to extract the pricing information.

Parsing the DOM to extract pricing data

The DOM is the collection of elements that form the structure a web page. If you have ever viewed the source of a web page, you have seen the components of the DOM. They include elements and tags such as `body`, `div`, `class`, and `id`. We'll need to work with these elements to extract the data we need.

Let's take a look at the DOM for our Google page. To see it, right-click on the page and click on **Inspect element**. This should be the same for Firefox or Chrome. This will open the developer tab that allows you to see the page source information. Once this is open, choose the element selector in the upper left corner, and click on one of the price bars to jump to that element.

Image from https://www.google.com/flights/explore/

The first thing that you are likely to notice is that there isn't any pricing data in the `div` tags. If you hover over the bars, a tooltip will display the fare, but this is all done with JavaScript and is not available with the DOM. In fact, the only thing available is the height of the bar that represents the fare. So, how can we get data that isn't there? We deduce it!

The page does give us just enough clues to infer the price using the height of the bars. You'll notice that the one fare listed for each city is the best fare. You can see it to the left-hand side of the bar graph. This `div` provides you with the pricing as text, as shown in the following screenshot:

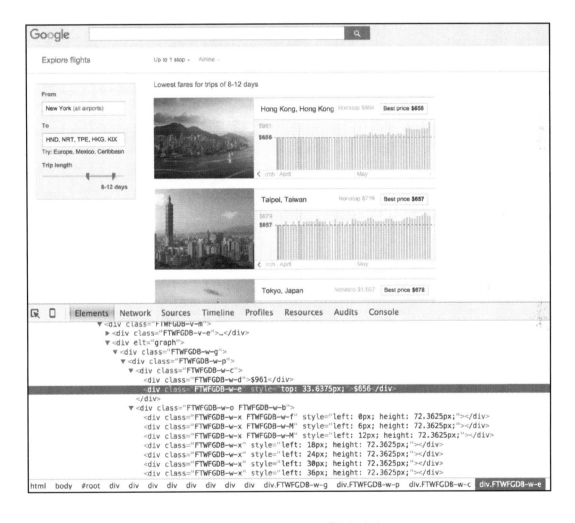

Image from https://www.google.com/flights/explore/

You will also notice that each city has a bar that matches the lowest fare. It's highlighted in a darker shade than the other bars. As it has a unique class that generates this coloring, we can find it. Once we find it, we can use its height divided by its price to determine the price per pixel. Using this, it becomes a simple exercise to derive the price for each flight.

Let's code this now.

The first step is to feed the page source to `BeautifulSoup`:

```
s = BeautifulSoup(driver.page_source, "lxml")
```

We can then retrieve a list of all the best prices:

```
best_price_tags = s.findAll('div', 'FTWFGDB-w-e')
best_prices = []
for tag in best_price_tags:
    best_prices.append(int(tag.text.replace('$','')))
```

As the city with the cheapest fare rises to the top, we can just use it:

```
best_price = best_prices[0]
```

Next, we'll get the list of bar heights for each:

```
best_height_tags = s.findAll('div', 'FTWFGDB-w-f')
best_heights = []
for t in best_height_tags:
    best_heights.append(float(t.attrs['style']\
    .split('height:')[1].replace('px;','')))
```

Again, we'll only need the first one:

```
best_height = best_heights[0]
```

Then we can calculate the price per pixel of the height:

```
pph = np.array(best_price)/np.array(best_height)
```

Next, we'll retrieve the bar heights for all flights in each city:

```
cities = s.findAll('div', 'FTWFGDB-w-o')

hlist=[]
for bar in cities[0]\
    .findAll('div', 'FTWFGDB-w-x'):
    hlist.append(float(bar['style']\
                     .split('height: ')[1]\
                     .replace('px;',''))*pph)
```

```
fares = pd.DataFrame(hlist, columns=['price'])
```

This completed, we now have a DataFrame with the cheapest fare for a two-month period. Let's take a look:

```
fares.min()
```

The preceding code generates the following output:

```
price     656
dtype: float64
```

Our minimum fare should match the one that we see on the page, and it does. Let's now take a look at the full list.

	price
0	656.000000
1	656.000000
2	656.000000
3	656.000000
4	656.000000
5	656.000000
6	656.000000
7	656.000000
8	656.000000
9	656.000000

Everything looks good. We can now move on to setting up our outlier detection.

Identifying outlier fares with clustering techniques

Airfares are updated continually throughout the day. If we're trying to identify fares that are priced well below what they should be priced, how might we do this without machine learning? It seems like it would be fairly simple, but when you start to consider the options available, it quickly becomes more far complex than anticipated.

One option would be to get the prices for every city and set a threshold so that if they fell below that price, you would trigger an alert. This might work, but do you set a percentage alert below the currently lowest price? A strict dollar-level trigger? Then, where exactly do you place it? What if fares naturally decline due to seasonal factors? Maybe you could check each bar for deviation from the median bar. What if prices are nearly flat and then there is a minor drop? Maybe check each bar's height versus its neighboring bars. What if the mistake fare occurs across more than just one day?

As you can see, it's not as simple as it might appear. Given that, how do we avoid the headaches of storing pricing data for each city, dealing with seasonality, and trying to set thresholds? We use a clustering algorithm instead.

There are a number of clustering algorithms available, but for the type of data that we are working with here, we will use an algorithm known as **density-based spatial clustering of applications with noise (DBSCAN)**. It is an exceedingly effective algorithm that tends to identify clusters of points the same way in that humans do. The following image is a visualization taken from scikit-learn's documentation. It demonstrates DBSCAN's effectiveness across a range of different data distributions:

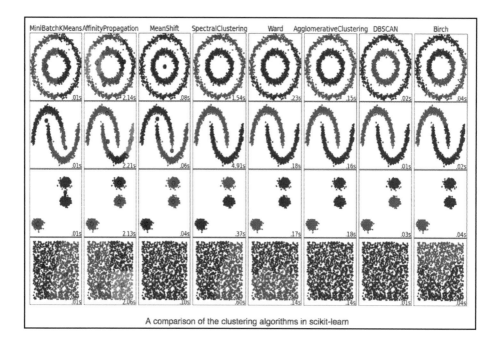

A comparison of the clustering algorithms in scikit-learn

Image from http://scikit-learn.org/stable/auto_examples/cluster/plot_cluster_comparison.html

As you can see, it is quite powerful. Let's now discuss how the algorithm works.

To understand the DBSCAN algorithm, first we need to discuss two parameters that must be set for the algorithm to work. The first parameter is called **epsilon.** This parameter determines the distance two points can be from each other and still be in the same cluster. If epsilon is large, then any two points are more likely to cluster together. The second parameter is called min points. This is the minimum number of points (including the current point) that are required to create a cluster. If min points are one, then every point will be one in a cluster. If min points are greater than one, then it's possible for some points to not be affiliated with any cluster. These then become the **noise**– the N in DBSCAN.

The DBSCAN algorithm proceeds as follows. Randomly select a point from the set of all points. Search epsilon distance in all directions from this point. If min points are within this epsilon distance, all points within epsilon become affiliated with a cluster (the colored areas seen in the preceding image). Repeat the procedure by checking all the new points that were added to the cluster. Continue this until no new points can be added to this current cluster. When this occurs, the first cluster is complete. Now begin again by randomly selecting a new point outside the closed cluster. Repeat this same procedure until no new clusters can be formed.

Now that we have an understanding of how the algorithm works, let's apply it to the airfare data. We'll begin by creating a simple graph of the fares to inspect:

```
fig, ax = plt.subplots(figsize=(10,6))
plt.scatter(np.arange(len(fares['price'])),fares['price'])
```

The output for the preceding code is shown as follows:

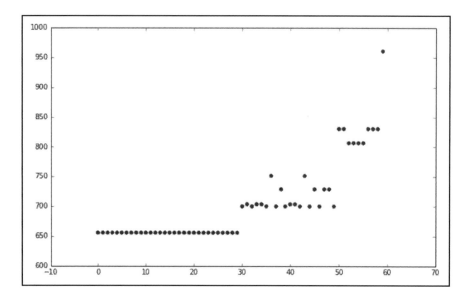

We can see that fares flatline for a number of weeks and then begin to rise dramatically. Most people would likely see this as four major clusters. Let's now set up our code to identify and display the clusters.

First, we will set up a price frame that we can pass to the DBSCAN object:

```
px = [x for x in fares['price']]
ff = pd.DataFrame(px, columns=['fare']).reset_index()
```

Then we'll need to import a couple libraries for the clustering:

```
from sklearn.cluster import DBSCAN
from sklearn.preprocessing import StandardScaler
```

Finally, the following code will apply the DBSCAN algorithm to our fare data and output a visualization:

```
X = StandardScaler().fit_transform(ff)
db = DBSCAN(eps=.5, min_samples=1).fit(X)

labels = db.labels_
clusters = len(set(labels))
unique_labels = set(labels)
colors = plt.cm.Spectral(np.linspace(0, 1, len(unique_labels)))
```

```
plt.subplots(figsize=(12,8))

for k, c in zip(unique_labels, colors):
    class_member_mask = (labels == k)
    xy = X[class_member_mask]
    plt.plot(xy[:, 0], xy[:, 1], 'o', markerfacecolor=c,
            markeredgecolor='k', markersize=14)

plt.title("Total Clusters: {}".format(clusters), fontsize=14,
        y=1.01)
```

Let's unpack this line by line. In the first line, we are utilizing `StandardScaler()`; this object will take our data, subtract the mean from each point, and divide each by the standard deviation. This step gets all of our data on the same basis and readies it for the algorithm. The standardized data is then passed to the DBSCAN object. Here, we are setting the two parameters that we discussed earlier. We set `eps`, or our epsilon distance, equal to .5, and set `min_samples` to 1. The next line sets `labels` equal to the array of the `labels` output from the algorithm. Every point (as `min_points` is set to 1) will be associated with a cluster ID. These clusters will be labeled from 0 to *n-1*, where *n* is the total number of clusters. The next two lines get the total number of clusters and their unique labels, and the line that begins with `colors` generates a color map for our graph. The remainder of the code then sets up our graph by applying a unique color to each cluster and setting a title for the graph with the total number of clusters.

Let's take a look at the output for our fare data:

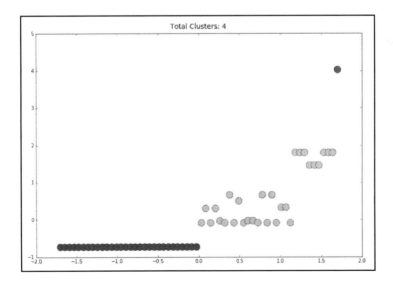

As you can see, the algorithm has identified four distinct clusters, which is exactly what we had hoped for. Now, having just told you how well it worked with these parameters, I'm going to suggest changing them. Why mess with perfection? Well, let's take a look at a few scenarios in which we introduce artificial fares.

With our current fare series and the same parameters, let's introduce a new fare into the mix.

We'll begin by replacing data point #10 in our series. We'll change it from $656 to $600:

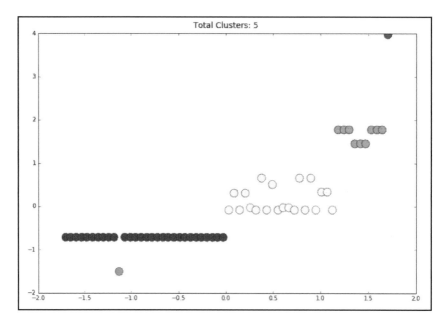

You'll notice that it becomes its own cluster near the bottom of the graph. However, while the fare has clear separation from the other fares, it is not far enough that we would want to be alerted to it.

Let's increase the epsilon parameter so that we are only clustering two groups: typical fares and extraordinary fares.

We'll now keep the same dummy fare, but increase the epsilon to 1.5:

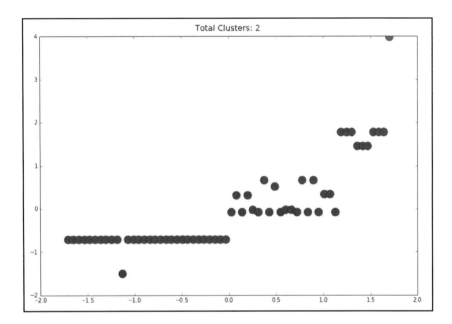

You can see that we now have two clusters. Our $600 fare has been placed in the main cluster, and the fare at the far right-hand side at the top of the graph has been placed in its own cluster. This looks reasonable as the far right-hand side fare is a clear outlier. Let's test this a bit more. How far would we need to drop our dummy fare to have it in its own cluster?

The following screenshot illustrates the results of dropping the dummy fare further.

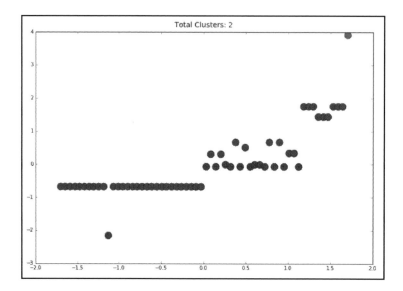

Dropping it to $550, we can see that it is still a part of the primary cluster:

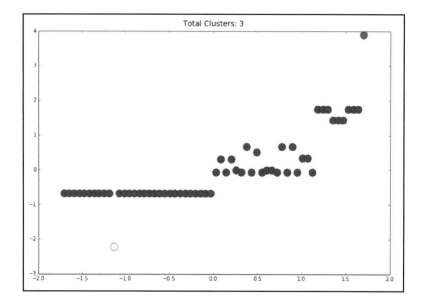

Dropping it to $545 puts it in its own cluster. This seems like a reasonable level, but let's now run a few other scenarios using other cities.

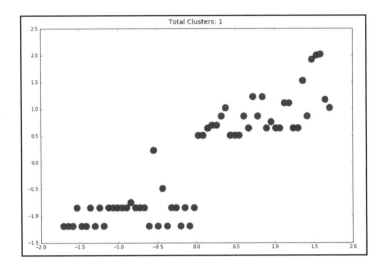

This is the Tokyo Narita Airport series. We have a single cluster, which is what we'd hope. Let's swap in a dummy fare now. We'll swap fare #45 in the series. We'll move it from $970 to $600. This is a major decline – far more than the $111 decline that triggered a new cluster in the other series – but it is clearly within the range of typical prices, so we wouldn't want a new cluster to form:

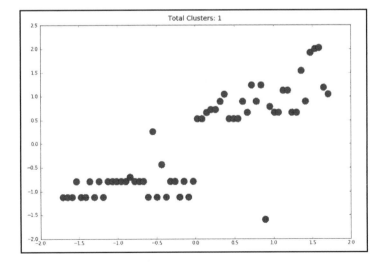

You can see that it didn't. Why is this the case if there is such a large distance between our dummy fare and the two fares to its left and right? This is because we are working with the entire series and not just the immediate neighbors for each point. Most likely, our dummy data point was recruited to the cluster by the points to its left. Let's try one more scenario. We'll swap a fare out to the right – further from our lower left cluster:

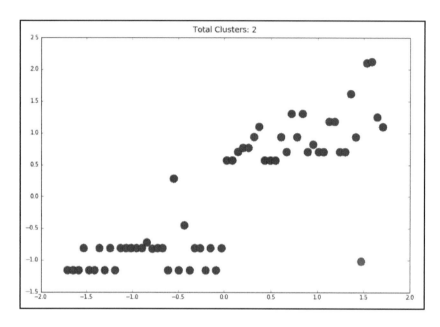

Here we have swapped fare #55 from $1176 to $700. This resulted in a new cluster. The fare is within the range of the other fares in the full series, but it is certainly an outlier at this point. We most likely don't want to be alerted to it, however.

As we don't want to be alerted every time there is more than a single cluster, we need to set up rules for the scenarios where we do want to be alerted.

First, as we are looking for mistake fares, we expect them to be equal to the lowest price displayed. We can group by cluster and retrieve the minimum price:

```
pf = pd.concat([ff, pd.DataFrame(db.labels_,
                           columns=['cluster'])], axis=1)
pf
```

The preceding code generates the following output:

	index	fare	cluster
0	0	678.000000	0
1	1	678.000000	0
2	2	678.000000	0
3	3	732.648361	0
4	4	678.000000	0
5	5	678.000000	0
6	6	732.648361	0
7	7	678.000000	0
8	8	732.648361	0
9	9	678.000000	0

The following code will aggregate by cluster and display the minimum price and count:

```
rf = pf.groupby('cluster')['fare'].agg(['min','count'])
rf
```

The preceding code generates the following output:

	min	count
cluster		
0	678	59
1	700	1

We also expect that the mistake cluster will be smaller than the main cluster. We'll set a limit on the size of our mistake cluster by requiring it to be less than the 10th percentile for count. In this case, it would be less than seven fares. This figure will vary depending on the number and size of clusters, but this should be a workable figure. To see the quantile breakdown, you can use the following line of code:

```
rf.describe([.10,.25,.5,.75,.9])
```

The preceding code generates the following output:

	min	count
count	2.000000	2.000000
mean	689.000000	30.000000
std	15.556349	41.012193
min	678.000000	1.000000
10%	680.200000	6.800000
25%	683.500000	15.500000
50%	689.000000	30.000000
75%	694.500000	44.500000
90%	697.800000	53.200000
max	700.000000	59.000000

Let's add one more condition. Let's set a minimum distance between the lowest priced cluster and the second lowest priced. Doing so will prevent a scenario like the one seen in the following output:

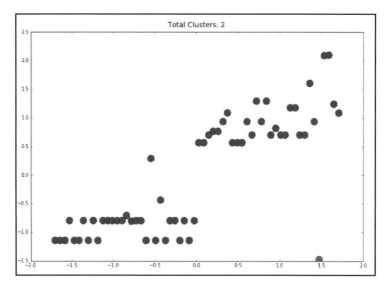

Here the fare is the lowest, but it is just below the range of the other cluster. Setting a minimum distance will cut down the false alerts that we receive. Let's set it at $100 initially.

Now that we have our outlier detection rules, let's move on to how we can put it all together with a real-time fare-alert app.

Sending real-time alerts using IFTTT

To have a chance at getting these cheap fares, we're going to need to know in near real time when they happen. To accomplish this, we'll use a service called **If This Then That (IFTTT)**. This is a free service that allows you to connect a huge number of services together with a series of triggers and actions. Want to save all the pictures that you've liked on Instagram to your iPhone Photos? Want to get an e-mail every time a particular person tweets? Want your Facebook updates posted to Twitter? IFTTT does all of this and more.

To get started with IFTTT:

1. Sign up for and account at `http://www.ifttt.com`
2. Sign up for the Maker channel at `https://ifttt.com/maker`
3. Sign up for the SMS channel at `https://ifttt.com/sms`

The Maker channel allows HTTP requests to be sent and received, and the SMS channel does the same for SMS messages.

Once you've created an account and activated the two channels, click on **My Recipes** from the home page, then click on **Create a Recipe**:

Image from https://ifttt.com/

Then search for and select the **Maker** channel:

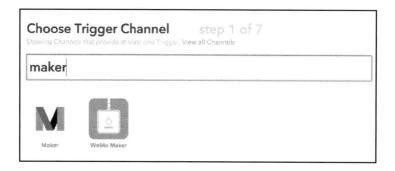

Image from https://ifttt.com/

Next, select **Receive a web request**:

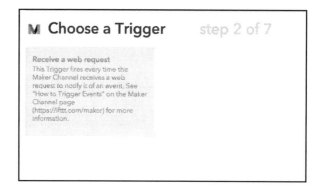

Image from https://ifttt.com/

Then we'll create an event called `fare_alert`:

Image from https://ifttt.com/

Next, we'll set up the **that**:

Image from https://ifttt.com/

Search for SMS and select it. Then choose **Send me an SMS**:

Image from https://ifttt.com/

After this, we'll fill in the field with `fare_alert`. Make sure to replace the curly braces:

Image from https://ifttt.com/

Once this is complete, you can customize your message with the city and airfare:

Image from https://ifttt.com/

To test the setup, go to `http://www.ifttt.com/maker`, and click on **How to Trigger Events**. Then fill in `fare_alert` for event, and place the test city and fare in the `value1` and `value2` boxes:

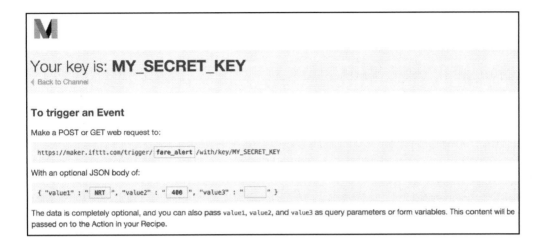

Your key is: **MY_SECRET_KEY**
◄ Back to Channel

To trigger an Event

Make a POST or GET web request to:

`https://maker.ifttt.com/trigger/` `fare_alert` `/with/key/MY_SECRET_KEY`

With an optional JSON body of:

`{ "value1" : "` `NRT` `", "value2" : "` `400` `", "value3" : "` `" }`

The data is completely optional, and you can also pass `value1`, `value2`, and `value3` as query parameters or form variables. This content will be passed on to the Action in your Recipe.

Image from https://ifttt.com/

Finally, click on **Test It**, and you should receive a text message in just a few seconds.

Now that we have all the pieces in place, it's time to pull it all together into a single script that will monitor fares 24/7.

Putting it all together

Up until this point, we've worked in the Jupyter notebook, but now to deploy our app, we'll move to working in a text editor. The notebook is excellent for exploratory analysis and visualization, but running a background job is best done with a simple `.py` file. So let's get started.

We'll begin with our imports. You may need to pip-install a few of these if you don't already have them installed:

```
import sys
import pandas as pd
import numpy as np

import requests

from selenium import webdriver
from selenium.webdriver.common.desired_capabilities import
DesiredCapabilities
from selenium.webdriver.common.by import By
```

```
from selenium.webdriver.support.ui import WebDriverWait
from selenium.webdriver.support import expected_conditions as EC

from bs4 import BeautifulSoup

from sklearn.cluster import DBSCAN
from sklearn.preprocessing import StandardScaler

import schedule
import time
```

Next, we'll create a function that pulls down the data and runs our clustering algorithm. Notice that we're including an explicit wait when we retrieve our data. As the page has an AJAX request, we need to add this wait time to ensure that the page's pricing data has been returned before we move on. If the scraping still fails for some reason, we'll send a text noting this failure:

```
def check_flights():
    url = "https://www.google.com/flights/explore/#explore;f=JFK,
        EWR,LGA;t=HND,NRT,TPE,HKG,KIX;s=1;li=8;lx=12;d=2016-04-01"

    driver = webdriver.PhantomJS()

    dcap = dict(DesiredCapabilities.PHANTOMJS)
    dcap["phantomjs.page.settings.userAgent"] = \
        ("Mozilla/5.0 (Macintosh; Intel Mac OS X 10_10_5)
AppleWebKit/537.36 (KHTML, like Gecko) Chrome/46.0.2490.80 Safari/537.36")

    driver = webdriver.PhantomJS(desired_capabilities=dcap,
                                 service_args=['--ignore-ssl-
                                 errors=true'])
    driver.get(url)

    wait = WebDriverWait(driver, 20)
    wait.until(EC.visibility_of_element_located((By.CSS_SELECTOR,
    "span.FTWFGDB-v-c")))

    s = BeautifulSoup(driver.page_source, "lxml")

    best_price_tags = s.findAll('div', 'FTWFGDB-w-e')

    # check if scrape worked - alert if it fails and shutdown
    if len(best_price_tags) < 4:
        print('Failed to Load Page Data')
requests.post('https://maker.ifttt.com/trigger/fare_alert/with/key/MY_SECRE
T_KEY',data={"value1": "script", "value2": "failed",
"value3": ""})
        sys.exit(0)
```

```
    else:
        print('Successfully Loaded Page Data')

    best_prices = []
    for tag in best_price_tags:
        best_prices.append(int(tag.text.replace('$', '')))

    best_price = best_prices[0]

    best_height_tags = s.findAll('div', 'FTWFGDB-w-f')
    best_heights = []
    for t in best_height_tags:
        best_heights.append(float(t.attrs['style']
                                    .split('height:')[1].replace('px;',
'')))

    best_height = best_heights[0]

    # price per pixel of height
    pph = np.array(best_price)/np.array(best_height)

    cities = s.findAll('div', 'FTWFGDB-w-o')

    hlist = []
    for bar in cities[0].findAll('div', 'FTWFGDB-w-x'):
        hlist.append(float(bar['style'].split('height: ')[1]
                                    .replace('px;', '')) * pph)

    fares = pd.DataFrame(hlist, columns=['price'])
    px = [x for x in fares['price']]
    ff = pd.DataFrame(px, columns=['fare']).reset_index()

    # begin the clustering
    X = StandardScaler().fit_transform(ff)
    db = DBSCAN(eps=1.5, min_samples=1).fit(X)

    labels = db.labels_
    clusters = len(set(labels))

    pf = pd.concat([ff, pd.DataFrame(db.labels_, columns=
['cluster'])], axis=1)

    rf = pf.groupby('cluster')['fare']\
            .agg(['min', 'count']).sort_values('min',
scending=True)
```

Now we'll check whether our rules have trigger. If yes, we'll send a request to receive a text:

```
# set up our rules
# must have more than one cluster
# cluster min must be equal to lowest price fare
# cluster size must be less than 10th percentile
# cluster must be $100 less the next lowest-priced cluster
if clusters > 1\
    and ff['fare'].min() == rf.iloc[0]['min']\
    and rf.iloc[0]['count'] < rf['count'].quantile(.10)\
    and rf.iloc[0]['fare'] + 100 < rf.iloc[1]['fare']:
        city = s.find('span', 'FTWFGDB-v-c').text
        fare = s.find('div', 'FTWFGDB-w-e').text
requests.post('https://maker.ifttt.com/trigger/fare_alert/with/key/MY_SECRE
T_KEY', data={"value1": city, "value2": fare, "value3": ""})
    else:
        print('no alert triggered')
```

Finally, we'll include a scheduler. This will run our code every 60 minutes:

```
# set up the scheduler to run our code every 60 min
schedule.every(60).minutes.do(check_flights)

while 1:
    schedule.run_pending()
    time.sleep(1)
```

That should do it. We can now save this as `fare_alerter.py`, and run it from the command line. It will continue running and check fares every 60 minutes. If a mistake fare occurs, we'll be one of the first to know!

 Note that this is a minimal implementation of this code. To create a proper implementation, good logging practices should be put in place in lieu of the print statements shown here. For more information on how to implement logging, see `https://docs.python.org/3.4/howto/loggi ng.html#logging-basic-tutorial`.

Summary

We've covered a lot of ground in this chapter. We've learned how to find the best airfare data on the Web, how to work with the DOM to find and parse the HTML elements, how to cluster data into meaningful groups, and finally how to send text alerts from code using web requests in IFTTT. While what we've covered here is for airfares, nearly everything that we've done could be reused for any type of pricing you'd like to be alerted to.

If you do decide to use it for airfares though, I hope it provides you with many happy travels!

In the next chapter, we'll cover how to use classification algorithms to help predict the IPO market.

4

Forecast the IPO Market using Logistic Regression

In the late 1990s, getting in on the right IPO was like winning the lottery. First day returns for some technology companies were many times their initial offering price. If you were lucky enough to get in an allocation, you were in for a windfall. Here are a few of the top first-day performers from the period:

- VA Linux up 697%, 12/09/99
- Globe.com up 606%, 11/13/98
- Foundry Networks up 525%, 9/28/99

While the days of dotcom mania are far behind us, IPOs can still have outsized first-day returns. Here are a just few that have risen over 100% on their first day of trading in the past year:

- Seres Therapeutics up 185%, 06/26/15
- Audro Biotech up 147%, 4/15/15
- Shake Shack up 118%, 1/30/15

As you can see, this is still a market worth paying attention to. In this chapter, we'll take a closer look at the IPO market. We'll see how we can use machine learning to help us decide which IPOs are worth a closer look and which ones we may want to take a pass on.

We'll cover the following topics in this chapter:

- The IPO market
- Data cleansing and feature engineering
- Binary classification with logistic regression

- Model evaluation
- Feature importance

The IPO market

Before we jump in and begin modeling, let's first discuss what an IPO, or initial public offering, is and what the research tells us about this market. After that, we'll discuss a number of strategies that we can apply.

What is an IPO?

An initial public offering is the process whereby a private company becomes a public company. Public offerings raise capital for the company and give the general public an opportunity to invest in the company by buying its shares.

Though there are variations in how this occurs, in the typical offering, a company enlists the aid of one or more investment banks to underwrite their offering. This means that the banks make a guarantee to the company that they will purchase all of the shares being offered at the IPO price on the day of the offering. The underwriters, of course, do not intend to keep all of the shares themselves. With the help of the offering company, they go on what's called a *roadshow* to drum up interest from institutional clients. These clients put in a *subscription* for the shares which indicates their interest in buying shares on the day of the IPO. This is a nonbinding contract since the price of the offering is not finalized until the day of the IPO. The underwriter will then set the offer price, given the level of interest expressed.

What is interesting from our perspective is that research has consistently shown a systematic underpricing of IPOs. There are a number of theories for why this happens, and why this level of underpricing seems to vary over time, but suffice it to say, studies have shown billions of dollars are left on the table every year.

In an IPO, "money left on the table" is the difference between the offering price of the shares and the first day's closing price.

One other point that should be mentioned before we move on is the difference between the offering price and the opening price. While you can occasionally get in on the deal through your broker and receive the IPO at its offering price, in nearly all instances you, as a member of the general public, will have to purchase the IPO at the (typically higher) opening price. We'll build our models under this assumption.

Recent IPO market performance

Let's now take a look at the performance of the IPO market. We are going to pull down data from `IPOScoop.com`. This is a service that provides ratings for upcoming IPOs. Go to `http s://www.iposcoop.com/scoop-track-record-from-2000-to-present/` and click on the button at the bottom of the page to download the spreadsheet. We'll load this into pandas and run a number of visualizations using our Jupyter notebook.

First, we'll set up the imports that we'll need throughout the chapter. Then, we'll pull in the data, as follows:

```
import numpy as np
import pandas as pd
import matplotlib.pyplot as plt
from patsy import dmatrix
from sklearn.ensemble import RandomForestClassifier
from sklearn import linear_model
%matplotlib inline
ipos = pd.read_csv(r'/Users/alexcombs/Downloads/ipo_data.csv',
encoding='latin-1')
ipos
```

The preceding code generates the following output:

	Date	Issuer	Symbol	Lead/Joint-Lead Mangager	Offer Price	Opening Price	1st Day Close	1st Day % Px Chng	$ Chg Opening	$ Chg Close	Star Ratings	Performed
0	2002-01-28	Synaptics	SYNA	Bear Stearns	$11.00	$13.11	$13.11	19.18%	$2.11	$2.11	2	NaN
1	2002-02-01	ZymoGenetics	ZGEN	Lehman Brothers/Merrill Lynch	$12.00	$12.01	$12.05	0.42%	$0.01	$0.05	1	NaN
2	2002-02-01	Carolina Group (Loews Corp.)	CG	Salomon Smith Barney/Morgan Stanley	$28.00	$30.05	$29.10	3.93%	$2.05	$1.10	3	NaN
3	2002-02-05	Sunoco Logistics Partners	SXL	Lehman Brothers	$20.25	$21.25	$22.10	9.14%	$1.00	$1.85	3	NaN
4	2002-02-07	ManTech International	MANT	Jefferies	$16.00	$17.10	$18.21	13.81%	$1.10	$2.21	3	NaN

Here, we can see that we have some great information on each IPO: the offering date, issuer, offering price, opening price, and price changes. Let's first explore the performance data by year.

We'll first need to perform some cleanup to properly format the columns. We'll get rid of the dollar signs and the percentage marks:

```
ipos = ipos.applymap(lambda x: x if not '$' in str(x) else
x.replace('$',''))
ipos = ipos.applymap(lambda x: x if not '%' in str(x) else
x.replace('%',''))
ipos
```

The preceding code generates the following output:

	Date	Issuer	Symbol	Lead/Joint-Lead Mangager	Offer Price	Opening Price	1st Day Close	1st Day % Px Chng	$ Chg Opening	$ Chg Close	Star Ratings	Performed
0	2002-01-28	Synaptics	SYNA	Bear Stearns	11.00	13.11	13.11	19.18	2.11	2.11	2	NaN
1	2002-02-01	ZymoGenetics	ZGEN	Lehman Brothers/Merrill Lynch	12.00	12.01	12.05	0.42	0.01	0.05	1	NaN
2	2002-02-01	Carolina Group (Loews Corp.)	CG	Salomon Smith Barney/Morgan Stanley	28.00	30.05	29.10	3.93	2.05	1.10	3	NaN
3	2002-02-05	Sunoco Logistics Partners	SXL	Lehman Brothers	20.25	21.25	22.10	9.14	1.00	1.85	3	NaN
4	2002-02-07	ManTech International	MANT	Jefferies	16.00	17.10	18.21	13.81	1.10	2.21	3	NaN

Next, we'll fix the data types for the columns. They are all objects currently, and we want numeric types for the aggregations and manipulations that we will perform:

```
ipos.info()
```

The preceding code generates the following output:

```
<class 'pandas.core.frame.DataFrame'>
Int64Index: 2335 entries, 0 to 2334
Data columns (total 12 columns):
Date                         2335 non-null object
Issuer                       2335 non-null object
Symbol                       2335 non-null object
Lead/Joint-Lead Mangager     2335 non-null object
Offer Price                  2335 non-null object
Opening Price                2335 non-null object
1st Day Close                2335 non-null object
1st Day % Px Chng            2335 non-null object
$ Chg Opening                2335 non-null object
$ Chg Close                  2335 non-null object
Star Ratings                 2335 non-null object
Performed                     259 non-null object
dtypes: object(12)
memory usage: 237.1+ KB
```

There are some `'N/C'` values in our data that we'll need to replace first. After this, we can change the data types:

```
ipos.replace('N/C',0, inplace=True)
ipos['Date'] = pd.to_datetime(ipos['Date'])
ipos['Offer Price'] = ipos['Offer Price'].astype('float')
ipos['Opening Price'] = ipos['Opening Price'].astype('float')
ipos['1st Day Close'] = ipos['1st Day Close'].astype('float')
ipos['1st Day % Px Chng '] = ipos['1st Day % Px Chng '].astype('float')
ipos['$ Chg Close'] = ipos['$ Chg Close'].astype('float')
ipos['$ Chg Opening'] = ipos['$ Chg Opening'].astype('float')
ipos['Star Ratings'] = ipos['Star Ratings'].astype('int')
```

Note that this throws an error, as seen in the following:

```
pandas/tslib.pyx in pandas.tslib.array_to_datetime (pandas/tslib.c:37155)()

pandas/tslib.pyx in pandas.tslib.array_to_datetime (pandas/tslib.c:35996)()

pandas/tslib.pyx in pandas.tslib.array_to_datetime (pandas/tslib.c:35724)()

pandas/tslib.pyx in pandas.tslib.array_to_datetime (pandas/tslib.c:35602)()

pandas/tslib.pyx in pandas.tslib.convert_to_tsobject (pandas/tslib.c:23563)()

pandas/tslib.pyx in pandas.tslib._check_dts_bounds (pandas/tslib.c:26809)()

OutOfBoundsDatetime: Out of bounds nanosecond timestamp: 120-11-01 00:00:00
```

This means one of our dates is not properly formatted. We find this based on the previous stack trace and fix it:

```
ipos[ipos['Date']=='11/120']
```

After fixing the error, we will observe the following output:

	Date	Issuer	Symbol	Lead/Joint-Lead Mangager	Offer Price	Opening Price	1st Day Close	1st Day % Px Chng	$ Chg Opening	$ Chg Close	Star Ratings	Performed
1660	11/120	Alon USA Partners, LP	ALDW	Goldman, Sachs/ Credit Suisse/ Citigroup	16	17	18.4	15	1	2.4	1	NaN

The proper date is 11/20/2012, so we'll set it and rerun the preceding data type fixes. After that, everything should go smoothly:

```
ipos.loc[1660, 'Date'] = '2012-11-20'
```

```
ipos['Date'] = pd.to_datetime(ipos['Date'])
```

```
ipos['Offer Price'] = ipos['Offer Price'].astype('float')
ipos['Opening Price'] = ipos['Opening Price'].astype('float')
ipos['1st Day Close'] = ipos['1st Day Close'].astype('float')
ipos['1st Day % Px Chng '] = ipos['1st Day % Px Chng']
.astype('float')
ipos['$ Chg Close'] = ipos['$ Chg Close'].astype('float')
ipos['$ Chg Opening'] = ipos['$ Chg Opening'].astype('float')
ipos['Star Ratings'] = ipos['Star Ratings'].astype('int')

ipos.info()
```

The preceding code generates the following output:

```
<class 'pandas.core.frame.DataFrame'>
Int64Index: 2335 entries, 0 to 2334
Data columns (total 12 columns):
Date                      2335 non-null datetime64[ns]
Issuer                    2335 non-null object
Symbol                    2335 non-null object
Lead/Joint-Lead Mangager  2335 non-null object
Offer Price               2335 non-null float64
Opening Price             2335 non-null float64
1st Day Close             2335 non-null float64
1st Day % Px Chng         2335 non-null float64
$ Chg Opening             2335 non-null float64
$ Chg Close               2335 non-null float64
Star Ratings              2335 non-null int64
Performed                 259 non-null object
dtypes: datetime64[ns](1), float64(6), int64(1), object(4)
memory usage: 237.1+ KB
```

Now, finally, we can start our exploration. Let's start with average first day percentage gain:

```
ipos.groupby(ipos['Date'].dt.year)['1st Day % Px Chng ']\
.mean().plot(kind='bar', figsize=(15,10), color='k', title='1st Day Mean
IPO Percentage Change')
```

The preceding code generates the following output:

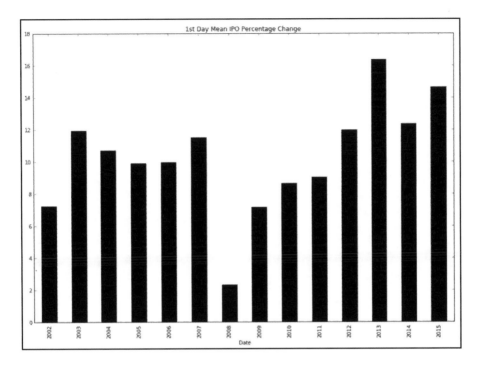

Those are some healthy percentages in recent years. Let's now take a look at how the median compares to the mean:

```
ipos.groupby(ipos['Date'].dt.year)['1st Day % Px Chng ']\
.median().plot(kind='bar', figsize=(15,10), color='k', title='1st Day
Median IPO Percentage Change')
```

The preceding code generates the following output:

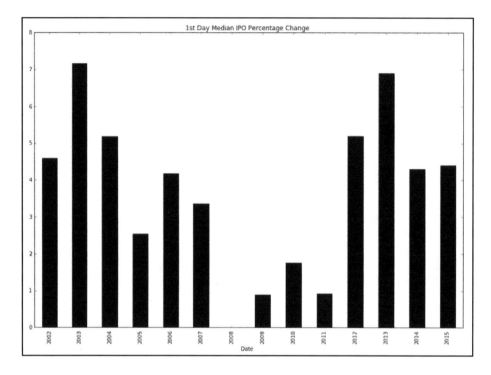

From this, we can clearly see that the distribution of returns is skewed by some large outliers. Let's now take a look at them:

```
ipos['1st Day % Px Chng '].describe()
```

The preceding code generates the following output:

```
count    2335.000000
mean       11.152599
std        22.924024
min       -35.220000
25%         0.000000
50%         3.750000
75%        16.715000
max       353.850000
Name: 1st Day % Px Chng , dtype: float64
```

Now we can plot it as well:

```
ipos['1st Day % Px Chng '].hist(figsize=(15,7), bins=100, color='grey')
```

The preceding code generates the following output:

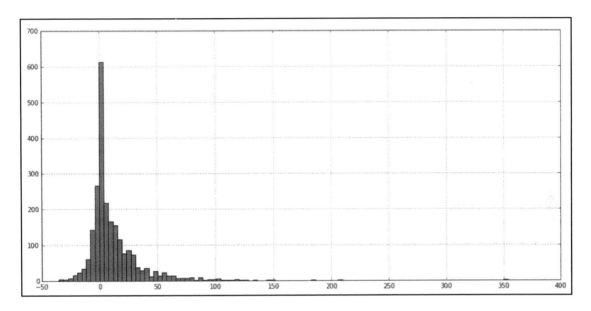

From this, we can see that most returns cluster around zero, but there is a long tail to the right with a number of true *homerun* offerings.

We've looked at the first day percentage change, which is the offering price to the closing price, but as I noted earlier, there is very little chance of getting in on the offering price. Since that's the case, let's now look at the returns for the opening price to the closing price. Do all of the gains go to those who get on the offering, or is there still an opportunity to jump in and capture an outsized return on the first day?

To answer this, we'll first create two new columns:

```
ipos['$ Chg Open to Close'] = ipos['$ Chg Close'] - ipos['$ Chg Opening']
ipos['% Chg Open to Close'] = (ipos['$ Chg Open to Close']/ipos['Opening
Price']) * 100
```

The preceding code generates the following output:

	Date	Issuer	Symbol	Lead/Joint-Lead Mangager	Offer Price	Opening Price	1st Day Close	1st Day % Px Chng	$ Chg Opening	$ Chg Close	Star Ratings	Performed	$ Chg Open to Close	% Chg Open to Close
0	2002-01-28	Synaptics	SYNA	Bear Stearns	11.00	13.11	13.11	19.18	2.11	2.11	2	NaN	0.00	0.000000
1	2002-02-01	ZymoGenetics	ZGEN	Lehman Brothers/Merrill Lynch	12.00	12.01	12.05	0.42	0.01	0.05	1	NaN	0.04	0.333056
2	2002-02-01	Carolina Group (Loews Corp.)	CG	Salomon Smith Barney/Morgan Stanley	28.00	30.05	29.10	3.93	2.05	1.10	3	NaN	-0.95	-3.161398
		Sunoco												

Next, we'll generate our statistics:

```
ipos['% Chg Open to Close'].describe()
```

```
count    2335.000000
mean        0.816079
std         9.401379
min       -98.522167
25%        -2.817541
50%         0.000000
75%         3.691830
max       113.333333
Name: % Chg Open to Close, dtype: float64
```

Immediately, this looks suspect. While IPOs can fall after their opening, a drop of nearly 99% seems unrealistic. After some investigating, it looks like the two worst performers were, in fact, bad data points. This is just a fact of life when working with real-world data, so we'll correct these and regenerate our data:

```
ipos.loc[440, '$ Chg Opening'] = .09
ipos.loc[1264, '$ Chg Opening'] = .01
ipos.loc[1264, 'Opening Price'] = 11.26

ipos['$ Chg Open to Close'] = ipos['$ Chg Close'] - ipos['$ Chg Opening']
ipos['% Chg Open to Close'] = (ipos['$ Chg Open to Close']/ipos['Opening
Price']) * 100

ipos['% Chg Open to Close'].describe()
```

The preceding code generates the following output:

```
count      2335.000000
mean          0.880407
std           9.114790
min         -40.383333
25%          -2.800000
50%           0.000000
75%           3.691830
max         113.333333
Name: % Chg Open to Close, dtype: float64
```

This down to a 40% loss, and still looks suspect, but after taking a closer look, it was the Zillow IPO. Zillow opened extremely hot, but quickly came back to earth before the closing bell. This tells us we appear to have cleaned out our bad data points.

We'll move forward now and hope that we have cleaned up the bulk of the errors:

```
ipos['% Chg Open to Close'].hist(figsize=(15,7), bins=100, color='grey')
```

The preceding code generates the following output:

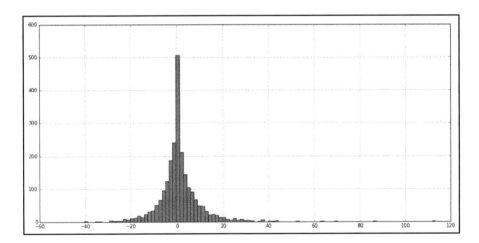

Finally, we can see the shape of the distribution for opening to closing prices. Compared to the distribution of offering to closing prices, there are noticeable differences. Both the mean and the median have fallen considerably, and the bars immediately to the right of zero look like they've had a healthy shave, while the ones to the left seem to have grown in equal proportion. Note that the long tail on the right-hand side is less pronounced, but still evident, so there is still a glimmer of hope.

Baseline IPO strategy

Now that we have a sense of the market, let's explore a few strategies. How would we fare if we were to purchase every IPO at its opening price and sell it at the close? We'll take a look at the 2015 year-to-date data:

```
ipos[ipos['Date']>='2015-01-01']['$ Chg Open to Close'].describe()
```

The preceding code generates the following output:

```
count    147.000000
mean       0.659105
std       11.334366
min      -28.729963
25%       -3.735019
50%        0.000000
75%        3.706447
max       63.903061
Name: % Chg Open to Close, dtype: float64
```

```
ipos[ipos['Date']>='2015-01-01']['$ Chg Open to Close'].sum()
```

The preceding code generates the following output:

```
33.739999999999995
```

Let's also break out the winning trades and losing trades:

```
ipos[(ipos['Date']>='2015-01-01')&(ipos['$ Chg Open to Close']>0)]['$ Chg
Open to Close'].describe()
```

The preceding code generates the following output:

```
count    73.000000
mean      1.574795
std       3.020735
min       0.010000
25%       0.200000
50%       0.670000
75%       1.340000
max      20.040000
Name: $ Chg Open to Close, dtype: float64
```

```
ipos[(ipos['Date']>='2015-01-01')&(ipos['$ Chg Open to Close']<0)]['$ Chg
Open to Close'].describe()
```

The preceding code generates the following output:

```
count     65.000000
mean      -1.249538
std        1.381957
min       -6.160000
25%       -1.580000
50%       -0.820000
75%       -0.220000
max       -0.010000
Name: $ Chg Open to Close, dtype: float64
```

So, we see that if we invested in every IPO this year, we would have been quite busy investing in 147 IPOs with about half making us money and half losing us money. On the whole, this would have been profitable as the gains from our winning IPOs would have ended up covering our losses and then a bit. This, of course, assumes there are no slippage or commission costs, which there inevitably are in the real world. However, this is clearly not a golden ticket to riches with a mean percentage return of less than 1%.

 Slippage is the difference between your attempted entry or exit price for a target stock and the price at which your order is actually fulfilled.

Let's see if we can use machine learning to help improve our results from a naive approach. A reasonable strategy would seem to be targeting that long right tail, so we'll focus on that.

Feature engineering

What might impact the performance of an offering as it begins trading? Perhaps the recent performance of the market in general or the prestige of the underwriters could impact it. Perhaps the day of the week or the month that it trades is important. The consideration and inclusion of these factors in a model is called **feature engineering**, and modeling this is nearly as important as the data that you use to build the model. If your features aren't informative, your model simply won't have value.

Let's begin this process by adding a few features that we expect may influence the performance of an IPO.

We'll begin by retrieving data for the S&P 500 index. This is perhaps the best proxy for the general U.S. market. We can download this from Yahoo! Finance at `https://finance.ya hoo.com/q/hp?s=%5EGSPC&a=00&b=1&c=2000&d=11&e=17&f=2015&g=d`. We can then import the data using pandas:

```
sp = pd.read_csv(r'/Users/alexcombs/Downloads/spy.csv')
sp.sort_values('Date', inplace=True)
sp.reset_index(drop=True, inplace=True)
sp
```

The preceding code generates the following output:

	Date	Open	High	Low	Close	Volume	Adj Close
0	2000-01-03	1469.250000	1478.000000	1438.359985	1455.219971	931800000	1455.219971
1	2000-01-04	1455.219971	1455.219971	1397.430054	1399.420044	1009000000	1399.420044
2	2000-01-05	1399.420044	1413.270020	1377.680054	1402.109985	1085500000	1402.109985
3	2000-01-06	1402.109985	1411.900024	1392.099976	1403.449951	1092300000	1403.449951
4	2000-01-07	1403.449951	1441.469971	1400.729980	1441.469971	1225200000	1441.469971
5	2000-01-10	1441.469971	1464.359985	1441.469971	1457.599976	1064800000	1457.599976
6	2000-01-11	1457.599976	1458.660034	1434.420044	1438.560059	1014000000	1438.560059
7	2000-01-12	1438.560059	1442.599976	1427.079956	1432.250000	974600000	1432.250000
8	2000-01-13	1432.250000	1454.199951	1432.250000	1449.680054	1030400000	1449.680054
9	2000-01-14	1449.680054	1473.000000	1449.680054	1465.150024	1085900000	1465.150024

Because broad market performance over the past week would be a logical influence on a stock, let's add this to our `DataFrame`. We'll take the closing price of the S&P 500 yesterday as a percent of its close seven days ago:

```
def get_week_chg(ipo_dt):
    try:
        day_ago_idx =  sp[sp['Date']==str(ipo_dt.date())].index[0]
- 1
        week_ago_idx = sp[sp['Date']==str(ipo_dt.date())].index[0] - 8
        chg = (sp.iloc[day_ago_idx]['Close'] - \
sp.iloc[week_ago_idx]['Close'])/(sp.iloc[week_ago_idx]['Close'])
        return chg * 100
    except:
        print('error', ipo_dt.date())

ipos['SP Week Change'] = ipos['Date'].map(get_week_chg)
```

The preceding code generates the following output:

```
error 2009-08-01
error 2013-11-16
error 2015-02-21
error 2015-02-21
```

Running this gives us several dates that fail, which tells us that our IPO dates may have a few errors. Checking the IPOs that have these dates indicates that they are off. Here's one example and the code to correct all of the errors:

```
ipos[ipos['Date']=='2009-08-01']
```

The preceding code generates the following output:

	Date	Issuer	Symbol	Lead/Joint-Lead Mangager	Offer Price	Opening Price	1st Day Close	1st Day % Px Chng	$ Chg Opening	$ Chg Close	Star Ratings	Performed	$ Chg Open to Close	% Chg Open to Close	SP Week Change
1175	2009-08-01	Emdeon	EM	Morgan Stanley	15	17.5	16.52	10.13	2.5	1.52	3	NaN	-0.98	-5.6	NaN

The actual IPO date for EM is 8/12/15, so we'll correct it and the others based upon what a bit of research shows us as their true offering dates:

```
ipos.loc[1175, 'Date'] = pd.to_datetime('2009-08-12')
ipos.loc[1660, 'Date'] = pd.to_datetime('2012-11-20')
ipos.loc[2251, 'Date'] = pd.to_datetime('2015-05-21')
ipos.loc[2252, 'Date'] = pd.to_datetime('2015-05-21')
```

Running the function again will correctly add the one week change for all offerings:

```
ipos['SP Week Change'] = ipos['Date'].map(get_week_chg)
```

Now, let's add the S&P 500 percentage change from the close the previous day of the IPO to the next day's opening of the IPO:

```
def get_cto_chg(ipo_dt):
    try:
        today_open_idx =  sp[sp['Date']==str(ipo_dt.date())].index[0]
        yday_close_idx = sp[sp['Date']==str(ipo_dt.date())].index[0] - 1
        chg = (sp.iloc[today_open_idx]['Open'] - \
sp.iloc[yday_close_idx]['Close'])/(sp.iloc[yday_close_idx]['Close'])
        return chg * 100
    except:
        print('error', ipo_dt)
```

```
ipos['SP Close to Open Chg Pct'] = ipos['Date'].map(get_cto_chg)
```

The preceding code generates the following output:

Symbol	Lead/Joint-Lead Mangager	Offer Price	Opening Price	1st Day Close	1st Day % Px Chng	$ Chg Opening	$ Chg Close	Star Ratings	Performed	$ Chg Open to Close	% Chg Open to Close	SP Week Change	SP Week Chg Pct	SP Close to Open Chg Pct
SYNA	Bear Steams	11.00	13.11	13.11	19.18	2.11	2.11	2	NaN	0.00	0.000000	-1.126333	-1.126333	0.000000
ZGEN	Lehman Brothers/Merrill Lynch	12.00	12.01	12.05	0.42	0.01	0.05	1	NaN	0.04	0.333056	0.972911	0.972911	0.000000
CG	Salomon Smith Barney/Morgan Stanley	28.00	30.05	29.10	3.93	2.05	1.10	3	NaN	-0.95	-3.161398	0.972911	0.972911	0.000000
	Lehman													

Now, let's tidy up the underwriter data. This is going to take some work. We'll perform a number of steps. First, we'll add a column for the lead underwriter or manager. Next, we'll standardize the data. Finally, we'll add a column representing the total count of underwriters involved.

First, we parse out the lead manager by splitting the data and removing white space:

```
ipos['Lead Mgr'] = ipos['Lead/Joint-Lead Mangager'].map(lambda x:
x.split('/')[0])
ipos['Lead Mgr'] = ipos['Lead Mgr'].map(lambda x: x.strip())
```

Next, printing out the different lead managers shows just how much cleanup is going to be required to standardize the bank's names:

```
for n in pd.DataFrame(ipos['Lead Mgr'].unique(),
columns=['Name']).sort('Name')['Name']:
    print(n)
```

The preceding code generates the following output:

```
A.G. Edwards
A.G. Edwrads & Sons
AG Edwards
AG Edwards & Sons
AG Edwrads
Adams Harkness
Advest
Aegis Capital
Aegis Capital Corp
Aegis Capital Corp.
Anderson & Strudrick
Axiom Capital Management
BB&T Capital Markets
BMO Capital Markets
Baird
Baird, BMO Capital Markets, Janney Montgomery Scott
Banc of America
Banc of America Securities
Barclay Capital
Barclays
```

There are two ways to do this if you're following along. The first way, and undoubtedly the easier of the two, is to trust that we have done the work for you and simply copy and paste the code on the following pages. The other is to perform a lot of iterative partial string matching and correcting by yourself. The first option is strongly recommended:

```python
ipos.loc[ipos['Lead Mgr'].str.contains('Hambrecht'),'Lead Mgr'] = 'WR
Hambrecht+Co.'
ipos.loc[ipos['Lead Mgr'].str.contains('Edwards'), 'Lead Mgr'] = 'AG
Edwards'
ipos.loc[ipos['Lead Mgr'].str.contains('Edwrads'), 'Lead Mgr'] = 'AG
Edwards'
ipos.loc[ipos['Lead Mgr'].str.contains('Barclay'), 'Lead Mgr'] = 'Barclays'
ipos.loc[ipos['Lead Mgr'].str.contains('Aegis'), 'Lead Mgr'] = 'Aegis
Capital'
ipos.loc[ipos['Lead Mgr'].str.contains('Deutsche'), 'Lead Mgr'] = 'Deutsche
Bank'
ipos.loc[ipos['Lead Mgr'].str.contains('Suisse'), 'Lead Mgr'] = 'CSFB'
ipos.loc[ipos['Lead Mgr'].str.contains('CS.?F'), 'Lead Mgr'] = 'CSFB'
ipos.loc[ipos['Lead Mgr'].str.contains('^Early'), 'Lead Mgr'] =
'EarlyBirdCapital'
ipos.loc[325,'Lead Mgr'] = 'Maximum Captial'
ipos.loc[ipos['Lead Mgr'].str.contains('Keefe'), 'Lead Mgr'] = 'Keefe,
Bruyette & Woods'
ipos.loc[ipos['Lead Mgr'].str.contains('Stan'), 'Lead Mgr'] = 'Morgan
Stanley'
ipos.loc[ipos['Lead Mgr'].str.contains('P. Morg'), 'Lead Mgr'] = 'JP
Morgan'
ipos.loc[ipos['Lead Mgr'].str.contains('PM'), 'Lead Mgr'] = 'JP Morgan'
ipos.loc[ipos['Lead Mgr'].str.contains('J\.P\.'), 'Lead Mgr'] = 'JP Morgan'
```

```
ipos.loc[ipos['Lead Mgr'].str.contains('Banc of'), 'Lead Mgr'] = 'Banc of
America'
ipos.loc[ipos['Lead Mgr'].str.contains('Lych'), 'Lead Mgr'] = 'BofA Merrill
Lynch'
ipos.loc[ipos['Lead Mgr'].str.contains('Merrill$'), 'Lead Mgr'] = 'Merrill
Lynch'
ipos.loc[ipos['Lead Mgr'].str.contains('Lymch'), 'Lead Mgr'] = 'Merrill
Lynch'
ipos.loc[ipos['Lead Mgr'].str.contains('A Merril Lynch'), 'Lead Mgr'] =
'BofA Merrill Lynch'
ipos.loc[ipos['Lead Mgr'].str.contains('Merril '), 'Lead Mgr'] = 'Merrill
Lynch'
ipos.loc[ipos['Lead Mgr'].str.contains('BofA$'), 'Lead Mgr'] = 'BofA
Merrill Lynch'
ipos.loc[ipos['Lead Mgr'].str.contains('SANDLER'), 'Lead Mgr'] = 'Sandler
O'neil + Partners'
ipos.loc[ipos['Lead Mgr'].str.contains('Sandler'), 'Lead Mgr'] = 'Sandler
O'Neil + Partners'
ipos.loc[ipos['Lead Mgr'].str.contains('Renshaw'), 'Lead Mgr'] = 'Rodman &
Renshaw'
ipos.loc[ipos['Lead Mgr'].str.contains('Baird'), 'Lead Mgr'] = 'RW Baird'
ipos.loc[ipos['Lead Mgr'].str.contains('Cantor'), 'Lead Mgr'] = 'Cantor
Fitzgerald'
ipos.loc[ipos['Lead Mgr'].str.contains('Goldman'), 'Lead Mgr'] = 'Goldman
Sachs'
ipos.loc[ipos['Lead Mgr'].str.contains('Bear'), 'Lead Mgr'] = 'Bear
Stearns'
ipos.loc[ipos['Lead Mgr'].str.contains('BoA'), 'Lead Mgr'] = 'BofA Merrill
Lynch'
ipos.loc[ipos['Lead Mgr'].str.contains('Broadband'), 'Lead Mgr'] =
'Broadband Capital'
ipos.loc[ipos['Lead Mgr'].str.contains('Davidson'), 'Lead Mgr'] = 'DA
Davidson'
ipos.loc[ipos['Lead Mgr'].str.contains('Feltl'), 'Lead Mgr'] = 'Feltl &
Co.'
ipos.loc[ipos['Lead Mgr'].str.contains('China'), 'Lead Mgr'] = 'China
International'
ipos.loc[ipos['Lead Mgr'].str.contains('Cit'), 'Lead Mgr'] = 'Citigroup'
ipos.loc[ipos['Lead Mgr'].str.contains('Ferris'), 'Lead Mgr'] = 'Ferris
Baker Watts'
ipos.loc[ipos['Lead Mgr'].str.contains('Friedman|Freidman|FBR'), 'Lead
Mgr'] = 'Friedman Billings Ramsey'
ipos.loc[ipos['Lead Mgr'].str.contains('^I-'), 'Lead Mgr'] = 'I-Bankers'
ipos.loc[ipos['Lead Mgr'].str.contains('Gunn'), 'Lead Mgr'] = 'Gunn Allen'
ipos.loc[ipos['Lead Mgr'].str.contains('Jeffer'), 'Lead Mgr'] = 'Jefferies'
ipos.loc[ipos['Lead Mgr'].str.contains('Oppen'), 'Lead Mgr'] =
'Oppenheimer'
ipos.loc[ipos['Lead Mgr'].str.contains('JMP'), 'Lead Mgr'] = 'JMP
```

```
Securities'
ipos.loc[ipos['Lead Mgr'].str.contains('Rice'), 'Lead Mgr'] = 'Johnson
Rice'
ipos.loc[ipos['Lead Mgr'].str.contains('Ladenburg'), 'Lead Mgr'] =
'Ladenburg Thalmann'
ipos.loc[ipos['Lead Mgr'].str.contains('Piper'), 'Lead Mgr'] = 'Piper
Jaffray'
ipos.loc[ipos['Lead Mgr'].str.contains('Pali'), 'Lead Mgr'] = 'Pali
Capital'
ipos.loc[ipos['Lead Mgr'].str.contains('Paulson'), 'Lead Mgr'] = 'Paulson
Investment Co.'
ipos.loc[ipos['Lead Mgr'].str.contains('Roth'), 'Lead Mgr'] = 'Roth
Capital'
ipos.loc[ipos['Lead Mgr'].str.contains('Stifel'), 'Lead Mgr'] = 'Stifel
Nicolaus'
ipos.loc[ipos['Lead Mgr'].str.contains('SunTrust'), 'Lead Mgr'] = 'SunTrust
Robinson'
ipos.loc[ipos['Lead Mgr'].str.contains('Wachovia'), 'Lead Mgr'] =
'Wachovia'
ipos.loc[ipos['Lead Mgr'].str.contains('Wedbush'), 'Lead Mgr'] = 'Wedbush
Morgan'
ipos.loc[ipos['Lead Mgr'].str.contains('Blair'), 'Lead Mgr'] = 'William
Blair'
ipos.loc[ipos['Lead Mgr'].str.contains('Wunderlich'), 'Lead Mgr'] =
'Wunderlich'
ipos.loc[ipos['Lead Mgr'].str.contains('Max'), 'Lead Mgr'] = 'Maxim Group'
ipos.loc[ipos['Lead Mgr'].str.contains('CIBC'), 'Lead Mgr'] = 'CIBC'
ipos.loc[ipos['Lead Mgr'].str.contains('CRT'), 'Lead Mgr'] = 'CRT Capital'
ipos.loc[ipos['Lead Mgr'].str.contains('HCF'),'Lead Mgr'] = 'HCFP Brenner'
ipos.loc[ipos['Lead Mgr'].str.contains('Cohen'), 'Lead Mgr'] = 'Cohen &
Co.'
ipos.loc[ipos['Lead Mgr'].str.contains('Cowen'), 'Lead Mgr'] = 'Cowen &
Co.'
ipos.loc[ipos['Lead Mgr'].str.contains('Leerink'), 'Lead Mgr'] = 'Leerink
Partners'
ipos.loc[ipos['Lead Mgr'].str.contains('Lynch\xca'), 'Lead Mgr'] = 'Merrill
Lynch'
```

After this process is complete, you can run the following again to see the updated list:

```
for n in pd.DataFrame(ipos['Lead Mgr'].unique(),
columns=['Name']).sort_values('Name')['Name']:
    print(n)
```

The preceding code generates the following output:

```
AG Edwards
Adams Harkness
Advest
Aegis Capital
Anderson & Strudrick
Axiom Capital Management
BB&T Capital Markets
BMO Capital Markets
Banc of America
Barclays
Bear Stearns
BofA Merrill Lynch
Broadband Capital
Burnham Securities
C&Co
C.E. Unterberg, Towbin
CIBC
CRT Capital
CSFB
Canaccord Genuity
```

As we can see, the list is tidy now. With this completed, we'll add a count of underwriters:

```
ipos['Total Underwriters'] = ipos['Lead/Joint-Lead Mangager'].map(lambda x:
len(x.split('/')))
```

Next, we'll add a couple of date features. We'll add the day of the week and the month:

```
ipos['Week Day'] = ipos['Date'].dt.dayofweek.map({0:'Mon', 1:'Tues',
2:'Wed',\
3:'Thurs', 4:'Fri', 5:'Sat', 6:'Sun'})
ipos['Month'] = ipos['Date'].map(lambda x: x.month)
ipos['Month'] = ipos['Month'].map({1:'Jan', 2:'Feb', 3:'Mar', 4:'Apr',
5:'May', 6:'Jun',7:'Jul',\
8:'Aug', 9:'Sep', 10:'Oct', 11:'Nov', 12:'Dec'})
ipos
```

The preceding code generates the following output:

	Performed	$ Chg Open to Close	% Chg Open to Close	SP Week Change	SP Week Chg Pct	SP Close to Open Chg Pct	Lead Mgr	Total Underwriters	Week Day	Month
..	NaN	0.00	0.000000	-1.126333	-1.126333	0.000000	Bear Stearns	1	Mon	Jan
..	NaN	0.04	0.333056	0.972911	0.972911	0.000000	Lehman Brothers	2	Fri	Feb
..	NaN	-0.95	-3.161398	0.972911	0.972911	0.000000	Salomon Smith Barney	2	Fri	Feb

If all goes as expected, our `DataFrame` should look like the preceding image. We'll now add a couple final features that relate to the change between the offer price and the opening and closing prices:

```
ipos['Gap Open Pct'] = (ipos['$ Chg Opening'].astype('float')/ipos['Opening
Price'].astype('float')) * 100
ipos['Open to Close Pct'] = (ipos['$ Chg Close'].astype('float') -\
ipos['$ Chg Opening'].astype('float'))/\
ipos['Opening Price'].astype('float') * 100
```

That should do it for our features for now. We can always add more if we come across useful data that we think would improve the model, but this should get us started.

However, before we start feeding these features to the model, we need to consider which features to select. We have to be extremely careful not to "leak" information when adding features. This is a common mistake that happens when information is provided to the model from data that would not be available at the time. For example, adding the closing price to our model would completely invalidate the results. By doing this, we would be essentially giving the model the answer it is trying to predict. Usually, leakage mistakes are more subtle than this, but they are a concern nonetheless.

We'll add the following as features:

- Month
- Day of the week
- Lead manager
- Total underwriters
- Offer to open gap percentage
- Dollar change from offer to open

- Offering price
- Opening price
- S&P close to open percent
- S&P prior week change

With all of our model's features completed, we'll next prepare them for use by our model. We're going to use the `Patsy` library for this. `Patsy` can be pip-installed if needed. `Patsy` takes data in its raw form and transforms it into a matrix that is appropriate for the building of statistical models:

```
from patsy import dmatrix
X = dmatrix('Month + Q("Week Day") + Q("Total Underwriters") + Q("Gap Open
Pct") + Q("$ Chg Opening") +\
Q("Lead Mgr") + Q("Offer Price") + Q("Opening Price") +\
Q("SP Close to Open Chg Pct") + Q("SP Week Change")', data=ipos,
return_type='dataframe')
X
```

The preceding code generates the following output:

.Jun]	Month[T.Mar]	Month[T.May]	Month[T.Nov]	...	Q("Lead Mgr") [T.WestPark Capital]	Q("Lead Mgr") [T.William Blair]	Q("Lead Mgr") [T.Wunderlich]	Q("Total Underwriters")	Q("Gap Open Pct")
0	0	0	...	0	0	0	1	16.094584
0	0	0	...	0	0	0	2	0.083264
0	0	0	...	0	0	0	2	6.821963
0	0	0	...	0	0	0	1	4.705882
0	0	0	...	0	0	0	1	6.432749
0	0	0	...	0	0	0	1	11.363636
0	0	0	...	0	0	0	1	7.692308
0	0	0	...	0	0	0	1	15.620105

We can see that Patsy has reconfigured our categorical data into multiple columns while keeping our continuous data in a single column. This is called **dummy coding**. In this format, each month except one will get its own column. The same is true for each broker. For example, if the particular IPO instance (row) was in `May`, then `May` will have 1 in the `May` column while all the other month columns are for this row. There are always *n-1* feature columns for each categorical feature. The one that is excluded becomes the baseline that the others are compared against.

Finally, `Patsy` also adds an intercept column. This is a column of 1s that is needed for regression models to function properly.

With this completed, we'll move on to to the modeling phase.

Binary classification

Instead of attempting to predict exactly what the total first day return will be, we are going to attempt to predict if the IPO will be one we should buy for a trade or not. It is here that we should point out this is not investment advice and that this is for illustrative purposes only. Please don't run out and start day trading IPOs with this model willy-nilly. It will end badly. Now, to predict a binary outcome (that's a 1 or 0, yes or no), we will start with a model called a **logistic regression**. A logistic regression utilizes a logistic function. This is ideal as it has several mathematical properties that make it easy to work with:

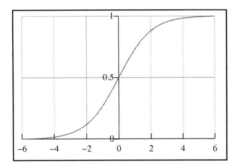

Due to the logistic function's form, it is particularly suited to providing probability estimates, and from these estimates, binary responses. Anything greater than **0.5** is classified as **1**, and everything below **0.5** is classified as 0. These 1s and 0s can correspond to anything we would like to classify, but in this application, it will determine if we buy the offering (1) or do not (0).

Let's go ahead and apply this model to our data. We're going to split our data in a somewhat unusual way. The standard practice in machine learning models is to randomize which instances are fed to the model as training data and which are used as test data. However, because this data is time-based, we are going to use everything but the current year for training. We will then test on the 2015 year-to-date data:

```
# 2188 is the first index of 2015 data - data is date sorted
X_train, X_test = X[:2188], X[2188:]
y_train = ipos['$ Chg Open to Close'][:2188].map(lambda x: 1 if x >= 1 else
```

```
0)
y_test = ipos['$ Chg Open to Close'][2188:].map(lambda x: 1 if x >= 1 else
0)
```

With the preceding code, we split our data into training and test sets. Note that we have also arbitrarily set a $1 threshold for the positive outcome. This is intended to align with our strategy of targeting the long-tail winners rather than just any positive close.

We'll now fit the model, as follows:

```
clf = linear_model.LogisticRegression()
clf.fit(X_train, y_train)
```

The preceding code will generate the following output:

```
LogisticRegression(C=1.0, class_weight=None, dual=False, fit_intercept=True,
          intercept_scaling=1, max_iter=100, multi_class='ovr', n_jobs=1,
          penalty='l2', random_state=None, solver='liblinear', tol=0.0001,
          verbose=0, warm_start=False)
```

We can now evaluate the model on our hold-out 2015 data:

```
clf.score(X_test, y_test)
```

The preceding code will generate the following output:

```
0.8231292517006803
```

From this, we can see about 82% of our predictions were accurate. This is certainly looking better than our baseline rate for 2015, but this can also be misleading as the actual percentage of IPOs that gained more than $1 is very low. This means guessing zero for all would give us about the same result, but let's compare the two.

First our baseline is as follows:

```
ipos[(ipos['Date']>='2015-01-01')]['$ Chg Open to Close'].describe()
```

The preceding code generates the following output:

```
count     147.000000
mean        0.229524
std         2.686850
min        -6.160000
25%        -0.645000
50%         0.000000
75%         0.665000
max        20.040000
```

Next, we'll get our predicted result. We'll set up a DataFrame with our results first, then output them:

```
pred_label = clf.predict(X_test)
results=[]
for pl, tl, idx, chg in zip(pred_label, y_test, y_test.index,
ipos.ix[y_test.index]['$ Chg Open to Close']):
    if pl == tl:
        results.append([idx, chg, pl, tl, 1])
    else:
        results.append([idx, chg, pl, tl, 0])
rf = pd.DataFrame(results, columns=['index', '$ chg', 'predicted',
'actual', 'correct'])
rf
```

The preceding code generates the following output:

	index	$ chg	predicted	actual	correct
0	2188	0.01	0	0	1
1	2189	3.03	0	1	0
2	2190	-1.06	0	0	1
3	2191	-2.67	0	0	1
4	2192	2.74	0	1	0
5	2193	-4.05	0	0	1
6	2194	-1.10	0	0	1
7	2195	0.35	0	0	1
8	2196	-0.50	0	0	1
9	2197	-0.65	0	0	1

```
rf[rf['predicted']==1]['$ chg'].describe()
```

The preceding code generates the following output:

```
count       6.000000
mean        2.986667
std         8.512992
min        -2.800000
25%        -1.080000
50%        -0.015000
75%         1.605000
max        20.040000
Name: $ chg, dtype: float64
```

So, the total went from 147 buys to 6. Our mean went from $0.23 to $2.99, but our median went down from $0 to $-0.02. Let's look at a plot of our returns:

```
fig, ax = plt.subplots(figsize=(15,10))
rf[rf['predicted']==1]['$ chg'].plot(kind='bar')
ax.set_title('Model Predicted Buys', y=1.01)
ax.set_ylabel('$ Change Open to Close')
ax.set_xlabel('Index')
```

The preceding code generates the following output:

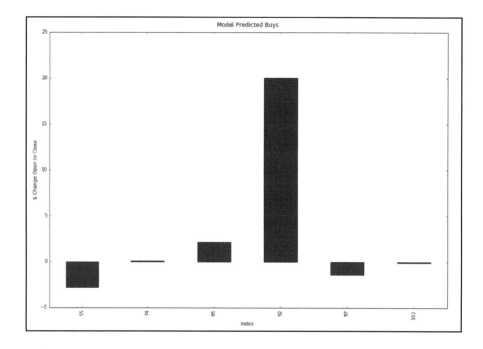

From this, it looks like we got the big winner of the year along with a couple other minor wins and losses. This isn't a lot to go on as far as a test of our model. We could have just been very lucky to catch this win. We need to assess the robustness of our model. We can do this in several ways, but let's do just two things. We'll first drop our threshold from $1 to $0.25 to see how the model holds up:

```
X_train, X_test = X[:2188], X[2188:]
y_train = ipos['$ Chg Open to Close'][:2188].map(lambda x: 1 if x >= .25
else 0)
y_test = ipos['$ Chg Open to Close'][2188:].map(lambda x: 1 if x >= .25
else 0)
clf = linear_model.LogisticRegression()
clf.fit(X_train, y_train)
clf.score(X_test, y_test)
```

The preceding code generates the following output:

```
0.59863945578231292
```

Now we'll examine our results:

```
pred_label = clf.predict(X_test)
results=[]
for pl, tl, idx, chg in zip(pred_label, y_test, y_test.index,
ipos.ix[y_test.index]['$ Chg Open to Close']):
    if pl == tl:
        results.append([idx, chg, pl, tl, 1])
    else:
        results.append([idx, chg, pl, tl, 0])
rf = pd.DataFrame(results, columns=['index', '$ chg', 'predicted',
'actual', 'correct'])
rf[rf['predicted']==1]['$ chg'].describe()
```

The preceding code generates the following output:

```
count     25.000000
mean       1.820800
std        5.520852
min       -6.160000
25%       -1.000000
50%        0.090000
75%        2.120000
max       20.040000
Name: $ chg, dtype: float64
```

Looking at the results, our accuracy dropped, as did our mean. However, our count went from 9 to 25, and we're still far above the baseline approach. Let's do one more test. Let's now remove 2014 from our training data and include it in our test:

```
X_train, X_test = X[:1900], X[1900:]
y_train = ipos['$ Chg Open to Close'][:1900].map(lambda x: 1 if x >= .25
else 0)
y_test = ipos['$ Chg Open to Close'][1900:].map(lambda x: 1 if x >= .25
else 0)
clf = linear_model.LogisticRegression()
clf.fit(X_train, y_train)
clf.score(X_test, y_test)
```

The preceding code generates the following output:

```
0.62068965517241381
```

Once again, we'll examine the results:

```
pred_label = clf.predict(X_test)
results=[]
for pl, tl, idx, chg in zip(pred_label, y_test, y_test.index,
ipos.ix[y_test.index]['$ Chg Open to Close']):
    if pl == tl:
        results.append([idx, chg, pl, tl, 1])
    else:
        results.append([idx, chg, pl, tl, 0])
rf = pd.DataFrame(results, columns=['index', '$ chg', 'predicted',
'actual', 'correct'])
rf[rf['predicted']==1]['$ chg'].describe()
```

The preceding code generates the following output:

```
count    72.000000
mean      0.876944
std       4.643477
min      -6.960000
25%      -1.570000
50%      -0.150000
75%       2.320000
max      20.040000
Name: $ chg, dtype: float64
```

With the 2014 included in our test data, we can see that our mean dropped, but the model continues to appear better than the naive approach of investing in every IPO as seen in the proceeding table:

Model	Trades	Total Gain	Avg. Per Trade
2014-2015 naive	435	61	0.14
2104-2015 .25 LR	72	63.14	0.88
2015 naive	147	33.74	0.23
2015 .25 LR	25	45.52	1.82
2015 1 LR	6	25.20	4.20

Let's now move on to examine which features were most important in our model.

Feature importance

Which features increase the probability that an offering will be successful? There is, unfortunately, no simple answer to this. However, we'll take a look at two ways of assessing this. Because we built our model using a logistic regression, one thing we can examine is the coefficient for each parameter. Remember that the logistic function takes the following form:

$ln(p/1-p) = B0 + B_1 x$

Here, p represents the probability of our positive outcome, B is our intercept, and B_1 is the coefficient for our feature. Once we fit our model, these coefficients can be examined. Let's retrieve them now:

```
f fv = pd.DataFrame(X_train.columns, clf.coef_.T).reset_index()
fv.columns = ['Coef', 'Feature']
fv.sort_values('Coef', ascending=0).reset_index(drop=True)
```

The preceding code generates the following output:

	Coef	Feature
0	1.043891	Q("Lead Mgr")[T.C.E. Unterberg, Towbin]
1	1.022947	Q("Lead Mgr")[T.Morgan Keegan]
2	1.016990	Q("Lead Mgr")[T.Wachovia]
3	0.815448	Q("Lead Mgr")[T.China International]
4	0.684503	Q("Lead Mgr")[T.Merrill Lynch]
5	0.672572	Q("Lead Mgr")[T.Burnham Securities]
6	0.642754	Q("Lead Mgr")[T.Anderson & Strudrick]
7	0.627048	Q("Lead Mgr")[T.BMO Capital Markets]
8	0.595898	Q("Lead Mgr")[T.FIG Partners]
9	0.538498	Q("Lead Mgr")[T.Sanders Morris Harris]

For categorical features, a positive sign on the feature' coefficient tells us that when present, this feature increases the probability of a positive outcome versus the baseline. For continuous features, a positive sign tells us that an increase in the value of this feature corresponds to an increase in the probability of a positive outcome. The size of the coefficient tells us the magnitude of the increase in probability. Let's examine this by looking at the days of the week:

```
fv[fv['Feature'].str.contains('Week Day')]
```

The preceding code generates the following output:

	Coef	Feature
12	-0.132437	Q("Week Day")[T.Mon]
13	0.053885	Q("Week Day")[T.Thurs]
14	-0.062727	Q("Week Day")[T.Tues]
15	-0.039074	Q("Week Day")[T.Wed]

From the preceding screenshot, we can see that Friday is missing. This means that Friday is the baseline against which all other treatments are compared. We also see that only Thursday has increased odds of having a successful IPO based on our model.

It is important to note that the coefficient does not represent the actual increase in odds over the baseline. To get this value, we must take the exponential of it. For Thursday, the increase in odds over Friday is $e(0.053885) = 1.055$. This means that holding all else constant, the odds that Thursday will have a successful IPO are 5.5% greater than Friday. We can also see that Monday is the worst day of the week for IPOs with $e(-0.132437) = 0.876$ or about a 12.4% decrease in the odds of a successful IPO.

Coming back to feature importance, you most likely think at this point that you can take the features with the largest positive coefficients, throw them into a model, and you'll have everything that you' need to dominate the new issue market. Not so fast.

Let's look at top two features based on the size of their positive coefficient:

```
ipos[ipos['Lead Mgr'].str.contains('Keegan|Towbin')]
```

The preceding code generates the following output:

	Date	Issuer	Symbol	Lead/Joint-Lead Mangager	Offer Price	Opening Price	1st Day Close	1st Day % Px Chng	$ Chg Opening	$ Chg Close	...	$ Chg Open to Close	% Chg Open to Close	SP Week Change	SP Close to Open Chg Pct	
33	2002-05-21	Computer Programs and Systems	CPSI	Morgan Keegan/Raymond James	16.5	17.50	18.12	9.82	1.00	1.62	...	0.62	3.542857	2.480647	0.000000	
518	2005-08-04	Advanced Life Sciences	ADLS	C.E. Unterberg, Towbin/ThinkEquity Partners	5.0	5.03	6.00	20.00	0.03	1.00	...	0.97	19.284294	1.777992	0.000000	
884	2007-02-26	Rosetta Genomics	ROSG	C.E. Unterberg, Towbin	7.0	7.02	7.32	4.57	0.02	0.32	...	0.30	4.273504	0.363086	-0.010330	
1467	2011-06-22	Fidus Investment	FDUS	Morgan Keegan	15.0	14.75	15.00	0.00	-0.25	0.00	...	0.25	1.694915	-3.693126	-0.003091	

Our top two features represent a sum total of four IPOs. This is why it is difficult to extract this information from logistic regression models, especially ones of this complexity.

All is not lost, however. We can utilize another model known as a random forest classifier to get our importance measures. This chapter won't go into depth about how this model works, but it should give similar results to the logistic regression model, and as bonus, it will provide a very nice summary of which features have the highest influence on a positive outcome.

Using the same training and test data as earlier, we'll fit the random forest classifier:

```
clf_rf = RandomForestClassifier(n_estimators=1000)
clf_rf.fit(X_train, y_train)
f_importances = clf_rf.feature_importances_
f_names = X_train
f_std = np.std([tree.feature_importances_ for tree in clf_rf.estimators_],
axis=0)
zz = zip(f_importances, f_names, f_std)
zzs = sorted(zz, key=lambda x: x[0], reverse=True)
imps = [x[0] for x in zzs[:20]]
labels = [x[1] for x in zzs[:20]]
errs = [x[2] for x in zzs[:20]]
plt.subplots(figsize=(15,10))
plt.bar(range(20), imps, color="r", yerr=errs, align="center")
plt.xticks(range(20), labels, rotation=-70);
```

The preceding code generates the following output:

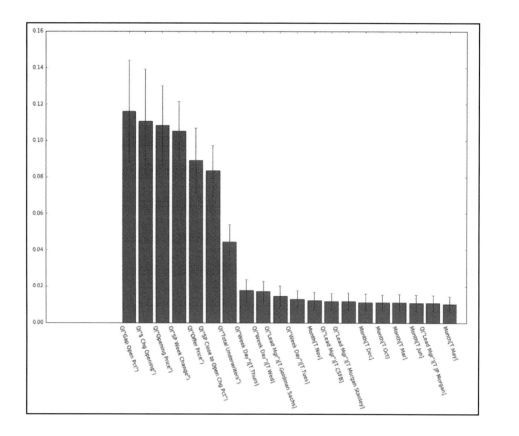

The output from this gives us a ranked list of feature importance along with error bars for each. Looking at the list, these rankings would seem to make sense with gap opening percentage and dollar change from opening leading the pack.

Summary

We've covered a lot of ground this chapter, but we've only just cracked the surface for how to build this type of model. Hopefully, you've gained a better understanding of the modeling process from cleaning the data, to engineering the features, to testing. Hopefully, you'll use this information to extend the model on your own and improve upon it.

In the next chapter, we'll turn our attention to a very different domain as we move from numerical data to text-based data.

5

Create a Custom Newsfeed

I read *a lot*. Some might even say compulsively. I've been known to consume more than a hundred articles on some days. Despite this, I frequently find myself searching for more to read. I suffer from this sneaking suspicion that I have missed something interesting and will forever suffer a gap in my knowledge!

If you suffer from similar symptoms, fear not, because in this chapter, I'm going to reveal one simple trick to finding all the articles that you want to read without having to dig through the dozens that you don't.

By the end of this chapter, you'll have learned how to build a system that understands your taste in news, and will send you a personally tailored newsletter each day.

Here's what we'll cover in this chapter:

- Creating a supervised training set with the Pocket app
- Leveraging the Pocket API to retrieve stories
- Using the embed.ly API to extract story bodies
- Natural language processing basics
- Support vector machines
- IFTTT integration with RSS feeds and Google Sheets
- Setting up a daily personal newsletter

Creating a supervised training set with the Pocket app

Before we can create a model of our taste in news articles, we need training data. This training data will be fed into our model in order to teach it to discriminate between the articles that we'd be interested in and the ones that we would not. To build this corpus, we will need to annotate a large number of articles that correspond to these interests. For each article, we'll label it either "y" or "n". This will indicate whether the article is the one that we would want to have sent to us in our daily digest or not.

To simplify this process, we will use the Pocket app. Pocket is an application that allows you to save stories to read later. You simply install the browser extension, and then click on the Pocket icon in your browser's toolbar when you wish to save a story. The article is saved to your personal repository. One of the great features of Pocket for our purposes is its ability to save the article with a tag of your choosing. We'll use this feature to mark interesting articles as "y" and non-interesting articles as "n".

Installing the Pocket Chrome extension

We use Google Chrome here, but other browsers should work similarly. For Chrome, go into the **Google App Store** and look for the **Extensions** section:

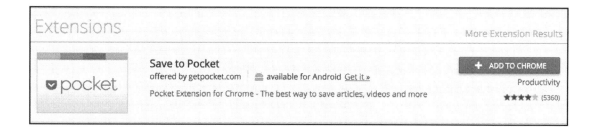

Image from https://chrome.google.com/webstore/search/pocket

Click on the blue **Add to Chrome** button. If you already have an account, log in, and if you do not have an account, go ahead and sign up (it's free). Once this is complete, you should see the Pocket icon in the upper right-hand corner of your browser. It will be greyed out, but once there is an article you wish to save, you can click on it. It will turn red once the article has been saved.

The greyed out icon can be seen in the upper right-hand corner. When the icon is clicked, it turns red to indicated the article has been saved.

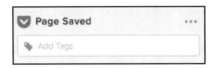

Image from https://www.wsj.com

Now comes the fun part! Begin saving articles all the that you come across. Tag the interesting ones with "y", and the non-interesting ones with "n". This is going to take some work. Your end results will only be as good as your training set, so you're going to to need to do this for hundreds of articles. If you forget to tag an article when you save it, you can always go to the site, `http://www.get.pocket.com`, to tag it there.

Using the Pocket API to retrieve stories

Now that you've diligently saved your articles to Pocket, the next step is to retrieve them. To accomplish this, we'll use the Pocket API. You can sign up for an account at `https://getpocket.com/developer/apps/new`. Click on **Create New App** in the upper left-hand side and fill in the details to get your API key. Make sure to click all of the permissions so that you can add, change, and retrieve articles.

APPS
My Apps
Create a New App

DOCUMENTATION
Overview
Add
Modify
Retrieve
Authentication
Objective-C SDK
Article View API
Preferences API

GETTING STARTED
iOS/Mac
Android
Windows 8
Web
Other Mobile
Adding URLs
Existing Developers

ADDITIONAL INFO
Rate Limits
Error Handling
Migrating Accounts to OAuth
Application Naming
Terms of Service
Security
Developer FAQ
Developer Support

How to Save   Blog   Support   My List

Create an Application

Application Name:
This is the name of your application that will be displayed to users. 80 character max.

Application Description:
This is the description of your application that will be displayed to users. 120 character max.

Permissions:
Please select one or more permissions for your application below.
Important: You cannot change permissions once they are set without generating a new set of keys.

- **Add:** Add items to a user's list.
- **Modify:** Modify items in a user's list.
- **Retrieve:** Retrieve items from a user's list.

Platforms:
We'll generate keys for the platforms you select below. You must select at least one platform to get started and you can always add or remove platforms later.

iPhone	iPad	Mac
Android - Mobile	Android - Tablet	Extension
Windows - Mobile	Windows - Desktop	Web
Mobile (other)	Desktop (other)	

I accept the Terms of Service.

CREATE APPLICATION

Image from https://getpocket.com/developer

Once you have filled this in and submitted it, you will receive your **CONSUMER KEY**. You can find this in the upper left-hand corner under **My Apps**. This will look like the following screen, but obviously with a real key:

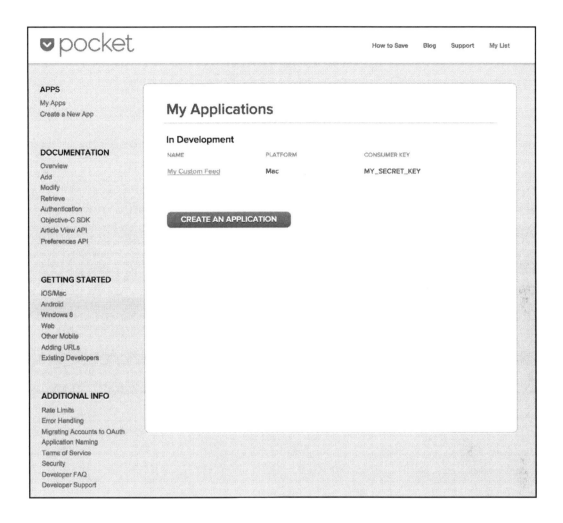

Image from https://getpocket.com/developer

Once this is set, you are ready to move on the the next step, which is to set up the authorizations. We'll do this now. It requires that you input your consumer key and a redirect URL. The redirect URL can be anything. Here I have used my Twitter account:

```
import requests
auth_params = {'consumer_key': 'MY_CONSUMER_KEY', 'redirect_uri':
    'https://www.twitter.com/acombs'}
    tkn = requests.post('https://getpocket.com/v3/oauth/request',
    data=auth_params)
tkn.content
```

This results in the following output:

```
b'code=some_long_code'
```

The output will have the code that you'll need for the next step. Place the following in your browser bar:

```
https://getpocket.com/auth/authorize?request_token=some_long_code&redir
ect_uri=https%3A//www.twitter.com/acombs
```

If you change the redirect URL to one of your own, make sure to URL encode it. There are a number of resources for this. One option is to use the Python library **urllib**, another is to use a free online source.

At this point, you should be presented with an authorization screen. Go ahead and approve it, and we can move on to the next step:

```
usr_params = {'consumer_key':'my_consumer_key', 'code':
    'some_long_code'}
usr = requests.post('https://getpocket.com/v3/oauth/authorize',
data=usr_params)
usr.content
```

We'll use the following output code here to move on to retrieving the stories:

```
b'access_token=some_super_long_code&username=someuser@somewhere.com'
```

First, we retrieve the stories tagged "n":

```
no_params = {'consumer_key':'my_consumer_key', 'access_token':
    'some_super_long_code',
    'tag': 'n'}
no_result = requests.post('https://getpocket.com/v3/get',
data=no_params)
no_result.text
```

The preceding code generates the following output:

```
u'{"status":1,"complete":1,"list":{"1167823383":{"item_id":"1167823383","resolved_id":"116782
3383","given_url":"http:\\/\\/www.businessinsider.com\\/gates-dont-expect-the-nuclear-agreeme
nt-to-lead-to-a-more-moderate-iran-2016-1","given_title":"GATES: Nuclear agreement won\'t lea
d to moderate Iran - Business Insider","favorite":"0","status":"0","time_added":"145325519
8","time_updated":"1453255217","time_read":"0","time_favorited":"0","sort_id":0,"resolved_tit
le":"GATES: Don\'t expect the nuclear agreement to lead to a more moderate Iran","resolved_ur
l":"http:\\/\\/www.businessinsider.com\\/gates-dont-expect-the-nuclear-agreement-to-lead-to-a
-more-moderate-iran-2016-1","excerpt":"Former US defense secretary Robert Gates isn\'t optimi
stic that the landmark July 2015 nuclear deal with Iran will lead the country\\u00a0to halt a
ny of its disruptive policies in the Middle East or its support for terrorist groups.","is_ar
ticle":"1","is_index":"0","has_video":"0","has_image":"1","word_count":"963"},"1167877560":
```

Note that we have a long JSON string on all the articles that we tagged "n". There are several keys in this, but we are really only interested in the URL at this point. We'll go ahead and create a list of all the URLs from this:

```
no_jf = json.loads(no_result.text)
no_jd = no_jf['list']
no_urls=[]
for i in no_jd.values():
    no_urls.append(i.get('resolved_url'))
no_urls
```

The preceding code generates the following output:

```
['http://www.slate.com/articles/double_x/doublex/2016/01/kermit_gosnell_s_atrocities_aren_t_an_argument_for_stricte
r_abortion_laws.html',
 'http://bleacherreport.com/articles/2608872-australian-open-2016-results-winners-scores-stats-from-monday-singles-br
acket',
 'http://www.slate.com/blogs/xx_factor/2016/01/14/rihanna_ahead_of_beyonc_in_the_celebrity_endorsement_game.html',
 'http://www.nzherald.co.nz/nz/news/article.cfm?c_id=1&objectid=11576760',
 'https://blogs.msdn.microsoft.com/oldnewthing/20160114-00/?p=92851',
 'https://www.washingtonpost.com/national/energy-environment/conservation-groups-demand-end-to-refuge-occupation/201
6/01/19/bb83a94e-beff-11e5-98c8-7fab78677d51_story.html',
 'http://www.ultimatepp.org/index.html',
```

This list contains all the URLs of stories that we aren't interested in. Now, let's put this in a `DataFrame` object and tag it as such:

```
import pandas
no_uf = pd.DataFrame(no_urls, columns=['urls'])
no_uf = no_uf.assign(wanted = lambda x: 'n')
no_uf
```

The preceding code generates the following output:

	urls	wanted
0	http://netboot.xyz/	n
1	https://theconversation.com/how-do-you-build-a-mirror-for-one-of-the-worlds-biggest-telescopes-4...	n
2	http://www.wsj.com/articles/alcoa-to-delay-idling-of-washington-smelting-operation-1453235716	n
3	http://www.nzherald.co.nz/nz/news/article.cfm?c_id=1&objectid=11576760	n
4	http://www.businessinsider.com/r-islamic-state-frees-270-of-400-people-it-kidnapped-from-syrias-...	n
5	http://www.wsj.com/articles/johnson-johnson-plans-to-cut-6-of-workforce-1453205772	n
6	https://ramcloud.atlassian.net/wiki/display/RAM/RAMCloud+Papers	n
7	http://mmajunkie.com/2016/01/ronda-rousey-targets-holly-holm-rematch-in-2016-thats-what-i-want-t...	n

Now, we're all set with the unwanted stories. Let's do the same thing with the stories that we are interested in:

```
ye_params = {'consumer_key': 'my_consumer_key', 'access_token':
    'some_super_long_token',
    'tag': 'y'}
yes_result = requests.post('https://getpocket.com/v3/get',
data=yes_params)
yes_jf = json.loads(yes_result.text)
yes_jd = yes_jf['list']
yes_urls=[]
for i in yes_jd.values():
    yes_urls.append(i.get('resolved_url'))
yes_uf = pd.DataFrame(yes_urls, columns=['urls'])
yes_uf = yes_uf.assign(wanted = lambda x: 'y')
yes_uf
```

The preceding code generates the following output:

	urls	wanted
0	https://medium.com/the-development-set/the-reductive-seduction-of-other-people-s-problems-3c07b3...	y
1	http://www.fastcompany.com/3054847/work-smart/can-exercise-really-make-you-grow-new-brain-cells	y
2	http://www.bbc.com/news/magazine-35290671	y
3	http://mobile.nytimes.com/2016/01/08/fashion/mens-style/new-york-bachelors-yearn-for-more.html	y
4	http://www.fastcompany.com/3055019/how-to-be-a-success-at-everything/the-secret-to-making-anxiet...	y
5	https://mentalfloss.atavist.com/secrets-of-the-mit-poker-course	y
6	https://medium.com/@amimran/usability-as-the-enemy-badf5ed6453a#.jxrdu7xub	y
7	http://www.fastcompany.com/3055282/why-its-totally-legal-to-dock-employees-pay-for-going-to-the-...	y
8	http://thenextweb.com/insider/2016/01/11/tinder-is-secretly-scoring-your-desirability-and-pickin...	y
9	http://www.theatlantic.com/science/archive/2016/01/fiber-gut-bacteria-microbiome/423903/	y

Now that we have both types of stories for our training data, let's join them together into a single `DataFrame`:

```
df = pd.concat([yes_uf, no_uf])
df.dropna(inplace=1)
df
```

The preceding code generates the following output:

26	http://www.slideshare.net/ChristopherMoody3/wo...	y
27	http://www.fastcompany.com/3055118/most-creati...	y
28	http://mobile.nytimes.com/blogs/bits/2016/01/1...	y
29	http://lifehacker.com/the-akrasia-effect-why-w...	y
...	...	...
58	http://www.huffingtonpost.com/tim-ward/7-advan...	n
59	http://www.cnn.com/2016/01/19/asia/peshawar-at...	n
60	http://www.nytimes.com/2016/01/24/travel/green...	n

Now that we're set with all our URLs and their corresponding tags in a single frame, we'll move on to downloading the HTML for each article. We'll use another free service for this called **embed.ly**.

Using the embed.ly API to download story bodies

We have all the URLs for our stories, but unfortunately this isn't enough to train on. We'll need the full article body. This could become an enormous challenge if we needed to build our own scraper for dozens of sites. We would need to write code to target the article body while carefully avoiding all the other site gunk that surrounds it. Fortunately, there are a number of free services that will do this for us. We're going to be using `embed.ly` to do this, but there are a number of other services that you also could use.

The first step is to sign up for embed.ly API access. You can do this at `https://app.embed.ly/signup`. This is a straightforward process. Once you confirm your registration, you will receive an API key. This is really all you'll need. You just use this key in your HTTP request. Let's do this now:

```
import urllib
def get_html(x):
    qurl = urllib.parse.quote(x)
    rhtml = requests.get('https://api.embedly.com/1/extract?url=' +
    qurl + '&key=some_api_key')
    ctnt = json.loads(rhtml.text).get('content')
return ctnt
df.loc[:,'html'] = df['urls'].map(get_html)
df.dropna(inplace=1)
df
```

The preceding code generates the following output:

	urls	wanted	html
0	https://medium.com/the-development-set/the-red...	y	<div>\n<section><h3>The Reductive Seduction of...
1	http://www.fastcompany.com/3054847/work-smart/...	y	<div>\n<p><a href="http://suzukilab.com/">Wend...
2	http://www.bbc.com/news/magazine-35290671	y	<div>\n<figure><img src="http://ichef.bbci.co....
3	http://mobile.nytimes.com/2016/01/08/fashion/m...	y	<div>\n<p>Jean-Marc Choffel, a 42-year-old Fre...
4	http://www.fastcompany.com/3055019/how-to-be-a...	y	<div>\n<p>Alison Wood Brooks, a colleague of m...
5	https://mentalfloss.atavist.com/secrets-of-the...	y	<div>\n<i>This story originally appeared in th...
6	https://medium.com/@amimran/usability-as-the-e...	y	<div>\n<h3>Usability as the enemy</h3>\n<figur...
7	http://www.fastcompany.com/3055282/why-its-tot...	y	<div>\n<p>Last week, 6,000 workers of a Pennsy...

With that, we have the HTML of each story.

We need to feed plain text to our model rather than HTML, so we will use a parser to strip out the markup tags:

```
from bs4 import BeautifulSoup
def get_text(x):
    soup = BeautifulSoup(x, 'lxml')
    text = soup.get_text()
    return text
df.loc[:, 'text'] = df['html'].map(get_text)
df
```

The preceding code generates the following output:

	urls	wanted	html	text
0	http://ramiro.org/vis/hn-most-linked-books/	y	<div>\n<h3>Top 30 books ranked by total number...	\nTop 30 books ranked by total number of links...
1	http://www.vox.com/2014/7/15/5881947/myers-bri...	y	<div>\n<p>The Myers-Briggs Type Indicator is p...	\nThe Myers-Briggs Type Indicator is probably ...
2	https://medium.com/@karppinen/how-i-ended-up-p...	y	<div>\n<h3>How I ended up paying $150 for a si...	\nHow I ended up paying $150 for a single 60GB...
3	http://www.businessinsider.com/the-scientific-...	y	<div>\n<figure><img src="http://static1.busine...	\nshutterstockA wise Shakespeare mug once said...
4	http://www.vox.com/2016/1/14/10760622/nutritio...	y	<div>\n<p>There was a time, in the distant pas...	\nThere was a time, in the distant past, when ...

With this, we have our training set ready. We can now move on to a discussion of how to transform our text into something that our model can work with.

Natural language processing basics

If machine learning models only operate on numerical data, how can we transform our text into a numerical representation? This is the focus of natural language processing, or NLP. We'll need to get a brief overview of the principles of NLP before we can work our data. And rather than using the data we have already collected from Pocket, we'll work with a minimal example to keep it simple enough to illustrate the principles. Once those are clear, we can then apply them to our newsfeed corpus.

We'll begin with a small corpus of three sentences:

- The new kitten played with the other kittens
- She ate lunch
- She loved her kitten

We'll first convert our corpus into a **bag-of-words** (**BOW**) representation. We'll skip preprocessing for now. Converting our corpus into bag-of-words representation involves taking each word and its count to create a **term-document matrix**. In a term-document matrix, each unique word is assigned to a column, and each document is assigned to a row. At the intersection of the two is the count:

	the	new	kitten	played	with	other	kittens	she	ate	lunch	loved	her
1	1	1	1	1	1	1	1	0	0	0	0	0
2	0	0	0	0	0	0	0	1	1	1	0	0
3	0	0	1	0	0	0	0	1	0	0	1	1

Note that for these three short sentences, we already have 12 features. As you can imagine, if we were dealing with true documents, such as news articles or even books, the number of features would explode into the hundreds of thousands. To mitigate this, we can take a number of steps to remove features that add little to no informational value to our analysis.

The first step that we can take is to remove **stop words**. These are words that are so common that they typically tell you nothing about the content of the document. Common examples of English stop words are "the", "is", "at", "which", and "on". We'll remove these and re-compute our term-document matrix:

	new	kitten	played	kittens	ate	lunch	loved
1	1	1	1	1	0	0	0
2	0	0	0	0	1	1	0
3	0	1	0	0	0	0	1

As you can see, the number of features was reduced from 12 to seven. This is great, but we can take it even further. We can perform stemming or **lemmatization** to further reduce the features. Note that in our matrix we have both "kitten" and "kittens". Using stemming or lemmatization, we can consolidate this into just "kitten":

	new	kitten	play	eat	lunch	love
1	1	2	1	0	0	0
2	0	0	0	1	1	0
3	0	1	0	0	0	1

Our new matrix consolidated "kittens" and "kitten", but something else happened as well. We lost the suffixes to "played" and "loved", but "ate" was transformed to "eat". Why? This is what lemmatization does. If you remember your grade school grammar classes, we've gone from the inflectional form to the base form of the word. Now, if lemmatization is the transformation to the base form of a word, what is stemming? Stemming has the same goal, but it uses a less sophisticated approach. This approach can sometimes produce pseudo-words rather than the actual base form. For example, in lemmatization, if you were to reduce the word "ponies", you would get "pony"; with stemming, you'd get "poni".

Now, let's go further to apply another transformation to our matrix. So far, we used a simple count of each word, but we can apply an algorithm that will act like a filter on our data to enhance the words that are unique to each document. This algorithm is called **term frequency-inverse document frequency** or **tf-idf**.

We calculate this *tf-idf* ratio for each term in our matrix. Let's calculate it for a couple of examples. For the word "new" in document one, the term frequency is just the count, which is 1. The inverse document frequency is calculated as the log of the number of documents in the corpus over the number of documents the term appears in. For "new" this is $log (3/1)$, or *.4471*. So for the complete *tf-idf* value, we have *tf * idf*, or here it is *1 x .4471*, or just *.4471*. For the word "kitten" in document one, the *tf-idf* is *2 * log (3/2)*, or *.3522*.

Completing this for the remainder of terms and documents, we have the following:

	new	kitten	play	eat	lunch	love
1	.4471	.3522	.4471	0	0	0
2	0	0	0	.4471	.4471	0
3	0	.1761	0	0	0	.4471

Why do all of this? To obtain a high *tf-idf* value, a term would need to have a high number of occurrences in low number of documents. In this way, documents can be said to be represented by terms with high *tf-idf* values.

With this framework, we'll now convert our training set into a *tf-idf* matrix:

```
from sklearn.feature_extraction.text import TfidfVectorizer
vect = TfidfVectorizer(ngram_range=(1,3), stop_words='english', min_df=3)
tv = vect.fit_transform(df['text'])
```

With these three lines, we have converted all our documents into a *tf-idf* vector. A couple of points to note. We passed in a number of parameters: `ngram_range`, `stop_words`, and `min_df`. Let's discuss each of these.

First, `ngram_range` is how the document is tokenized. In our prior examples, we used each word as a token, but here we are using every one to three word sequence as tokens. Let's take our second sentence, "She ate lunch." We'll ignore stop words for the moment. The ngrams for this sentence would be: "she", "she ate", "she ate lunch", "ate", "ate lunch", and "lunch".

Next, we have `stop_words`. We pass in "english" for this to remove all the English stop words. As discussed previously, this removes all terms that lack informational content.

Finally, we have `min_df`. This removes all words from consideration that don't appear in at least three documents. Adding this removes very rare terms and cuts down on the size of our matrix.

Now that our article corpus is in a workable numerical format, we'll move on to feeding it to our classifier.

Support vector machines

We're going to be utilizing a new classifier in this chapter, the linear support vector machine. A support vector machine is an algorithm that attempts to linearly separate data points into classes using a "maximum-margin hyperplane". This is a mouthful, so let's look at what this really means.

Suppose we have two classes of data, and we want to separate them with a line. (We'll just deal with two features, or dimensions, here.) What is the most effective way to place this line?

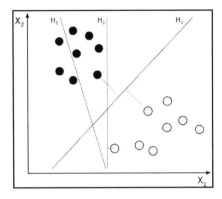

Image from https://commons.wikimedia.org/wiki/File:Svm_separating_hyperplanes_(SVG).svg

In the preceding figure, line H1 does not effectively discriminate between the two classes, so we can eliminate this one. Line H2 is able to discriminate between them cleanly, but H3 is the maximum-margin line. This means that the line is centered between the two nearest points of each class, which are known as the **support vectors**. These can be seen as the dotted lines in the following figure:

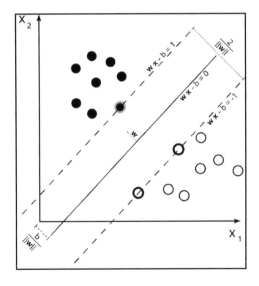

Image from https://commons.wikimedia.org/wiki/File:Svm_max_sep_hyperplane_with_margin.png

But, what if the data isn't able to be separated into classes so neatly? What if there is overlap between the points? In this situation there are still options. One is to use what's called a soft-margin SVM. This formulation still maximizes the margin, but with the tradeoff being a penalty for points that fall on the wrong side of the margin. The other option is to use what's called the **kernel trick**. This method transforms the data into a higher dimensional space where the data can be linearly separated.

Here we have two classes that cannot be separated with a single linear plane.

Image from https://www.cs.utah.edu/~piyush/teaching/15-9-print.pdf

But the implementation of a kernel maps our previous image into a higher dimension as seen in the following image. This allows the data to be linearly separated.

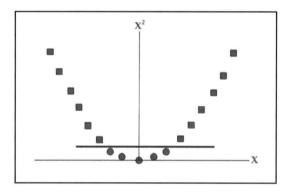

Image from https://www.cs.utah.edu/~piyush/teaching/15-9-print.pdf

We have taken a one dimensional feature space and mapped it onto a two dimensional feature space. The mapping simply takes each x value and maps it to x, $x2$. This transformation allows us to add a linear separating plane.

With this covered, let's now feed our *tf-idf* matrix into to our SVM:

```
from sklearn.svm import LinearSVC
clf = LinearSVC()
model = clf.fit(tv, df['wanted'])
```

The `tv` parameter is our matrix, and the `df['wanted']` method is our list of labels. Remember this is either 'y' or 'n' representing if we are interested in the article or not. Once this runs, or model is trained.

One thing we aren't doing in this chapter is formally evaluating our model. You should almost always have a hold out set to evaluate your model against, but because we are going to be continuously updating our model, and evaluating it daily, we'll skip this step for this chapter. Just remember this is generally a terrible idea.

Let's now move on to setting up our daily feed of news items.

IFTTT integration with feeds, Google Sheets, and e-mail

We used Pocket to build our training set, but now we need a streaming feed of articles to run our model against. To set this up, we'll use IFTT once again, as well as Google Sheets, and a Python library that will allow us to work with Google Sheets.

Setting up news feeds and Google Sheets through IFTTT

Hopefully, you have an IFTTT account set up at this point, but if not go ahead and set this up now. More details can be found in `Chapter 3`, *Build an App to Find Cheap Airfares*. Once this is done, you'll need to set up integration with feeds and with Google Sheets.

First click on **Channels**, search for feeds, and click to set this up:

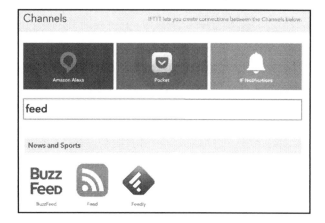

Image from https://www.iftt.com

You'll just need to click on **Connect**.

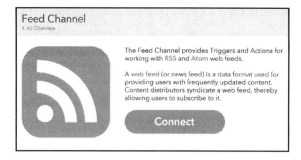

Image from https://www.iftt.com

Next, click on **Channels** again in the upper right-hand corner. This time search for Google Drive:

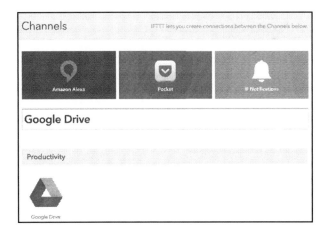

Image from https://www.iftt.com

Click on this. It should take you to a page where you select the Google account that you want to connect to. Choose the account and then click on **Allow** to enable IFTT to access your Google Drive account. Once this is done, you should see the following:

Image from https://www.iftt.com

Now with our channels connected, we can set up our feed. Click on **My Recipes**, and then on **Create a Recipe**. That will bring you here:

Image from https://www.iftt.com

Click on **this**. Search for `feed`, and then click on it. This should bring you here:

Image from https://www.iftt.com

From here, click on **New feed item**:

Image from https://www.iftt.com

Then, add the URL to the box and click on **Create Trigger**. Once this is done, you'll be brought back to add the **that** action:

Image from https://www.ifttt.com

Click on **that**, search for `Google Drive`, and then click on its icon. Once this is done, you'll find yourself here:

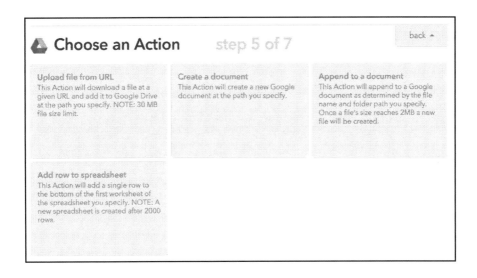

Image from https://www.ifttt.com

We want to our news items to flow into a Google Drive spreadsheet, so click on **Add row to spreadsheet**. You'll then have an opportunity to customize the spreadsheet:

Image from https://www.ifttt.com

I gave this spreadsheet the name **NewStories**, and placed it in a Google Drive folder called IFTTT. Click on **Create Action** to finish this recipe, and soon you'll start seeing news items flow into your Google Drive spreadsheet. Note that it will only add new items as they come in, not items that existed at the time you created the sheet. I recommend adding a number of feeds. You will need to create individual recipes for each. It is best if you add feeds for the sites that are in your training set, for example, the ones you saved with Pocket.

Give the stories a day or two to build up in the sheet. They should soon look something like the following:

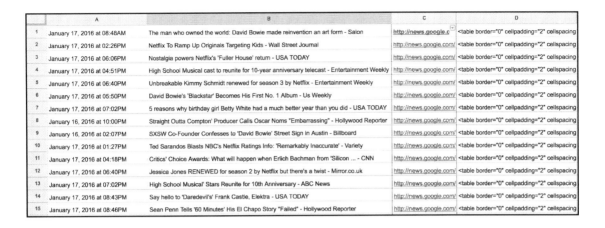

Image from https://docs.google.com

Fortunately, the full article HTML body is included. This means we won't have to use `embed.ly` to download it for each article. We will still need to download the articles from Google Sheets, and then process the text to strip out the HTML tags, but this can all be done rather easily.

To pull down the articles, we'll use a Python library called **gspread**. This can be `pip` installed. Once that's done, you'll need to follow the directions to set up `oauth2`. This can be found at `http://gspread.readthedocs.org/en/latest/oauth2.html`. You will end up downloading a JSON credentials file. Once you have this file, you can find the e-mail address in it with the `client_email` key. You then need to share the `NewStories` spreadsheet that you are sending the stories to with that e-mail. Just click on the blue **Share** button in the upper right-hand corner of the sheet, and paste the e-mail in here. You will end up receiving a failed to send message in your Gmail account, but this is expected. Make sure to swap in your path to the file and the name of the file in the following code:

```
import gspread
from oauth2client.client import SignedJwtAssertionCredentials
json_key = json.load(open(r'/PATH_TO_KEY/KEY.json'))
scope = ['https://spreadsheets.google.com/feeds']
credentials = SignedJwtAssertionCredentials(json_key['client_email'],
json_key['private_key'].encode(), scope)
gc = gspread.authorize(credentials)
```

Now, if everything went well, it should run without errors. Next, you can download the stories:

```
ws = gc.open("NewStories")
sh = ws.sheet1
zd = list(zip(sh.col_values(2),sh.col_values(3), sh.col_values(4)))
zf = pd.DataFrame(zd, columns=['title','urls','html'])
zf.replace('', pd.np.nan, inplace=True)
zf.dropna(inplace=True)
zf
```

	title	urls
0	The man who owned the world: David Bowie made ...	http://news.google.com/news/url?sa=t&fd=R&ct2=...
1	Netflix To Ramp Up Originals Targeting Kids - ...	http://news.google.com/news/url?sa=t&fd=R&ct2=...
2	Nostalgia powers Netflix's 'Fuller House' retu...	http://news.google.com/news/url?sa=t&fd=R&ct2=...
3	High School Musical cast to reunite for 10-yea...	http://news.google.com/news/url?sa=t&fd=R&ct2=...

With this, we downloaded all of the articles from our feed and placed them into a `DataFrame` object. We now need to strip out the HTML tags. We can use the function that we used earlier to retrieve the text. We'll then transform it using our *tf-idf* vectorizer:

```
zf.loc[:,'text'] = zf['html'].map(get_text) zf.reset_index(drop=True,
inplace=True)
test_matrix = vect.transform(zf['text'])
test_matrix
```

The preceding code generates the following output:

```
<488x4532 sparse matrix of type '<class 'numpy.float64'>'
        with 23361 stored elements in Compressed Sparse Row format>
```

Here, we see that our vectorization was successful. Let's now pass this into our model to get back the results:

```
results = pd.DataFrame(model.predict(test_matrix),
columns = ['wanted'])
```

The preceding code generates the following output:

	wanted
0	n
1	n
2	n
3	n
4	n
5	n
6	n
7	n
8	n

We can see that we have results for each story. Let's join this with the stories themselves so that we can evaluate the results:

```
rez = pd.merge(results,zf, left_index=True, right_index=True)
rez
```

n	Nostalgia powers Netflix's 'Fuller House return' - USA TODAY
n	High School Musical cast to reunite for 10-year anniversary telecast - Entertainment Weekly

Definitely nailed these two as my interests lie outside of High School Musical and Full House.

At this point, we can improve the model by going through the results and correcting errors. You'll need to do this for yourself, but here is how I made changes to my own:

```
change_to_no = [130, 145, 148, 163, 178, 199, 219, 222, 223, 226, 235, 279,
348, 357, 427, 440, 542, 544, 546, 568, 614, 619, 660, 668, 679, 686, 740,
829]
change_to_yes = [0, 9, 29, 35, 42, 71, 110, 190, 319, 335, 344, 371, 385,
399, 408, 409, 422, 472, 520, 534, 672]
for i in rez.iloc[change_to_yes].index:
    rez.iloc[i]['wanted'] = 'y'
for i in rez.iloc[change_to_no].index:
    rez.iloc[i]['wanted'] = 'n'
rez
```

The preceding code generates the following output:

	wanted	title	urls
0	n	The man who owned the world: David Bowie made reinvention an art form - Salon	http://news.google.com/news/url?sa=t&fd=R&ct2=us&usg=AFQjCNE_a3MZnPNJ_DL--w-_YaNx6lrrbw&clid=c3a7d30bb8a4878e06b80cf16b898331&cid=52779030852562&ei=PyCcVtDxCYaa3QHP5ogI&url=http://\
1	n	Netflix To Ramp Up Originals Targeting Kids -	http://news.google.com/news/url?sa=t&fd=R&ct2=us&usg=AFQjCNFcojfNfk-8kEXByj4x1dWEyPmiJw&clid=c3a7d30bb8a4878e06b80cf16b898331&cid=52779031941618&ei=ISOcVujuMYOT3AH8vpb4

This may look like a lot of changes, but for over 900 articles evaluated, I had to change very few. By making these corrections, we can now feed this back into our model to improve it even more. Let's add these results to our earlier training data and then rebuild the model:

```
combined = pd.concat([df[['wanted', 'text']], rez[['wanted',
'text']]])
combined
```

The preceding code generates the following output:

	wanted	text
0	y	\nTop 30 books ranked by total number of links to Amazon in Hacker News comments\nClick on a thumbnail image or bar to show the book details.\nAmazon product links were extracted and counted from ...
1	y	\nThe Myers-Briggs Type Indicator is probably the most widely used personality test in the world.\nAbout 2 million peopletake it annually, at the behest of corporate HR departments, colleges, and ...
2	y	\nHow I ended up paying $150 for a single 60GB download from Amazon Glacier\nIn late 2012, I decided that it was time for my last remaining music CDs to go. Between MacBook Airs and the just-intro...
3	y	\nshutterstockA wise Shakespeare mug once said that "love is merely madness" and when you're in the throws of it, that certainly seems to be so.\nLike Dimetapp, love tastes strange, is intoxicatin...
4	y	\nThere was a time, in the distant past, when studying nutrition was a relatively simple science.\nIn 1747, a Scottish doctor named James Lind wanted to figure out why so many sailors got scurvy, ...

Now we rebuild the model.

```
tvcomb = vect.fit_transform(combined['text'], combined['wanted'])
model = clf.fit(tvcomb, combined['wanted'])
```

We have now retrained our model with all available data. You may want to do this a number of times as you get more results over the days and weeks. The more that you add, the better your results will be.

We'll assume you have a well trained model at this point, and are ready to begin using it. Let's now see how we can deploy this to set up a personalized news feed.

Setting up your daily personal newsletter

In order to set up a personal e-mail with news stories, we're going to utilize IFTTT again. As we did before, in Chapter 3, *Build an App to Find Cheap Airfares*, we'll use the Maker Channel to send a POST request. This time, however, the payload will be our news stories. If you haven't set up the Maker Channel, do this now. Instructions can be found in Chapter 3, *Build an App to Find Cheap Airfares*. You should also set up the Gmail channel. Once that is complete, we'll add a recipe to combine the two.

First, click on **Create a Recipe** from the IFTTT home page. Then, search for the **Maker Channel**:

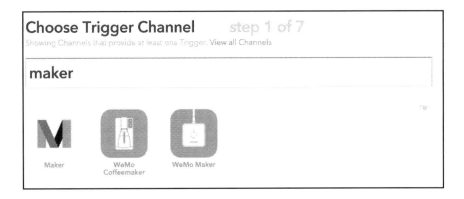

Image from https://www.iftt.com

Select **this**, then select **Receive a web request**:

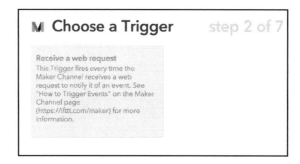

Image from https://www.iftt.com

Then, give the request a name. I'm using `news_event`:

Image from https://www.iftt.com

Finish by clicking on **Create Trigger**. Next, click on **that** to set up the e-mail piece. Search for Gmail and click on the icon seen as follows:

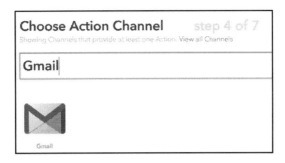

Image from https://www.ifttt.com

Once you have clicked on **Gmail**, click on **Send an e-mail**. From here, you can customize your e-mail message.

Image from https://www.ifttt.com

Input your e-mail address, a subject line, and finally, include **Value1** in the e-mail body. We will pass our story title and link into this with our POST request. Click on **Create Recipe** to finalize this.

Now, we're ready to generate the script that will run on a schedule automatically sending us articles of interest. We're going to create a separate script for this, but one last thing that we need to do in our existing code is serialize our vectorizer and our model:

```
import pickle
pickle.dump(model, open
(r'/Users/alexcombs/Downloads/news_model_pickle.p', 'wb'))
pickle.dump(vect, open
(r'/Users/alexcombs/Downloads/news_vect_pickle.p', 'wb'))
```

With this, we have saved everything that we need from our model. In our new script, we will read these in to generate our new predictions. We're going to use the same scheduling library to run the code that we used in Chapter 3, *Build an App to Find Cheap Airfares*. Putting it all together, we have the following script:

```
# get our imports.
import pandas as pd

from sklearn.feature_extraction.text import TfidfVectorizer
from sklearn.svm import LinearSVC

import schedule
import time

import pickle

import json

import gspread

import requests
from bs4 import BeautifulSoup

from oauth2client.client import SignedJwtAssertionCredentials


# create our fetching function
def fetch_news():
    try:
        vect = pickle.load(open(r'/Users/alexcombs/Downloads/
        news_vect_pickle.p', 'rb'))
        model = pickle.load(open(r'/Users/alexcombs/Downloads/
        news_model_pickle.p', 'rb'))

        json_key = json.load(open(r'/Users/alexcombs/Downloads/
```

```
        APIKEY.json'))
        scope = ['https://spreadsheets.google.com/feeds']
        credentials = SignedJwtAssertionCredentials(json_key
        ['client_email'], json_key['private_key'].encode(), scope)
        gc = gspread.authorize(credentials)

        ws = gc.open("NewStories")
        sh = ws.sheet1
        zd = list(zip(sh.col_values(2), sh.col_values(3),
        sh.col_values(4)))
        zf = pd.DataFrame(zd, columns=['title', 'urls', 'html'])
        zf.replace('', pd.np.nan, inplace=True)
        zf.dropna(inplace=True)

        def get_text(x):
            soup = BeautifulSoup(x, 'lxml')
            text = soup.get_text()
            return text

        zf.loc[:, 'text'] = zf['html'].map(get_text)

        tv = vect.transform(zf['text'])
        res = model.predict(tv)

        rf = pd.DataFrame(res, columns=['wanted'])
        rez = pd.merge(rf, zf, left_index=True, right_index=True)

        news_str = ''
        for t, u in zip(rez[rez['wanted'] == 'y']['title'],
        rez[rez['wanted'] == 'y']['urls']):
            news_str = news_str + t + '\n' + u + '\n'

        payload = {"value1": news_str}
        r = requests.post('https://maker.ifttt.com/trigger/
        news_event/with/key/IFTTT_KEY', data=payload)

        # cleanup worksheet
        lenv = len(sh.col_values(1))
        cell_list = sh.range('A1:F' + str(lenv))
        for cell in cell_list:
            cell.value = ""
        sh.update_cells(cell_list)
        print(r.text)
    except:
        print('Failed')

schedule.every(480).minutes.do(fetch_news)
```

```
while 1:
    schedule.run_pending()
    time.sleep(1)
```

What this script will do is run every 4 hours, pull down the news stories from Google Sheets, run the stories through the model, generate an e-mail by sending a POST request to IFTTT for the stories that are predicted to be of interest, and then finally, it will clear out the stories in the spreadsheet so that only new stories get sent in the next e-mail.

Congratulations! You now have your own personalize news feed!

Summary

In this chapter, we learned how to work with text data when training machine learning models. We also learned the basics of NLP and of Support Vector Machines. In the next chapter, we'll go further with these skills, and attempt to predict what sort of content will go viral.

6

Predict whether Your Content Will Go Viral

It all began with a wager. It was 2001, and Jonah Peretti, a graduate student at MIT at the time, was procrastinating. Instead of writing his thesis, he decided to take up Nike on their offer to personalize a pair of sneakers. Under a recently-launched program, anyone could do this from Nike's new website, NIKEiD. The only problem, at least from Nike's point of view, was that emblazoning a pair of their shoes with the word "sweatshop", as Peretti had requested, was a non-starter. Peretti, in a series of e-mails to the company, demurred pointing out that in no way did the word "sweatshop" fall into any of the categories of objectionable terms that they had outlined that should cause his request to be rejected.

Peretti, believing others might find the back-and-forth with Nike's customer service representatives as amusing as he did, forwarded the messages on to a number of his close friends. Within days, the e-mails had found their way into inboxes across the world. Major media outlets, such as Time, Salon, The Guardian, and even the Today Show had picked up on it. Peretti was at the center of a viral sensation.

Soon after, the question that began nagging at Peretti was whether this sort of thing could be replicated. His friend, Cameron Marlow, had been preparing to write his PhD thesis on viral phenomena, and was was sure that such things were far too complex for anyone to engineer. Marlow wagered Peretti that he could not repeat the success he had enjoyed with that original set of e-mails with Nike. Peretti took the bet.

Fast forward 15 years, and Jonah Peretti leads the website whose name has become synonymous with viral content—BuzzFeed. With more than 77 million unique visitors in 2015, it ranked higher than the New York Times in total reach. I think it's safe to say Peretti won the bet.

But how exactly did he do it? How did Peretti piece together the secret formula to create content that spreads like wildfire? In this chapter, we'll attempt to unravel some these mysteries. We'll examine some of the most-shared content and attempt to find the common elements that differentiate it from the content that people are less willing to share.

We'll cover the following topics in this chapter:

- What does research tell us about virality?
- Sourcing shared counts and content
- Exploring the features of shareability
- Building a predictive content scoring model

What does research tell us about virality?

Understanding sharing behavior is big business. As consumers become blind to traditional advertising, the push is on to go beyond simple pitches to tell engaging stories. Increasingly, the success of these endeavors is measured in social shares. Why go to so much trouble? Because as a brand, every share received represents another consumer that reached—all without spending an additional cent.

Due to this value, several researchers have examined sharing behavior in the hopes of understanding what motivates it.

Among the reasons researchers have found:

- To provide practical value to others (an altruistic motive)
- To associate ourselves with certain ideas and concepts (an identity motive)
- To bond with others around a common emotion (a communal motive)

With regard to the last motive, one particularly well-designed study looked at the 7,000 pieces of content from the New York Times to examine the effect of emotion on sharing. They found that simple emotional sentiment was not enough to explain sharing behavior, but when combined with emotional arousal, the explanatory power was greater. For example, while sadness has a strong negative valence, it is considered to be a low arousal state. Anger, on the other hand, has a negative valence paired with a high arousal state. As such, stories that sadden the reader tend to generate far fewer stories than anger-inducing stories:

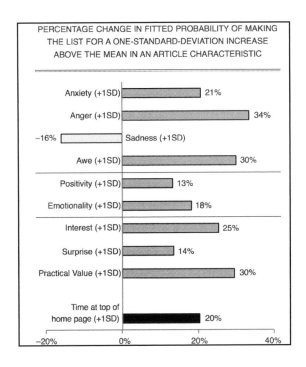

Figure taken from "What Makes Online Content Viral?" by Jonah Berger and Katherine L. Milkman. Journal of Marketing Research available at
http://jonahberger.com/wp-content/uploads/2013/02/ViralityB.pdf

This covers the motivational aspects. However, if we hold those factors constant, how do other attributes affect the virality of a piece of content? Some of these factors could include: headline wording, headline length, headline parts of speech, content length, social network of post, topic, timeliness of subject matter, and so on. Without a doubt, a person could spend their entire life studying this phenomenon. For now, however, we'll just spend the next 30 or so pages doing so.

Sourcing shared counts and content

Before we can begin exploring which features make content shareable, we need to get our hands on a fair amount of content. We'll also need the share counts for each piece of content from the various social networks. Fortunately, we can source this without too much difficulty. I'll be using the site `ruzzit.com`.

This is a relatively new site—it's still in beta, but it tracks the most-shared content over time, which is exactly what we need:

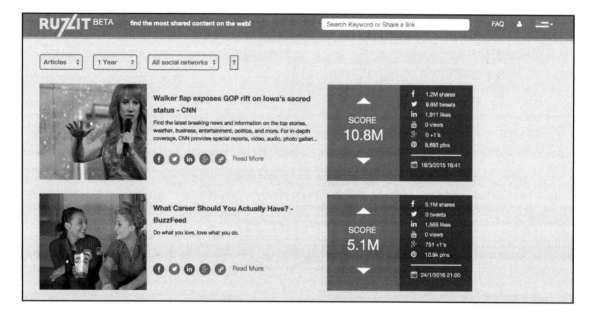

We're going to have to scrape the content from the page—there is no API, unfortunately. And because the site uses an infinite scroll, we'll need to use our old friends from Chapter 3, *Build an App to Find Cheap Airfares*, **Selenium** and **PhantomJS**. Let's get started with the scraping now.

We'll begin with the imports that we'll need initially:

```
import requests
import pandas as pd
import numpy as np
import json
import time
from selenium import webdriver
    pd.set_option('display.max_colwidth', 200)
```

Next, we'll set up our Selenium browser. We'll use the URL that is generated by selecting only articles from the past year from the site. We're going to size the browser so that we get the standard desktop appearance, and pace our calls at 15 seconds each as a matter of etiquette. We are also going to scroll down for the equivalent of 50 pages (there are 10 articles on each page):

```
browser = webdriver.PhantomJS()
browser.set_window_size(1080,800)
browser.get("http://www.ruzzit.com/en-US/Timeline?media=Articles&timeline=Y
ear1&networks=All")
time.sleep(3)
pg_scroll_count = 50
while pg_scroll_count:
    browser.execute_script("window.scrollTo(0,
    document.body.scrollHeight);")
    time.sleep(15)
    pg_scroll_count -= 1
titles = browser.find_elements_by_class_name("article_title")
link_class = browser.find_elements_by_class_name("link_read_more_article")
stats = browser.find_elements_by_class_name("ruzzit_statistics_area")
```

Finally, in the last section, we selected the elements of the page that we need for our analysis. We will need to parse them further to retrieve the text; we'll do that next.

I have chosen to exclude Twitter share counts from this analysis. The company made the decision in late 2015 to remove this count from their standard API. Due to this, the counts displayed may not be reliable. Better to exclude them rather than take the risk in tainting the data:

```
all_data = []
for title, link, stat in zip(titles, link_class, stats):
    all_data.append((title.text,\
                    link.get_attribute("href"),\
                    stat.find_element_by_class_name("col-md-
                    12").text.split(' shares')[0],
                    stat.find_element_by_class_name("col-md-
                    12").text.split('tweets\n')
                    [1].split('likes\n0')[0],
                    stat.find_element_by_class_name("col-md-
                    12").text.split('1's\n')[1].split(' pins')[0],
                    stat.find_element_by_class_name("col-md-
                    12").text.split('pins\n')[1]))
```

Next, we'll put this into a DataFrame:

```
df = pd.DataFrame(all_data, columns=['title', 'link', 'fb', 'lnkdn',
'pins', 'date'])
df
```

The preceding code generates the following output:

	title	link	fb	lnkdn	pins	date
0	Walker flap exposes GOP rift on Iowa's sacred status - CNN	http://www.ruzzit.com/en-US/Redirect/Link?media=653892	1.2M	1,911	8,693	18/3/2015 18:41
1	What Career Should You Actually Have? - BuzzFeed	http://www.ruzzit.com/en-US/Redirect/Link?media=1928328	5.1M	1,559	10.9k	24/1/2016 21:00
2	What State Do You Actually Belong In? - BuzzFeed	http://www.ruzzit.com/en-US/Redirect/Link?media=1927663	4.1M	76	5,465	24/1/2016 15:15
3	Which "Grease" Pink Lady Are You? - BuzzFeed	http://www.ruzzit.com/en-US/Redirect/Link?media=1960941	3M	0	2,760	1/2/2016 03:46

This is a good start, but we're going to need to clean this up. You'll notice that all the links are redirects from ruzzit.com. We'll fix this by following the link to retrieve the original site's link, as follows:

```
df = df.assign(redirect = df['link'].map(lambda x: requests.get(x).url))
```

This line uses the requests library to retrieve the true URL for the story (after the redirection):

link	fb	lnkdn	pins	date	redirect
http://www.ruzzit.com/en-US/Redirect/Link?media=653892	1.2M	1,911	8,693	18/3/2015 18:41	http://www.cnn.com/
http://www.ruzzit.com/en-US/Redirect/Link?media=1928328	5.1M	1,559	10.9k	24/1/2016 21:00	http://www.buzzfeed.com/ashleyperez/what-career-should-you-have
http://www.ruzzit.com/en-US/Redirect/Link?media=1927663	4.1M	76	5,465	24/1/2016 15:15	http://www.buzzfeed.com/awesomer/what-state-do-you-actually-belong-in
http://www.ruzzit.com/en-US/Redirect/Link?media=1960941	3M	0	2,760	1/2/2016 03:46	http://www.buzzfeed.com/louispeitzman/which-grease-pink-lady-are-you

If we examine our `DataFrame` now, we can see that we have the original link for the site. You will also notice that we have the homepage for CNN in the first row. After taking a look, there were 17 stories that directed to the homepage of a site. This is because the story had been removed. One other issue is that some links directed to images rather than articles.

The following code will identity both of these issues and remove the offending rows:

```
def check_home(x):
    if '.com' in x:
        if len(x.split('.com')[1]) < 2:
            return 1
        else:
            return 0
    else:
        return 0
def check_img(x):
    if '.gif' in x or '.jpg' in x:
        return 1
    else:
        return 0
df = df.assign(pg_missing = df['pg_missing'].map(check_home))
df = df.assign(img_link = df['redirect'].map(check_img))
dfc = df[(df['img_link']!=1)&(df['pg_missing']!=1)]
dfc
```

The preceding code generates the following output:

	title	link	fb	lnkdn	pins	date
1	What Career Should You Actually Have? - BuzzFeed	http://www.ruzzit.com/en-US/Redirect/Link?media=1928328	5.1M	1,559	10.9k	24/1/2016 21:00
2	What State Do You Actually Belong In? - BuzzFeed	http://www.ruzzit.com/en-US/Redirect/Link?media=1927663	4.1M	76	5,465	24/1/2016 15:15
3	Which "Grease" Pink Lady Are You? - BuzzFeed	http://www.ruzzit.com/en-US/Redirect/Link?media=1960941	3M	0	2,760	1/2/2016 03:46

Let's now take the next step and retrieve the full article and additional metadata. As in the last chapter, we'll use the API from embed.ly. If you need help getting set up, head back to the previous chapter for details. We'll use embed.ly to retrieve the article's title, HTML, and some additional data such as the entities referenced and images:

```
def get_data(x):
    try:
        data = requests.get('https://api.embedly.com/1/extract?
        key=SECRET_KEY7&url=' + x)
        json_data = json.loads(data.text)
```

```
        return json_data
    except:
        print('Failed')
        return None
dfc = dfc.assign(json_data = dfc['redirect'].map(get_data))
dfc
```

The preceding code generates the following output:

pg_missing	img_link	json_data
0	0	{'type': 'html', 'lead': None, 'favicon_colors': [{'weight': 0.6704101562, 'color': [233, 52, 37]}, {'weight': 0.3295898438, 'color': [249, 249, 249]}], 'original_url': 'http://www.buzzfeed.com/as...
0	0	{'type': 'html', 'lead': None, 'favicon_colors': [{'weight': 0.6704101562, 'color': [233, 52, 37]}, {'weight': 0.3295898438, 'color': [249, 249, 249]}], 'original_url': 'http://www.buzzfeed.com/aw...
0	0	{'type': 'html', 'lead': None, 'favicon_colors': [{'weight': 0.6704101562, 'color': [233, 52, 37]}, {'weight': 0.3295898438, 'color': [249, 249, 249]}], 'original_url': 'http://www.buzzfeed.com/lo...

We now have a column of JSON data for each article. We will now parse this out into individual columns for the features that we are interested in exploring. We'll start with the basics: site, title, HTML, and the number of images:

```
def get_title(x):
    try:
        return x.get('title')
    except:
        return None
def get_site(x):
    try:
        return x.get('provider_name')
    except:
        return None
def get_images(x):
    try:
        return len(x.get('images'))
    except:
        return None
def get_html(x):
    try:
```

```
        return x.get('content')
    except:
        return None
dfc = dfc.assign(title = dfc['json_data'].map(get_title))
dfc = dfc.assign(site = dfc['json_data'].map(get_site))
dfc = dfc.assign(img_count = dfc['json_data'].map(get_images))
dfc = dfc.assign(html = dfc['json_data'].map(get_html))
dfc
```

The preceding code generates the following output:

html
<div>\n<p>I've heard the assertion made time and time again: Being a stay-at-home mom is not akin to They're right. I'm not ...
<div>\n<p>Astronomers have spotted a strange mess of objects whirling around a distant star. Scientist closer look. </p>\n<p>...

The majority of the rows did retrieve the HTML of the page, but there were a fair number that returned nothing. After examining the blank ones, it appears they are primarily from BuzzFeed. This makes sense as the pages are primarily pictures and quizzes. This is a minor annoyance, but we'll have to make do.

Let's now take the HTML and convert it into text. We'll use the BeautifulSoup library to do this for us:

```
from bs4 import BeautifulSoup
def text_from_html(x):
    try:
        soup = BeautifulSoup(x, 'lxml')
        return soup.get_text()
    except:
        return None
dfc = dfc.assign(text = dfc['html'].map(text_from_html))
dfc
```

The preceding code generates the following output:

text
\nI've heard the assertion made time and time again: Being a stay-at-home mom is not akin to having a "real" job. And as a stay-at-home mom, I'm here to tell you... They're right. I'm not sure why...
\nAstronomers have spotted a strange mess of objects whirling around a distant star. Scientists who search for extraterrestrial civilizations are scrambling

Let's now add additional features. We'll add the most prominent color of the first image on the page. The colors for each image are listed by their RGB value in the JSON data that we got from embed.ly, so this will be a simple task:

```python
import matplotlib.colors as mpc
def get_rgb(x):
    try:
        if x.get('images'):
            main_color = x.get('images')[0].get('colors')
            [0].get('color')
            return main_color
    except:
        return None
def get_hex(x):
    try:
        if x.get('images'):
            main_color = x.get('images')[0].get('colors')
            [0].get('color')
            return mpc.rgb2hex([(x/255) for x in main_color])
    except:
        return None
dfc = dfc.assign(main_hex = dfc['json_data'].map(get_hex))
dfc = dfc.assign(main_rgb = dfc['json_data'].map(get_rgb))
dfc
```

The preceding code generates the following output:

text	main_rgb	main_hex
\nI've heard the assertion made time and time again: Being a stay-at-home mom is not akin to having a "real" job. And as a stay-at-home mom, I'm here to tell you... They're right. I'm not sure why...	[243, 245, 245]	#f3f5f5
\nAstronomers have spotted a strange mess of objects whirling around a distant star. Scientists who search for extraterrestrial civilizations are scrambling	[19, 19, 19]	#131313

We've pulled the most prominent color from the first image as an RGB value, but we have also transformed it into a HEX value as well. We'll use this later when we examine the image colors.

We're nearly done with our data manipulations, but we do need to convert some of the figures that we retrieved from Ruzzit. The share numbers that we have are for display purposes rather than for analysis as you can see in the following image:

	title	link	fb	lnkdn	pins	date
1	What Career Should You Actually Have? - BuzzFeed	http://www.ruzzit.com/en-US/Redirect/Link?media=1928328	5.1M	1,559	10.9k	24/1/2016 21:00
2	What State Do You Actually Belong In? - BuzzFeed	http://www.ruzzit.com/en-US/Redirect/Link?media=1927663	4.1M	76	5,465	24/1/2016 15:15
3	Which "Grease" Pink Lady Are You? - BuzzFeed	http://www.ruzzit.com/en-US/Redirect/Link?media=1960941	3M	0	2,760	1/2/2016 03:46

We'll need to clean up the `fb`, `lnkdn`, `pins`, and `date` columns by converting them from a string representation to a numeric one that we can work with as follows:

```python
def clean_counts(x):
    if 'M' in str(x):
        d = x.split('M')[0]
        dm = float(d) * 1000000
        return dm
    elif 'k' in str(x):
        d = x.split('k')[0]
        dk = float(d.replace(',','')) * 1000
        return dk
    elif ',' in str(x):
        d = x.replace(',','')
        return int(d)
    else:
        return x
dfc = dfc.assign(fb = dfc['fb'].map(clean_counts))
dfc = dfc.assign(lnkdn = dfc['lnkdn'].map(clean_counts))
dfc = dfc.assign(pins = dfc['pins'].map(clean_counts))
dfc = dfc.assign(date = pd.to_datetime(dfc['date'], dayfirst=True))
dfc
```

The preceding code generates the following output:

	title	link	fb	lnkdn	pins	date
1	What Career Should You Actually Have?	http://www.ruzzit.com/en-US/Redirect/Link?media=1928328	5100000	1559	10900	2016-01-24 21:00:00
2	What State Do You Actually Belong In?	http://www.ruzzit.com/en-US/Redirect/Link?media=1927663	4100000	76	5465	2016-01-24 15:15:00

Finally, we'll add our last feature, column-word count. We can derive this from splitting our text on whitespace and taking the count. Let's do this now:

```python
def get_word_count(x):
    if not x is None:
        return len(x.split(' '))
```

```
    else:
        return None
dfc = dfc.assign(word_count = dfc['text'].map(get_word_count))
dfc
```

The preceding code generates the following output:

text	word_count
\nI've heard the assertion made time and time again: Being a stay-at-home mom is not akin to having a "real" job. And as a stay-at-home mom, I'm here to tell you... They're right. I'm not sure why...	495
\nAstronomers have spotted a strange mess of objects whirling around a distant star. Scientists who search for extraterrestrial civilizations are scrambling to get a closer look. \n\n\n\nKevin Mor...	211
\nWhat would you say if you found out that our public schools were teaching children that it is not true that it's wrong to kill people for fun or cheat on tests? Would you be surprised?\nI was. A...	1360
\nAre you mindlessly twisting your hair or biting your nails as you read this article? New research from the University of Montreal suggests that compulsive behaviors like these might say more abo...	548

With our data now ready, we can begin to perform our analysis. We're going to attempt to find what makes content highly shareable.

Exploring the features of shareability

The stories that we have collected here represent approximately the 500 most shared pieces of content over the past year. We're going to try to deconstruct these articles to find the common traits that make them so shareable. We'll begin by looking at the image data.

Exploring image data

Let's begin by looking at the number of images that are included with each story. We'll run a value count and then plot the numbers:

```
dfc['img_count'].value_counts().to_frame('count')
```

The preceding code generates the following output:

	count
5	342
4	37
2	36
1	36
3	30
0	1

Now, let's plot that same information:

```
fig, ax = plt.subplots(figsize=(8,6))
y = dfc['img_count'].value_counts().sort_index()
x = y.sort_index().index
plt.bar(x, y, color='k', align='center')
plt.title('Image Count Frequency', fontsize=16, y=1.01)
ax.set_xlim(-.5,5.5)
ax.set_ylabel('Count')
ax.set_xlabel('Number of Images')
```

The preceding code generates the following output:

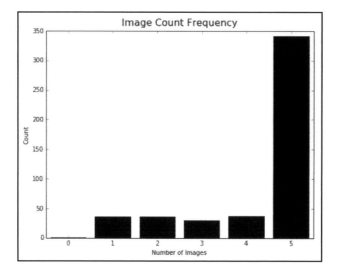

Already, the numbers are surprising. The vast majority of stories have five pictures in them, while having one or less is quite rare.

So, we see that people tend to share content with lots of images. Let's now take a look at the most common colors in those images:

```
mci = dfc['main_hex'].value_counts().to_frame('count')
mci
```

The preceding code generates the following output:

	count
#f8fbfa	3
#c4c4c4	3
#39546c	2
#f6fafb	2
#c6b7b5	2
#312c27	2
#f1f3f1	2
#070603	2
#3dd876	2
#f4f8f9	2

This isn't extremely helpful given that we don't see HEX values as colors. We can, however, use a new feature in pandas, called **conditional formatting**, to help us out:

```
mci['color'] = ' '
def color_cells(x):
    return 'background-color: ' + x.index
mci.style.apply(color_cells, subset=['color'], axis=0)
mci
```

The preceding code generates the following output:

	count	color
#f8fbfa	3	
#c4c4c4	3	
#39546c	2	
#f6fafb	2	
#c6b7b5	2	
#312c27	2	
#f1f3f1	2	
#070603	2	
#3dd876	2	
#f4f8f9	2	

This certainly helps. We can see a number of colors including a bit of blue and black and green (rendered here in grayscale), but the colors are so granular that we have over 450 unique in total. Let's use a bit of clustering to get this down to a more manageable range. As we have the RBG values for each color, we can create a three-dimensional space to cluster them using the K-means algorithm. I won't go into the details of the algorithm here, but this is a fairly simple iterative algorithm, which is based upon generating clusters by measuring the distance to centers and repeating this procedure iteratively. The algorithm does require that we select the k, or the number of clusters that we expect. As RGB ranges from 0 to 256, we'll use the square root of 256, which is 16. This should give us a manageable number while retaining the characteristics of our palette.

We'll first split our RGB values into individual columns as follows:

```
def get_csplit(x):
    try:
        return x[0], x[1], x[2]
    except:
        return None, None, None
dfc['reds'], dfc['greens'], dfc['blues'] =
zip(*dfc['main_rgb'].map(get_csplit))
```

Next, we'll use this to run our K-means model and retrieve the center values:

```
from sklearn.cluster import KMeans
clf = KMeans(n_clusters=16)
clf.fit(dfc[['reds', 'greens', 'blues']].dropna())
clusters = pd.DataFrame(clf.cluster_centers_, columns=['r', 'g', 'b'])
clusters
```

The preceding code generates the following output:

	r	g	b
0	191.235294	161.705882	135.941176
1	32.825397	31.507937	36.603175
2	213.357143	217.607143	215.017857
3	108.583333	105.000000	94.000000
4	82.583333	145.083333	152.666667
5	13.533333	14.733333	17.422222
6	238.509091	242.472727	242.309091
7	1.600000	82.000000	156.200000
8	132.714286	56.428571	30.857143
9	79.842105	69.026316	63.473684

We now have the sixteen most popular dominant colors from the first image in each picture. Let's see what they are using our pandas `DataFrame.style()` method and the function that we just created to color our cells. We'll need to set our index equal to the hex value of the three columns to use our `color_cells` function, so we'll do this as well:

```
def hexify(x):
    rgb = [round(x['r']), round(x['g']), round(x['b'])]
    hxc = mpc.rgb2hex([(x/255) for x in rgb])
    return hxc
clusters.index = clusters.apply(hexify, axis=1)
clusters['color'] = ' '
clusters.style.apply(color_cells, subset=['color'], axis=0)
```

The preceding code generates the following output:

	r	g	b	color
#bfa288	191.235294	161.705882	135.941176	
#212025	32.825397	31.507937	36.603175	
#d5dad7	213.357143	217.607143	215.017857	
#6d695e	108.583333	105.0	94.0	
#539199	82.583333	145.083333	152.666667	
#0e0f11	13.533333	14.733333	17.422222	
#eff2f2	238.509091	242.472727	242.309091	
#02529c	1.6	82.0	156.2	
#85381f	132.714286	56.428571	30.857143	
#50453f	79.842105	69.026316	63.473684	
#b0bec4	176.157895	190.315789	196.263158	
#d4beab	211.888889	189.555556	170.611111	
#96886f	149.818182	136.227273	111.136364	
#909a9d	144.434783	154.478261	156.521739	
#d93733	217.25	55.25	50.75	
#354967	52.545455	72.636364	103.272727	

So, there you have it. These are the most common colors seen (at least in the first image) in the most-shared content. A bit more on the drab side than expected: some blue and red, but mostly shades of brown.

Let's now move on to examine the headlines of our stories.

Exploring the headlines

We'll start by creating a function that we can use to examine the most common tuples. We'll set it up so that we can use it later as well on the body text:

```
from nltk.util import ngrams
from nltk.corpus import stopwords
import re
def get_word_stats(txt_series, n, rem_stops=False):
    txt_words = []
    txt_len = []
    for w in txt_series:
        if w is not None:
```

```
        if rem_stops == False:
            word_list = [x for x in ngrams(re.findall('[a-z0-
            9']+', w.lower()), n)]
        else:
            word_list = [y for y in ngrams([x for x in
            re.findall('[a-z0-9']+', w.lower())\
            if x not in stopwords.words('english')], n)]
            word_list_len = len(list(word_list))
            txt_words.extend(word_list)
            txt_len.append(word_list_len)
    return pd.Series(txt_words).value_counts().to_frame('count'),
    pd.DataFrame(txt_len, columns=['count'])
```

There is a lot in here, so let's unpack it. We created a function that takes in a `Series`, an integer, and a Boolean value. The integer determines the *n* we'll use for n-gram parsing, while the Boolean determines whether we exclude stop words. The function returns the number of tuples per row and the frequency for each tuple.

Let's run it now on our headlines keeping in the stop words. We'll begin with just single words:

```
hw,hl = get_word_stats(dfc['title'], 1, 0)
hl
```

The preceding code generates the following output:

	count
0	6
1	18
2	14
3	16
4	11
5	11
6	14
7	11
8	10
9	6

Now that we have the word count for each headline, let's see what the stats look like:

```
hl.describe()
```

The preceding code generates the following output:

	count
count	482.000000
mean	10.948133
std	3.436294
min	1.000000
25%	9.000000
50%	11.000000
75%	13.000000
max	25.000000

We can see the median headline length for our viral stories comes in at exactly 11 words. Let's take a look at the most frequently used words:

	count
(the,)	144
(to,)	130
(a,)	122
(of,)	86
(in,)	85
(is,)	68
(you,)	68
(and,)	65
(that,)	43
(will,)	42

That's not exactly useful, but it's in line with what we might expect. Let's take a look at the same information for bi-grams:

```
hw,hl = get_word_stats(dfc['title'], 2, 0)
hw
```

The preceding code generates the following output:

	count
(pictures, that)	11
(that, will)	9
(of, the)	8
(dies, at)	8
(people, who)	8
(in, the)	8
(in, a)	8
(that, are)	7
(how, to)	7
(donald, trump)	7

This is definitely more interesting. We can start to see some of the components of the headlines that we see over and over again. The two that stand out are (donald, trump) and (dies, at). Trump makes sense as he's made some headline-grabbing statements, but it's surprising to see the dies headlines. A quick look at the headlines over the past year reveals that a number of high-profile people died recently, so this makes some sense.

Let's now run it with the stop words removed:

```
hw,hl = get_word_stats(dfc['title'], 2, 1)
hw
```

The preceding code generates the following output:

	count
(donald, trump)	7
(year, old)	5
(community, post)	5
(fox, news)	4
(white, people)	4
(cnn, com)	4
(19, things)	4
(things, you'll)	4
(going, viral)	3
(23, things)	3

Again, we see many things that we might expect. It looks like if we changed how we parsed numbers (replacing each of them with a single identifier, such as [number]) that we would likely see more of these bubble up. I'll leave this as an exercise for you if you'd like to attempt it.

Let's now take a look at tri-grams:

```
hw,hl = get_word_stats(dfc['title'], 3, 0)
```

	count
(that, will, make)	4
(for, people, who)	4
(that, are, too)	3
(a, woman, is)	3
(ring, of, fire)	3
(dies, at, 83)	3
(are, too, real)	3
(you, need, to)	3
(of, fire, network)	3
(pictures, that, will)	3

It seems the more words that we include, the more the headlines come to resemble the classic **BuzzFeed** prototype. In fact, let's see if this is the case. We haven't looked at which sites produce the most viral stories; let's see whether **BuzzFeed** leads the charts:

```
dfc['site'].value_counts().to_frame()
```

The preceding code generates the following output:

	site
BuzzFeed	131
The Huffington Post	56
Nytimes	35
Upworthy	24
IFLScience	20
Washington Post	15
Mashable	13
Mic	11
Western Journalism	8
Business Insider	8
the Guardian	6
CNN	6
The Atlantic	6
BuzzFeed Community	5
Fox News	5
Rolling Stone	4

We can clearly see that **BuzzFeed** dominates list, and in a distant second place, we see **The Huffington Post**, which incidentally is another site that Jonah Peretti worked for. It seems that studying the science of virality can pay big dividends.

So far, we have examined images and headlines, let's now move on to examining the full text of the stories.

Exploring the story content

In the previous section, we created a function to examine the common n-grams found in our story headlines, now let's apply this to explore the full content of our stories.

We'll start by exploring bi-grams with the stop words removed. Because headlines are so short compared to the story bodies, it makes sense to look at them with the stop words intact, but within the story, it typically makes sense to eliminate them:

```
hw,hl = get_word_stats(dfc['text'], 2, 1)
hw
```

The preceding code generates the following output:

	count
(islamic, state)	160
(united, states)	126
(year, old)	121
(new, york)	91
(social, media)	60
(years, ago)	57
(white, people)	51
(first, time)	49
(bernie, sanders)	45
(don't, want)	44
(last, year)	43
(every, day)	43
(black, people)	40
(climate, change)	39
(don't, know)	39
(many, people)	38
(two, years)	37
(president, obama)	36

Interestingly, we see that the frivolity we saw in the headlines has completely disappeared. The text is now filled with content discussing terrorism, politics, and race relations.

How is it possible that the headlines are light-hearted while the text is dark and controversial? I would suggest that *13 Puppies Who Look Like Elvis* is going to have a lot less text than *The History of US Race Relations*.

Let's take a look at one more. We'll evaluate the tri-grams for the story bodies:

```
hw,hl = get_word_stats(dfc['text'], 3, 1)
hw
```

The preceding code generates the following output:

	count
(advertisement, story, continues)	32
(articles, buzzfeed, com)	27
(check, articles, buzzfeed)	27
(buzzfeed, com, tagged)	21
(new, york, times)	19
(via, upward, spiral)	17
(pic, twitter, com)	17
(new, york, city)	16
(every, single, day)	16
(follow, us, twitter)	15
(like, us, facebook)	14
(g, m, o)	13
(facebook, follow, us)	13
(us, facebook, follow)	13
(may, like, conversations)	12
(playstation, 5, xbox)	12
(5, xbox, two)	12

We appear to have suddenly entered the land of advertising and social pandering. With this, let's move on to building a predictive model for content scoring.

Building a predictive content scoring model

Let's now use what we learned to create a model that can estimate the share counts for a given piece of content. We'll use the features that we have already created, as well as a few additional features.

Ideally, we would have a much larger sample of content, especially content that had more typical share counts. Despite this, we'll make do with what we have here.

We're going to use an algorithm called **random forest regression**. In prior chapters, we looked at a more typical implementation of random forests, which is based upon classification. Here, we're going to use a regression and attempt to predict the share counts. We could bucket our share classes into ranges, but it is preferable to use regression when dealing with continuous variables.

To begin, we'll create a bare-bones model. We'll use the number of images, the site, and the word count. We'll train our model on the number of Facebook likes.

We'll first import the sci-kit learn library, then we'll prepare our data by removing the rows with nulls, resetting our index, and finally splitting the frame into our training and testing set:

```
from sklearn.ensemble import RandomForestRegressor
all_data = dfc.dropna(subset=['img_count', 'word_count'])
all_data.reset_index(inplace=True, drop=True)
train_index = []
test_index = []
for i in all_data.index:
    result = np.random.choice(2, p=[.65,.35])
    if result == 1:
        test_index.append(i)
    else:
        train_index.append(i)
```

We used a random number generator with a probability set for approximately 2/3 and 1/3 to determine which row items (based on their index) would be placed in each set. Setting the probabilities like this ensures that we get approximately twice the number of rows in our training set as compared to the test set. We can print this out as seen in the following:

```
print('test length:', len(test_index), '\ntrain length:', len(train_index))
```

The preceding code generates the following output:

```
test length: 140
train length: 245
```

Now, we'll continue on with preparing our data. Next, we need to set up categorical encoding for our sites. Currently, our `DataFrame` object has the name for each site represented with a string. We need to use dummy encoding. This creates a column for each site. If the row is for that particular site, then that column will be filled in with 1; all the other site columns be filled in with 0. Let's do that now:

```
sites = pd.get_dummies(all_data['site'])
sites
```

The preceding code generates the following output:

	ABC News	Asbury Park Press	BBC News	Bloomberg.com	Boredom Therapy	Breitbart	Business Insider	BuzzFeed	BuzzFeed Community	CNN	...	Well	Western Journalism	Windsor News - Breaking News & Latest Headlines	Windsor Star	Wise Mind Healthy Body
0	0	0	0	0	0	0	0	1	0	0	...	0	0	0	0
1	0	0	0	0	0	0	0	1	0	0	...	0	0	0	0
2	0	0	0	0	0	0	0	0	0	0	...	0	0	0	0
3	0	0	0	0	0	0	0	0	0	0	...	0	0	0	0
4	0	0	0	0	0	0	0	1	0	0	...	0	0	0	0
5	0	0	0	0	0	0	0	0	0	0	...	0	0	0	0
6	0	0	0	0	0	0	0	1	0	0	...	0	0	0	0
7	0	0	0	0	0	0	0	0	0	0	...	0	0	0	0
8	0	0	0	0	0	0	0	0	0	0	...	0	0	0	0
9	0	0	0	0	0	0	0	0	0	0	...	0	0	0	0
10	0	0	1	0	0	0	0	0	0	0	...	0	0	0	0
11	0	0	0	0	0	0	0	1	0	0	...	0	0	0	0
12	0	0	0	0	0	0	0	0	0	0	...	0	0	0	0
13	0	0	0	0	0	0	0	1	0	0	...	0	0	0	0
14	0	0	0	0	0	0	0	0	0	0	...	0	0	0	0
15	0	0	0	0	0	0	0	0	0	0	...	0	0	0	0

The dummy encoding can be seen in the preceding image.

We'll now continue by splitting our data into training and test sets as follows:

```
y_train = all_data.iloc[train_index]['fb'].astype(int)
X_train_nosite = all_data.iloc[train_index][['img_count', 'word_count']]
X_train = pd.merge(X_train_nosite, sites.iloc[train_index],
left_index=True, right_index=True)
y_test = all_data.iloc[test_index]['fb'].astype(int)
X_test_nosite = all_data.iloc[test_index][['img_count', 'word_count']]
X_test = pd.merge(X_test_nosite, sites.iloc[test_index], left_index=True,
right_index=True)
```

With this, we've set up our X_test, X_train, y_test, and y_train variables. We'll use this now to build our model:

```
clf = RandomForestRegressor(n_estimators=1000)
clf.fit(X_train, y_train)
```

With these two lines of code, we have trained our model. Let's now use it to predict the Facebook likes for our testing set:

```
y_actual = y_test
deltas = pd.DataFrame(list(zip(y_pred, y_actual, (y_pred -
y_actual)/(y_actual))), columns=['predicted', 'actual', 'delta'])
deltas
```

The preceding code generates following output:

	predicted	actual	delta
0	290888.000000	395000	-0.263575
1	336476.000000	386000	-0.128301
2	276856.000000	383000	-0.277138
3	278293.000000	378000	-0.263775
4	208898.000000	352000	-0.406540
5	259866.000000	363000	-0.284116
6	262380.500000	1100000	-0.761472
7	318108.000000	360000	-0.116367
8	251200.000000	337000	-0.254599
9	310909.750000	336000	-0.074673

Here we see side by side the predicted value, the actual value, and the difference as a percentage. Let's take a look at the descriptive stats for this:

```
deltas['delta'].describe()
```

The preceding code generates the following output:

```
count    140.000000
mean       0.053903
std        0.587523
min       -0.774626
25%       -0.297857
50%        0.000637
75%        0.277858
max        2.982869
Name: delta, dtype: float64
```

This looks amazing. Our median error is 0! Well, unfortunately, this isn't a particularly useful bit of information as errors are on both sides—positive and negative, and they tend to average out, which is what we see here. Let's now look at a more informative metric to evaluate our model. We're going to look at root mean square error as a percentage of the actual mean.

To first illustrate why this is more useful, let's run the following scenario on two sample series:

```
a = pd.Series([10,10,10,10])
b = pd.Series([12,8,8,12])
np.sqrt(np.mean((b-a)**2))/np.mean(a)
```

This results in the following output:

```
0.20000000000000001
```

Now compare this to the mean:

```
(b-a).mean()
```

This results in the following output:

```
0.0
```

Clearly the former is the more meaningful statistic. Let's now run this for our model:

```
np.sqrt(np.mean((y_pred-y_actual)**2))/np.mean(y_actual)
```

The preceding code generates the following output:

```
0.6934545982263226
```

Suddenly, our awesome model is a lot less awesome. Let's now add another feature to our model. Let's see whether adding the counts for words will help our model. We'll use a count vectorizer to do this. Much like what we did with the site names, we'll transform individual words and n-grams into features:

```
from sklearn.feature_extraction.text import CountVectorizer
vect = CountVectorizer(ngram_range=(1,3)) X_titles_all =
vect.fit_transform(all_data['title'])
X_titles_train = X_titles_all[train_index]
X_titles_test = X_titles_all[test_index]
X_test = pd.merge(X_test, pd.DataFrame(X_titles_test.toarray(),
index=X_test.index), left_index=True, right_index=True)
X_train = pd.merge(X_train, pd.DataFrame(X_titles_train.toarray(),
index=X_train.index), left_index=True, right_index=True)
```

In these lines, we joined our existing features to our new n-gram features. Let's now train our model and see if we have any improvement:

```
clf.fit(X_train, y_train)
y_pred = clf.predict(X_test)
deltas = pd.DataFrame(list(zip(y_pred, y_actual, (y_pred -
y_actual)/(y_actual))), columns=['predicted', 'actual', 'delta'])
deltas
```

The preceding code generates the following output:

	predicted	actual	delta
0	296150.000000	395000	-0.250253
1	261650.000000	392000	-0.332526
2	305240.000000	386000	-0.209223
3	212840.000000	378000	-0.436931
4	308080.000000	378000	-0.184974
5	254168.571429	374000	-0.320405
6	262640.000000	371000	-0.292075
7	224250.000000	366000	-0.387295
8	213500.000000	340000	-0.372059
9	273950.000000	337000	-0.187092

Checking our errors again, we see the following:

```
np.sqrt(np.mean((y_pred-y_actual)**2))/np.mean(y_actual)
```

This results in the following output:

```
0.64352892438189691
```

It appears that we have a modestly improved model. Let's add one more feature to our model now. Let's add the word count of the title, as follows:

```
all_data = all_data.assign(title_wc = all_data['title'].map(lambda x:
len(x.split(' '))))
X_train = pd.merge(X_train, all_data[['title_wc']], left_index=True,
right_index=True)
X_test = pd.merge(X_test, all_data[['title_wc']], left_index=True,
```

```
right_index=True)
clf.fit(X_train, y_train)
y_pred = clf.predict(X_test)
np.sqrt(np.mean((y_pred-y_actual)**2))/np.mean(y_actual)
```

The preceding code generates the following output:

0.64134526362902999

It appears that each feature has modestly improved our model. There are certainly more features that we could add to our model. For example, we could add the day of the week and the hour of the posting, we could determine if the article is a listicle by running a regex on the headline, or we could examine the sentiment of each article. This only begins to touch on the features that could be important to model virality. We would certainly need to go much further to continue reducing the error in our model.

I should also note that we have performed only the most cursory testing of our model. Each measurement should be run multiple times to get a more accurate representation of the true error rate. It is possible that there is no statistically discernable difference between our last two models, as we only performed one test.

Summary

In this chapter, we examined the common features of viral content, and how we can build a model to predict virality using a random forest regression. We also learned how to combine multiple types of features and how to split our model into training and testing sets.

Hopefully, you will take what you've learned here to build the next viral empire. If this doesn't work out, perhaps the next chapter on mastering the stock market will be be useful…

7

Forecast the Stock Market with Machine Learning

In biology, there is fairly well-known phenomenon called the **Red Queen's race.** The idea is that every organism is engaged in a race not to gain some outsized advantage, but merely to keep pace with an ever-changing environment filled with opposing organisms.

The term comes from a quote in Lewis Carol's *Through the Looking Glass*: "Now, here, you see, it takes all the running you can do, to keep in the same place".

One example of this phenomenon can be seen with the rise of antibiotic-resistant superbugs such as MRSA. As we've developed stronger and stronger antibiotics, these bacteria have developed better and better defenses to defeat our drugs.

This may seem like it has little to do with the stock market, but this same phenomenon is at play every day in the financial markets. Just like living organisms, markets evolve, and what works one day quickly fails to work to next.

For example, occasionally a paper will be published that alerts the financial world to the existence of a phenomenon that is based upon some profitable anomaly. Frequently this phenomenon is the downstream effect of some outside-imposed, real-world constraint. Take for example year-end tax loss sales. Due to the nature of the tax laws, it makes sense for traders to sell their losses at the end of the year. This causes downward price pressure appears on the losing stocks toward year-end that causes the stocks to be discounted beyond their fair market value. This also means that in January, the downward pressure is gone, and in its place is upward pressure as new money is put to work in these now undervalued assets. Once this phenomenon has been broadcast, however, it only makes sense for traders to attempt to get ahead of it and begin buying those stocks in late December and selling to other traders in January. These new traders seeking to gain an early edge now dilute the effect by entering the market.

They are relieving the year-end selling pressure and decreasing the January buying pressure. The effect is essentially arbitraged away right along with the profitability. What once worked no longer works, and traders begin to abandon the strategy and move on to the next new thing. To stay in the same place, traders must quickly adapt.

In this chapter, we'll spend some time discussing how to build and test a trading strategy. We'll spend even more time, however, on how *not* to do this. There are countless pitfalls to avoid when trying to devise your own system, and it is quite nearly an impossible task. However, it can be a lot of fun – and sometimes, it can even be profitable.

We'll cover the following topics in this chapter:

- Types of market analysis
- What does research tell us about the stock market?
- How to develop a trading system

- Building and evaluating your machine learning models

Please don't do dumb things with the information in this chapter. Do not risk money that you can't afford to lose. If you do decide to use anything that you learned here to trade, you're on your own. This shouldn't be deemed investment advice of any kind, and I accept no responsibility for your actions.

Types of market analysis

Let's begin with a discussion of some key terms and methods of analysis when dealing with the financial markets. Though there are countless financial instruments such as stocks, bonds, ETFs, currencies, swaps, and so on, we'll limit our discussion to stocks and the stock market. A stock is simply a fractional share of ownership in a public company. The price of a stock is expected to increase when future prospects for the company rise, and decrease as these prospects decline.

Investors generally fall into one of two camps. The first camp believes in fundamental analysis. Fundamental analysts pour through company financials looking for information that indicates that somehow the market is undervaluing the shares of a company. These investors look at various factors such as revenue, earnings, and cash flow. They also examine numerous ratios relating to these values. Many times this involves looking at how one company's financials compare to another's.

The second camp of investors are the technical analysts. Technical analysts believe that the share price of a stock already reflects all the available public information, and that looking through the fundamentals is largely a waste of time. They believe that by looking at historical prices—stock charts—one can see areas where prices are likely to rise, fall, or stagnate. Generally, they feel that these charts reveal clues to investor psychology.

What both groups have in common is an underlying belief that the right analysis can lead to profits. Is this true, however?

What does research tell us about the stock market?

Perhaps the most influential theory of the stock market over the last 50 years is the efficient-market hypothesis. This theory was developed by Eugene Fama, and it states that markets are rational and all available information is adequately reflected in stock prices. As such, it is impossible for an investor to consistently "beat the market" on a risk-adjusted basis. The efficient-market hypothesis is often discussed as having three forms: a weak form, a semi-strong form, and a strong form.

In the weak form, the market is efficient in the sense that one cannot use past information from prices to predict future prices. Information is reflected in stocks relatively quickly. Also, while technical analysis would be ineffective, in some scenarios, a fundamental analysis could be effective.

In the semi-strong form, prices immediately reflect all the relevant new public information in an unbiased manner. Here, neither technical nor fundamental analysis would be effective. Finally, in the strong form, stock prices reflect all public and private information.

Based on these theories, there isn't a lot of hope of making money by exploiting patterns in the market. Fortunately, while the market operates in a largely efficient manner on the whole, distinct pockets of inefficiency have been uncovered. Most of these tend to be ephemeral, but some do persist. One of the most pervasive—even according to Fama—is the outperformance of momentum strategies.

So, what exactly is a momentum strategy? There are a number of variations on the theme, but the basic idea is that stocks are ranked from the highest to lowest according to their return over some prior period. The top performers are bought and held for some period of time, and then the process is repeated after some fixed holding period. A typical long-only momentum strategy may involve buying the top 25 performing stocks in the S&P 500 over the past year, holding them for a year, and then repeating the process.

This may sound like an absurdly simple strategy—and it is. However, it has consistently returned results that defy expectation. Why? As you can imagine, a lot of research has examined this effect, and the hypothesis is that there is something inherently, systemically biased about how humans deal with new information. Research suggests that they underreact to news in the short term and then overreact to news in the long term.

Will this effect be arbitraged away as more traders learn of it and pile in? There has been some evidence of this in recent years, but it remains unclear. Regardless, the effect was real and persisted far longer than can be currently be accounted for by the efficient-market hypothesis, so there is hope. With this slight glimmer of hope, let's now move on to seeing how we may go about finding our own anomalies.

How to develop a trading strategy

We'll begin our strategy development by focusing on the technical aspects. Let's take a look at the S&P 500 over the last several years. We'll use the functionality of pandas to import our data. This will give us access to several sources of stock data, including Yahoo! and Google.

First, we'll need to install the `datareader` package. This can be pip-installed from the command line using `pip install pandas_datareader`.

Then, we'll go ahead an set our imports, as follows:

```
import pandas as pd
from pandas_datareader import data, wb
import matplotlib.pyplot as plt

%matplotlib inline
pd.set_option('display.max_colwidth', 200)
```

Now, we'll get our data for the SPY ETF. This instrument represents the stocks of the S&P 500. We'll pull data from the start of 2010 through the beginning of March 2016:

```
import pandas_datareader as pdr

start_date = pd.to_datetime('2010-01-01')
stop_date = pd.to_datetime('2016-03-01')

spy = pdr.data.get_data_yahoo('SPY', start_date, stop_date)
```

The preceding code generates the following output:

	Open	High	Low	Close	Volume	Adj Close
Date						
2010-01-04	112.370003	113.389999	111.510002	113.330002	118944600	100.323436
2010-01-05	113.260002	113.680000	112.849998	113.629997	111579900	100.589001
2010-01-06	113.519997	113.989998	113.430000	113.709999	116074400	100.659822
2010-01-07	113.500000	114.330002	113.180000	114.190002	131091100	101.084736
2010-01-08	113.889999	114.620003	113.660004	114.570000	126402800	101.421122
2010-01-11	115.080002	115.129997	114.239998	114.730003	106375700	101.562763
2010-01-12	113.970001	114.209999	113.220001	113.660004	163333500	100.615564
2010-01-13	113.949997	114.940002	113.370003	114.620003	161822000	101.465387
2010-01-14	114.489998	115.139999	114.419998	114.930000	115718800	101.739807

We can now plot our data. We'll select only the closing price, as follows:

```
spy_c = spy['Close']

fig, ax = plt.subplots(figsize=(15,10))
spy_c.plot(color='k')
plt.title("SPY", fontsize=20)
```

The preceding code generates the following output:

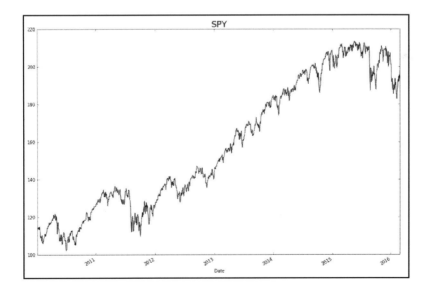

In the preceding figure, we see the price chart of the daily closing price of the S&P 500 for the period that we selected. Let's run a bit of analysis to see what the returns over this period could have been if we had invested in this ETF.

We'll pull data for the first open first:

```
first_open = spy['Open'].iloc[0]
first_open
```

The preceding code generates the following output:

```
112.370003
```

Next, let's get the closing price on the final day of the period:

```
last_close = spy['Close'].iloc[-1]
last_close
```

This will result in the following output:

```
198.11000100000001
```

And finally, let's see the change over the full period:

```
last_close - first_open
```

The preceding code generates the following output:

```
85.739998000000014
```

So, it appears that a purchase of 100 shares at the start of the period would have cost us approximately $11,237, and at the end of the period, that same 100 shares would have been valued at roughly $19,811. This transaction would have given us a gain of over 76% over the period. Not bad at all.

Let's now take a look at the return over the same period for just the intraday gains. This assumes that we buy the stock at the open of each day and sell it at the close of that same day:

```
spy['Daily Change'] = pd.Series(spy['Close'] - spy['Open'])
```

This will give us the change from the open to the close each day. Let's take a look at this:

```
spy['Daily Change']
```

The preceding code generates the following output:

```
Date
2010-01-04     0.959999
2010-01-05     0.369995
2010-01-06     0.190002
2010-01-07     0.690002
2010-01-08     0.680001
2010-01-11    -0.349999
2010-01-12    -0.309997
2010-01-13     0.670006
2010-01-14     0.440002
2010-01-15    -1.090004
2010-01-19     1.439995
2010-01-20    -0.390000
2010-01-21    -2.220001
2010-01-22    -1.989998
2010-01-25    -0.440002
2010-01-26    -0.029998
2010-01-27     0.660004
2010-01-28    -1.620002
2010-01-29    -1.650002
2010-02-01     0.909996
2010-02-02     1.119995
2010-02-03    -0.049995
```

Let's now sum those changes over the period:

```
spy['Daily Change'].sum()
```

The preceding code generates the following output:

```
41.460173000000196
```

So, as you can see, we have gone from a gain of over 85 points to one of just over 41 points. Ouch! More than half the market's gains came from holding overnight during the period.

The overnight returns were better than the intraday returns, but how about the volatility? Returns are always judged on a risk-adjusted basis, so let's take a look at how the overnight trades compared to the intraday trades on the basis of their standard deviation.

We can use NumPy to calculate this for us, as follows:

```
np.std(spy['Daily Change'])
```

The preceding code generates the following output:

```
1.1449966111357177
```

Now, let's get the standard deviation.

```
spy['Overnight Change'] = pd.Series(spy['Open'] - spy['Close'].shift(1))
np.std(spy['Overnight Change'])
```

The preceding code generates the following output:

```
0.95281601518051173
```

So, our overnight trading had lower volatility as compared to the intraday trading as well. However, not all volatility is created equal. Let's compare the mean change on downside days versus upside days for both strategies .

First, let's look at the upside days:

```
spy[spy['Daily Change']<0]['Daily Change'].mean()
```

The preceding code generates the following output:

```
-0.90606707692307742
```

Now, we'll look at the downside days:

```
spy[spy['Overnight Change']<0]['Overnight Change'].mean()
```

The preceding code generates the following output:

```
-0.66354681502086243
```

Again, we see that the average downside move is less for our overnight trading strategy versus our intraday trading strategy.

So far, we looked at everything in terms of points, but let's now move to looking at returns. This will help put our gains and losses in a more realistic context. Continuing with our three strategies, we'll construct a pandas series for each scenario: daily returns (close to close change), intraday returns (open to close), and overnight returns (close to open) as follows:

```
daily_rtn = ((spy['Close'] -
spy['Close'].shift(1))/spy['Close'].shift(1))*100
id_rtn = ((spy['Close'] - spy['Open'])/spy['Open'])*100
on_rtn = ((spy['Open'] - spy['Close'].shift(1))/spy['Close'].shift(1))*100
```

What we've done is use the pandas .shift() method to subtract each series from the prior day's series. For example, for the first Series in the preceding code, we subtracted the close one day ago from the current closing price for each day. A new Series is generated that contains one less data point due to the differencing. If you print out the new Series, you can see the following:

```
daily_rtn
```

The preceding code generates the following output:

Date	
2010-01-04	NaN
2010-01-05	0.264709
2010-01-06	0.070406
2010-01-07	0.422129
2010-01-08	0.332777
2010-01-11	0.139655
2010-01-12	-0.932624
2010-01-13	0.844623
2010-01-14	0.270456
2010-01-15	-1.122423
2010-01-19	1.249559
2010-01-20	-1.016860
2010-01-21	-1.922910
2010-01-22	-2.229184
2010-01-25	0.512772
2010-01-26	-0.419057
2010-01-27	0.475715

Let's now take a look at the statistics for all three strategies. We'll create a function that can take in each series of returns, and will print out the summary results. We're going to get statistics for each of our winning, losing, and breakeven trades, and something called the **Sharpe ratio**. I said earlier that returns are judged on a risk-adjusted basis. This is exactly what the Sharpe ratio provides us. It is a method of comparing returns by accounting for the volatility of these returns. Here, we use the Sharpe ratio with an adjustment to annualize the ratio:

```
def get_stats(s, n=252):
    s = s.dropna()
```

```
wins = len(s[s>0])
losses = len(s[s<0])
evens = len(s[s==0])
mean_w = round(s[s>0].mean(), 3)
mean_l = round(s[s<0].mean(), 3)
win_r = round(wins/losses, 3)
mean_trd = round(s.mean(), 3)
sd = round(np.std(s), 3)
max_l = round(s.min(), 3)
max_w = round(s.max(), 3)
sharpe_r = round((s.mean()/np.std(s))*np.sqrt(n), 4)
cnt = len(s)
print('Trades:', cnt,\
        '\nWins:', wins,\
        '\nLosses:', losses,\
        '\nBreakeven:', evens,\
        '\nWin/Loss Ratio', win_r,\
        '\nMean Win:', mean_w,\
        '\nMean Loss:', mean_l,\
        '\nMean', mean_trd,\
        '\nStd Dev:', sd,\
        '\nMax Loss:', max_l,\
        '\nMax Win:', max_w,\
        '\nSharpe Ratio:', sharpe_r)
```

Let's now run each strategy to see the stats. We'll start with the buy and hold strategy (daily returns) and then move to the other two, as follows:

```
get_stats(daily_rtn)
```

The preceding code generates the following output:

```
Trades: 1549
Wins: 844
Losses: 699
Breakeven: 6
Win/Loss Ratio 1.207
Mean Win: 0.691
Mean Loss: -0.743
Mean 0.041
Std Dev: 1.009
Max Loss: -6.512
Max Win: 4.65
Sharpe Ratio: 0.6477
```

```
get_stats(id_rtn)
```

The preceding code generates the following output:

```
Trades: 1550
Wins: 851
Losses: 689
Breakeven: 10
Win/Loss Ratio 1.235
Mean Win: 0.517
Mean Loss: -0.59
Mean 0.021
Std Dev: 0.758
Max Loss: -4.175
Max Win: 3.683
Sharpe Ratio: 0.4472
```

```
get_stats(on_rtn)
```

The preceding code generates the following output:

```
Trades: 1549
Wins: 821
Losses: 720
Breakeven: 8
Win/Loss Ratio 1.14
Mean Win: 0.421
Mean Loss: -0.437
Mean 0.02
Std Dev: 0.63
Max Loss: -5.227
Max Win: 4.09
Sharpe Ratio: 0.5071
```

As you can see, the buy and hold strategy has the highest mean return as well as the highest standard deviation of the three. This also has the largest daily drawdown (loss). Also notice that even though the overnight-only strategy has nearly the same mean return as the intraday strategy, it has substantially less volatility. This, in turn, gives it a Sharpe ratio that is higher than the intraday strategy.

At this point, we have a solid baseline to compare our future strategies. Now, I am going to tell you about a strategy that blows all three of these strategies out of the water.

Let's take a look at the statistics for this new mystery strategy:

```
Trades: 1549
Wins: 454
Losses: 340
Breakeven: 755
Win/Loss Ratio 1.335
Mean Win: 0.684
Mean Loss: -0.597
Mean 0.07
Std Dev: 0.663
Max Loss: -3.46
Max Win: 5.93
Sharpe Ratio: 1.6675
```

With this strategy, I have nearly tripled the Sharpe ratio over buy and hold, lowered the volatility substantially, increased the max win, and reduced the max loss by nearly half.

How did I devise this market-trouncing strategy? Wait for it.... I did this by generating 1,000 trials of random overnight signals (either to buy or not) for the test period and then picked the best performing one. This gave me the strategy with the best 1,000 random signals.

This is obviously not the way to beat the market. So then, why did I do this? I did it to demonstrate that if you test enough strategies, the fact is that just by random chance, you will come across a few strategies that appear to be amazing. This is the called the **data mining fallacy**, and it is a real risk in trading strategy development. This is why it is so important that a strategy is anchored in real-world behavior—behavior that is systematically biased due to some real-world constraint. If you want an edge in trading, you don't trade the markets, you trade with the people who trade markets.

Our edge comes from thoughtfully understanding how people might react to certain situations.

Extending our analysis period

Let's now extend our analysis. First, we'll pull data for the index starting from the year 2000:

```
start_date = pd.to_datetime('2000-01-01')
stop_date = pd.to_datetime('2016-03-01')
sp = pdr.data.get_data_yahoo('SPY', start_date, stop_date)
```

Let's have a look at our chart now:

```
fig, ax = plt.subplots(figsize=(15,10))
sp['Close'].plot(color='k')
```

```
plt.title("SPY", fontsize=20)
```

The preceding code generates the following output:

Here, we see the price action for the SPY from the start of 2000 through March 1, 2016. There has certainly been a lot of movement in that period as the market has experienced both highly positive and highly negative regimes.

Let's get our baseline for our new expanded period for our three base strategies.

First, let's set up our variables for each of them, as follows:

```
long_day_rtn = ((sp['Close'] -
sp['Close'].shift(1))/sp['Close'].shift(1))*100

long_id_rtn = ((sp['Close'] - sp['Open'])/sp['Open'])*100
long_on_rtn = ((sp['Open'] -
sp['Close'].shift(1))/sp['Close'].shift(1))*100
```

Now, let's see what the point totals are for each of them.

1. First, close to close:

```
(sp['Close'] - sp['Close'].shift(1)).sum()
```

The preceding code generates the following output:

```
52.67250100000001
```

2. Then, open to close:

```
(sp['Close'] - sp['Open']).sum()
```

The preceding code generates the following output:

```
-36.91226699999963
```

3. Finally, close to open:

```
(sp['Open'] - sp['Close'].shift(1)).sum()
```

The preceding code generates the following output:

```
86.77226799999964
```

Now, let's look at the statistics for each of them.

4. First, we get the statistic for close to close:

```
get_stats(long_day_rtn)
```

The preceding code generates the following output:

```
Trades: 4064
Wins: 2168
Losses: 1881
Breakeven: 15
Win/Loss Ratio 1.153
Mean Win: 0.819
Mean Loss: -0.91
Mean 0.016
Std Dev: 1.275
Max Loss: -9.845
Max Win: 14.52
Sharpe Ratio: 0.1958
```

5. Next, we retrieve the intra-day return statistics:

```
get_stats(long_id_rtn)
```

The preceding code generates the following output:

```
Trades: 4065
Wins: 2128
Losses: 1908
Breakeven: 29
Win/Loss Ratio 1.115
Mean Win: 0.686
Mean Loss: -0.766
Mean -0.0
Std Dev: 1.052
Max Loss: -8.991
Max Win: 8.435
Sharpe Ratio: -0.0063
```

6. Finally, we get the overnight return statistics:

```
get_stats(long_on_rtn)
```

The preceding code generates the following output:

```
Trades: 4064
Wins: 2152
Losses: 1878
Breakeven: 34
Win/Loss Ratio 1.146
Mean Win: 0.436
Mean Loss: -0.466
Mean 0.016
Std Dev: 0.696
Max Loss: -8.322
Max Win: 6.068
Sharpe Ratio: 0.3541
```

We can see that the differences between the three are even more pronounced over a longer period. If we only held this S&P ETF during the day over the past 16 years, we would have lost money. If we held the ETF only overnight, we would have improved our returns by more than 50%! Obviously this presumes no trading costs and no taxes along with perfect fills, but regardless, this is a remarkable finding.

Building our model with a support vector regression

Now that we have a baseline to compare to, let's build our first regression model. We're going to start with a very basic model using only the stock's prior closing values to predict the next day's close. We're going to build this model using a support vector regression. With this, let's set up our model.

The first step is to set up a `DataFrame` object that contains price history for each day. We're going to include the past 20 closes in our model, as follows:

```
for i in range(1, 21, 1):
    sp.loc[:,'Close Minus ' + str(i)] = sp['Close'].shift(i)
sp20 = sp[[x for x in sp.columns if 'Close Minus' in x or x ==
'Close']].iloc[20:,]
sp20
```

The preceding code generates the following output:

	Close	Close Minus 1	Close Minus 2	Close Minus 3	Close Minus 4	Close Minus 5	Close Minus 6	Close Minus 7	Close Minus 8	Close Minus 9	...	Close Minus 11
Date												
2000-02-01	140.937500	139.562500	135.875000	140.250000	140.812500	141.937500	140.343704	144.437500	144.750000	147.000000	...	146.968704
2000-02-02	141.062500	140.937500	139.562500	135.875000	140.250000	140.812500	141.937500	140.343704	144.437500	144.750000	...	145.812500
2000-02-03	143.187500	141.062500	140.937500	139.562500	135.875000	140.250000	140.812500	141.937500	140.343704	144.437500	...	147.000000
2000-02-04	142.593704	143.187500	141.062500	140.937500	139.562500	135.875000	140.250000	140.812500	141.937500	140.343704	...	144.750000
2000-02-07	142.375000	142.593704	143.187500	141.062500	140.937500	139.562500	135.875000	140.250000	140.812500	141.937500	...	144.437500

This code gives us each day's closing price along with the prior 20 all on the same line.

This will form the basis of the *X* array that we will feed our model. However, before we're ready for this, there are a few additional steps.

First, we'll reverse our columns so that time runs left to right, as follows:

```
sp20 = sp20.iloc[:,::-1]
sp20
```

The preceding code generates the following output:

	Close Minus 20	Close Minus 19	Close Minus 18	Close Minus 17	Close Minus 16	Close Minus 15	Close Minus 14	Close Minus 13	Close Minus 12	Close Minus 11	...	Close Minus 9
Date												
2000-02-01	145.437500	139.750000	140.000000	137.750000	145.750000	146.250000	144.500000	143.062500	145.000000	146.968704	...	147.000000
2000-02-02	139.750000	140.000000	137.750000	145.750000	146.250000	144.500000	143.062500	145.000000	146.968704	145.812500	...	144.750000
2000-02-03	140.000000	137.750000	145.750000	146.250000	144.500000	143.062500	145.000000	146.968704	145.812500	147.000000	...	144.437500
2000-02-04	137.750000	145.750000	146.250000	144.500000	143.062500	145.000000	146.968704	145.812500	147.000000	144.750000	...	140.343704
2000-02-07	145.750000	146.250000	144.500000	143.062500	145.000000	146.968704	145.812500	147.000000	144.750000	144.437500	...	141.937500

Now, let's import our support vector machine and set our our training and test matrices and our target vectors for each:

```
from sklearn.svm import SVR
clf = SVR(kernel='linear')
X_train = sp20[:-1000]
y_train = sp20['Close'].shift(-1)[:-1000]
X_test = sp20[-1000:]
y_test = sp20['Close'].shift(-1)[-1000:]
```

We had just a bit over 4,000 data points to work with, and choose to use the last 1,000 for testing. Let's now fit our model and use it to test out out-of-sample data, as follows:

```
model = clf.fit(X_train, y_train)
preds = model.predict(X_test)
```

Now that we have our predictions, let's compare them to our actual data:

```
tf = pd.DataFrame(list(zip(y_test, preds)), columns=['Next Day Close',
'Predicted Next Close'], index=y_test.index)
tf
```

The preceding code generates the following output:

Date	Next Day Close	Predicted Next Close
2012-03-09	137.580002	137.711754
2012-03-12	140.059998	137.845997
2012-03-13	139.910004	139.961618
2012-03-14	140.720001	139.878612
2012-03-15	140.300003	140.680807
2012-03-16	140.850006	140.359465
2012-03-19	140.440002	140.792090
2012-03-20	140.210007	140.356091
2012-03-21	139.199997	140.104833

Evaluating our model's performance

Let's now look at the performance of our model. We're going to buy the next day's open if the close is predicted to be higher than the open. We'll then sell at the close that same day.

We'll next add a few extra data points to our `DataFrame` object to calculate our results, as follows:

```
cdc = sp[['Close']].iloc[-1000:]
ndo = sp[['Open']].iloc[-1000:].shift(-1)
tf1 = pd.merge(tf, cdc, left_index=True, right_index=True)
tf2 = pd.merge(tf1, ndo, left_index=True, right_index=True)
tf2.columns = ['Next Day Close', 'Predicted Next Close', 'Current Day
Close', 'Next Day Open']
tf2
```

The preceding code generates the following output:

	Next Day Close	Predicted Next Close	Current Day Close	Next Day Open
Date				
2012-03-09	137.580002	137.711754	137.570007	137.550003
2012-03-12	140.059998	137.845997	137.580002	138.320007
2012-03-13	139.910004	139.961618	140.059998	140.100006
2012-03-14	140.720001	139.878612	139.910004	140.119995
2012-03-15	140.300003	140.680807	140.720001	140.360001
2012-03-16	140.850006	140.359465	140.300003	140.210007
2012-03-19	140.440002	140.792090	140.850006	140.050003
2012-03-20	140.210007	140.356091	140.440002	140.520004
2012-03-21	139.199997	140.104833	140.210007	139.179993

Here we'll add the following code to get our signal and our profit and loss for the signal:

```
def get_signal(r):
    if r['Predicted Next Close'] > r['Next Day Open']:
        return 1
    else:
        return 0
def get_ret(r):
    if r['Signal'] == 1:
        return ((r['Next Day Close'] - r['Next Day Open'])/r['Next
        Day Open']) * 100
    else:
        return 0
tf2 = tf2.assign(Signal = tf2.apply(get_signal, axis=1))
tf2 = tf2.assign(PnL = tf2.apply(get_ret, axis=1))
tf2
```

The preceding code generates the following output:

Date	Next Day Close	Predicted Next Close	Current Day Close	Next Day Open	Signal	PnL
2012-03-09	137.580002	137.711754	137.570007	137.550003	1	0.021810
2012-03-12	140.059998	137.845997	137.580002	138.320007	0	0.000000
2012-03-13	139.910004	139.961618	140.059998	140.100006	0	0.000000
2012-03-14	140.720001	139.878612	139.910004	140.119995	0	0.000000
2012-03-15	140.300003	140.680807	140.720001	140.360001	1	-0.042746
2012-03-16	140.850006	140.359465	140.300003	140.210007	1	0.456457
2012-03-19	140.440002	140.792090	140.850006	140.050003	1	0.278471
2012-03-20	140.210007	140.356091	140.440002	140.520004	0	0.000000
2012-03-21	139.199997	140.104833	140.210007	139.179993	1	0.014373

Let's now see whether we were able to successfully predict the next day's price using just the price history. We'll start by calculating the points gained, as follows:

```
(tf2[tf2['Signal']==1]['Next Day Close'] - tf2[tf2['Signal']==1]['Next Day
Open']).sum()
```

The preceding code generates the following output:

```
1.989974000000018
```

Ouch! Not looking too hot so far. But what about the period that we tested? We never evaluated it in isolation. How many points would our basic intraday strategy have generated during this last 1,000 days:

```
(sp['Close'].iloc[-1000:] - sp['Open'].iloc[-1000:]).sum()
```

The preceding code generates the following output:

```
30.560202000000288
```

So, it looks as if our strategy has failed to even match the basic intraday buying strategy. Let's get the full stats to compare the two.

First, the basic intraday strategy for the period is as follows:

```
get_stats((sp['Close'].iloc[-1000:] -
sp['Open'].iloc[-1000:])/sp['Open'].iloc[-1000:] * 100)
```

The preceding code generates the following output:

```
Trades: 1000
Wins: 546
Losses: 448
Breakeven: 6
Win/Loss Ratio 1.219
Mean Win: 0.458
Mean Loss: -0.512
Mean 0.021
Std Dev: 0.656
Max Loss: -4.175
Max Win: 2.756
Sharpe Ratio: 0.5016
```

Now, the results for our model are as follows:

```
get_stats(tf2['PnL'])
```

The preceding code generates the following output:

```
Trades: 1000
Wins: 254
Losses: 222
Breakeven: 524
Win/Loss Ratio 1.144
Mean Win: 0.468
Mean Loss: -0.523
Mean 0.003
Std Dev: 0.453
Max Loss: -2.135
Max Win: 2.756
Sharpe Ratio: 0.0957
```

This looks bad. What if we modified our trading strategy? What if we only took trades that were expected to be greater by a point or more instead of just being any amount greater than the open. Would this help? Let's try it out. We'll re-run our strategy with a modified signal, as follows:

```
def get_signal(r):
    if r['Predicted Next Close'] > r['Next Day Open'] + 1:
        return 1
    else:
        return 0
def get_ret(r):
    if r['Signal'] == 1:
        return ((r['Next Day Close'] - r['Next Day Open'])/r['Next
        Day Open']) * 100
```

```
    else:
        return 0
tf2 = tf2.assign(Signal = tf2.apply(get_signal, axis=1))
tf2 = tf2.assign(PnL = tf2.apply(get_ret, axis=1))
(tf2[tf2['Signal']==1]['Next Day Close'] - tf2[tf2['Signal']==1]['Next Day
Open']).sum()
```

The preceding code generates the following output:

```
-12.610090000000127
```

Now the stats are as follows:

```
get_stats(tf2['PnL'])
```

The preceding code generates the following output:

```
Trades: 1000
Wins: 50
Losses: 52
Breakeven: 898
Win/Loss Ratio 0.962
Mean Win: 0.586
Mean Loss: -0.676
Mean -0.006
Std Dev: 0.256
Max Loss: -1.966
Max Win: 2.756
Sharpe Ratio: -0.3636
```

We have gone from bad to worse. It appears that if past price history suggests good things to come, you can expect precisely the opposite. We seem to have developed a contrarian indicator with our model. What if we explore this? Let's see what our gains would look like if we flipped our model so that when we predict strong gains, we don't trade, but otherwise we do, as follows:

```
def get_signal(r):
    if r['Predicted Next Close'] > r['Next Day Open'] + 1:
        return 0
    else:
        return 1
def get_ret(r):
    if r['Signal'] == 1:
        return ((r['Next Day Close'] - r['Next Day Open'])/r['Next
        Day Open']) * 100
```

```
    else:
        return 0
tf2 = tf2.assign(Signal = tf2.apply(get_signal, axis=1))
tf2 = tf2.assign(PnL = tf2.apply(get_ret, axis=1))
(tf2[tf2['Signal']==1]['Next Day Close'] - tf2[tf2['Signal']==1]['Next Day
Open']).sum()
```

The preceding code generates the following output:

```
42.900288000000415
```

Let's get our stats:

```
get_stats(tf2['PnL'])
```

This will result in the following output:

```
Trades: 999
Wins: 495
Losses: 396
Breakeven: 108
Win/Loss Ratio 1.25
Mean Win: 0.446
Mean Loss: -0.491
Mean 0.026
Std Dev: 0.605
Max Loss: -4.175
Max Win: 1.969
Sharpe Ratio: 0.6938
```

It looks like we do have a contrarian indicator here. When our model predicts strong next day gains, the market significantly underperforms (at least for our test period). Would this hold true in most scenarios? Not likely. Markets tend to flip from regimes of mean reversion to regimes of trend persistence. Let's re-run our model for a different period to test it further:

```
X_train = sp20[:-2000]
y_train = sp20['Close'].shift(-1)[:-2000]
X_test = sp20[-2000:-1000]
y_test = sp20['Close'].shift(-1)[-2000:-1000]
model = clf.fit(X_train, y_train)
preds = model.predict(X_test)
tf = pd.DataFrame(list(zip(y_test, preds)), columns=['Next Day Close',
'Predicted Next Close'], index=y_test.index)
cdc = sp[['Close']].iloc[-2000:-1000]
```

```
ndo = sp[['Open']].iloc[-2000:-1000].shift(-1)
tf1 = pd.merge(tf, cdc, left_index=True, right_index=True)
tf2 = pd.merge(tf1, ndo, left_index=True, right_index=True)
tf2.columns = ['Next Day Close', 'Predicted Next Close', 'Current Day
Close', 'Next Day Open']
def get_signal(r):
    if r['Predicted Next Close'] > r['Next Day Open'] + 1:
        return 0
    else:
        return 1
def get_ret(r):
    if r['Signal'] == 1:
        return ((r['Next Day Close'] - r['Next Day Open'])/r['Next
        Day Open']) * 100
    else:
        return 0
tf2 = tf2.assign(Signal = tf2.apply(get_signal, axis=1))
tf2 = tf2.assign(PnL = tf2.apply(get_ret, axis=1))
(tf2[tf2['Signal']==1]['Next Day Close'] - tf2[tf2['Signal']==1]['Next Day
Open']).sum()
```

The preceding code generates the following output:

```
33.60002899999989
```

So, we can see that our new model and testing period returned over 33 points. Let's compare this to the intraday strategy for this same time period:

```
(sp['Close'].iloc[-2000:-1000] - sp['Open'].iloc[-2000:-1000]).sum()
```

This results in the following output:

```
-7.089998000000051
```

So, it appears that our contrarian model significantly outperformed during our new testing period as well.

At this point, there are a number of extensions that we could make to this model. We haven't even touched on using technical indicators or the fundamental data in our model, and we have limited our trades to one day. All of this could be tweaked and extended upon. However, at this point, I want to introduce another model that uses a completely different algorithm. This algorithm is called **dynamic time warping**. What it does is give you a metric that represents the similarity between two time series.

Modeling with Dynamic Time Warping

To get started, we'll need to pip install the fastdtw library from the command line using `pip install fastdtw`.

Once this is done, we'll import the additional libraries that we'll need, as follows:

```
from scipy.spatial.distance import euclidean
from fastdtw import fastdtw
```

Next, we'll create the function that will take in two series and return the distance between them:

```
def dtw_dist(x, y):
    distance, path = fastdtw(x, y, dist=euclidean)
    return distance
```

Now, we'll split our 16 years of time series data into distinct five day periods. We'll pair together each period with one additional point. This will serve to create our x and y data, as follows:

```
tseries = []
tlen = 5
for i in range(tlen, len(sp), tlen):
    pctc = sp['Close'].iloc[i-tlen:i].pct_change()[1:].values * 100
    res = sp['Close'].iloc[i-tlen:i+1].pct_change()[-1] * 100
    tseries.append((pctc, res))
```

We can take a look at our first series to get an idea of what the data looks like:

```
tseries[0]
```

The preceding code generates the following output:

```
(array([-3.91061453,  0.17889088, -1.60714286,  5.8076225 ]),
 0.34305317324185847)
```

Now that we have each series, we can run them through our algorithm to get the distance metric for each series against every other series:

```
dist_pairs = []
for i in range(len(tseries)):
    for j in range(len(tseries)):
        dist = dtw_dist(tseries[i][0], tseries[j][0])
        dist_pairs.append((i,j,dist,tseries[i][1], tseries[j][1]))
```

Once we have this, we can place it into a `DataFrame` object. We'll drop series that have zero distance as they represent the same series. We'll also sort by the date of the series and look only at the ones where the first series is chronologically before the second:

```
dist_frame = pd.DataFrame(dist_pairs, columns=['A','B','Dist', 'A Ret', 'B
Ret'])
sf =
dist_frame[dist_frame['Dist']>0].sort_values(['A','B']).reset_index(drop=1)
sfe = sf[sf['A']<sf['B']]
```

Finally, we'll limit our trades to where the distance is less than 1 and the first series has a positive return:

```
winf = sfe[(sfe['Dist']<=1)&(sfe['A Ret']>0)]
winf
```

The preceding code generates the following output:

	A	B	Dist	A Ret	B Ret
3312	4	69	0.778629	1.360843	-1.696072
3439	4	196	0.608377	1.360843	0.410595
3609	4	366	0.973193	1.360843	0.040522
3790	4	547	0.832545	1.360843	-1.447712
3891	4	648	0.548913	1.360843	-0.510458
4035	4	792	0.719260	1.360843	0.819056
5463	6	598	0.678313	1.180863	2.896685
5489	6	624	0.897108	1.180863	0.757222
7769	9	471	0.932647	2.333028	-0.212983
13002	16	27	0.849448	0.754885	-0.571339

Let's see what one of our top patterns looks like when plotted:

```
plt.plot(np.arange(4), tseries[6][0])
```

The preceding code generates the following output:

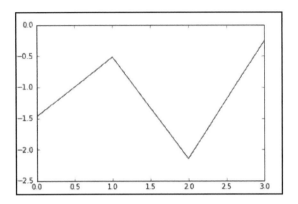

Now, we'll plot the second one:

```
plt.plot(np.arange(4), tseries[598][0])
```

The preceding code will generate the following output:

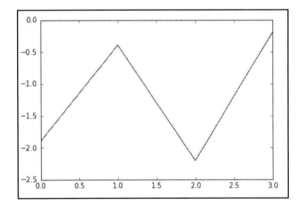

As we can see, the curves are nearly identical, which is exactly what we want. We're going to try to find all of the curves that have positive next-day gains. Then, once we have a curve that is highly similar to one of these profitable curves, we'll buy it in anticipation of another gain.

Let's now construct a function to evaluate our trades. We'll buy the similar curves unless they fail to return a positive result. If this happens, we'll eliminate them:

```
excluded = {}
return_list = []
def get_returns(r):
    if excluded.get(r['A']) is None:
        return_list.append(r['B Ret'])
        if r['B Ret'] < 0:
            excluded.update({r['A']:1})
winf.apply(get_returns, axis=1);
```

Now that we have all the returns from our trades stored in `return_list`, let's evaluate the results:

```
get_stats(pd.Series(return_list))
```

The preceding code generates the following output:

```
Trades: 569
Wins: 352
Losses: 217
Breakeven: 0
Win/Loss Ratio 1.622
Mean Win: 0.572
Mean Loss: -0.646
Mean 0.108
Std Dev: 0.818
Max Loss: -2.999
Max Win: 3.454
Sharpe Ratio: 2.0877
```

These results are by far the best that we've seen. The win/loss ratio and the mean are far above our other models. It appears that we may be on to something with this new model, especially compared to the others that we've seen.

At this point, to further vet our model, we should explore its robustness by examining other time periods for our matches. Does extending beyond the four days improve the model? Should we always exclude the patterns that generate a loss? There are many additional questions we could explore at this point, but I'll leave it as an exercise for the reader. If you do utilize these techniques, know that we have just scratched the surface, and that far more testing is required over additional windows to appropriately test these models.

Summary

In this chapter, we took a look at the stock market. We learned how to formulate a trading strategy using machine learning. We built the first strategy using a support vector regression and the second using dynamic time warping.

There is no doubt that the material of this chapter could fill a book in itself. Many of the most important components of a trading strategy, we didn't even cover. These include portfolio construction, risk mitigation, and money management. These are fundamental to any real strategy—arguably more important than trade signals.

Hopefully, this will serve as a jumping point for your own explorations. However, again I caution you that "beating the market" is a nearly impossible game. It is one in which you are competing against the brightest minds in the world. If you do decide to try, I wish you the best of luck. Just remember that I warned you if it doesn't turn out like you hoped!

In the next chapter we will examine how to build an image similarity engine.

8
Build an Image Similarity Engine

So far in our journey, we have worked exclusively with numbers and text. In this chapter, we'll jump into the world of images. While this might seem to require some next-level wizardry, I can assure you that transforming images into a machine-readable format is just as simple as transforming text is.

We'll start out simply with what is arguably the "hello world" of image-based machine learning: **digit recognition**. By the end of the chapter, however, we will have constructed an advanced, image-based deep learning application. To what noble end will we build this highly advanced application? Why finding our spirit animal, of course!

We'll also spend a fair amount of time covering deep learning algorithms to understand why they are so important and why there is so much hype surrounding them.

We'll cover the following topics in this chapter:

- Machine learning on images
- Working with images
- Finding similar images
- Understanding deep learning
- Building an image similarity engine

Machine learning on images

While the applications of machine learning for text and numerical data tend to be the most discussed, there are similarly a large number of applications for images. Many of these tend to be in areas of cutting-edge research with profound implications.

We are quite accustomed today to running a Google search to find some odd snippet of text from a news story that we read three weeks ago and having the first result be just what we wanted. Now, imagine if we could do the same thing for pictures, movies, and GIFs. For example, let's say you saw a GIF six months ago that is perfectly apropos for your current Slack conversation, but all you can remember is that it involved a llama and a man trying to feed him. Right now, you'd have a tough time locating it because most image searches involve hashtags and the text surrounding the image. Over the last few years, however, companies such as Google have made amazing progress in having machines label the contents of images. When this research is fully released and out "in the wild," it will radically transform how we search for images.

In this blog post from Google Research (`http://googleresearch.blogspot.com/2014/11/a-picture-is-worth-thousand-coherent.html`), they describe their progress toward this goal and explain some of the technical challenges in accomplishing it. For example, in the following image, we see two pizzas on top of a stove:

Image from https://research.googleblog.com/2014/11/a-picture-is-worth-thousand-coherent.html

In order to label the image as such requires not just an understanding of each of the objects, but their relationship to one another. And even then, the label needs to match up with a natural-sounding phrase—one that would likely match a human's description. For example, even though it is technically correct, a person would never label it "an oven under a pizza next to a pizza".

Another application of machine learning for images is facial recognition. You may have seen the recent news stories discussing Facebook's DeepFace technology. It was reported that this application was so advanced, it could actually recognize a person even if the image was of *back* of their head—and it did this with near-perfect accuracy.

While this may seem to have frightening implications for society at large, for Facebook, this is invaluable technology. Once a person has been tagged in a single photo, no additional tagging is needed—all future photos tagging takes place automatically.

It should be noted how difficult a task this is. Changes to a person's hair, clothing, age—not to mention the varying photo angles and lighting in each photo—make this an extraordinarily challenging task, even for people. In fact, just as computers have begun to surpassing people on games such as Go, they are also beginning to best us on these types of recognition tasks as well.

This new level of machine mastery comes from a relatively new class of algorithms that fall under the umbrella term **"Deep Learning"**. We'll explore deep learning in depth later in this chapter in order to understand how it differs from other algorithms and why it's so successful. For now, however, we will start at the beginning; we'll take a look at the basics of how to work with images.

Working with images

When we first introduced natural language processing, we learned that we would need to perform some sort of transformation in order to represent the words numerically. We did this by creating a term-document matrix. Now that we're dealing with pictures, we'll need to perform another sort of transformation to render the images in a numeric form.

Let's take a look at an image of a few handwritten digits:

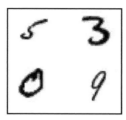

These particular digits are taken from the MNIST database of handwritten digits. (Yes, this really is a thing.) This database contains tens of thousands digits like this collected from the handwriting samples of US Census Bureau employees and high school students.

Let's suppose now that we wanted to use machine learning to recognize these digits. How might we represent them numerically from the data that we have?

One way might be to map each pixel in our image to a value in a numeric matrix of the same size. We could then represent some property of that pixel as a value in our matrix. In fact, this is exactly how it's done.

Each digit image is scaled and centered to a given canvas size (28×28 or 64×64 pixels), and then the color intensity of each pixel is represented as a value between 0 and 1 in our matrix where 1 is pure black and 0 is pure white. This procedure is known as gray scaling.

With this simple method, we turn a real world "thing" into a numerical representation that can utilized in our machine learning algorithms.

Let's now take a look at a sample of this. We'll load the MNIST database available within scikit-learn:

```
from sklearn import datasets
import matplotlib.pyplot as plt
import numpy as np
%matplotlib inline
digits = datasets.load_digits()
def display_img(img_no):
    fig, ax = plt.subplots()
    ax.set_xticklabels([])
    ax.set_yticklabels([])
    ax.matshow(digits.images[img_no], cmap = plt.cm.binary);
display_img(0)
```

The preceding code generates the following output:

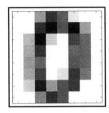

In the preceding code, we loaded the necessary packages, followed by the digits dataset, and finally, we displayed the first digit using `matplotlib`. This is a crude representation because it is scaled to 8×8, or 64 total pixels. The actual matrix representation can be seen by running the following command:

```
digits.images[0]
```

The preceding code generates the following output:

```
array([[  0.,   0.,   5.,  13.,   9.,   1.,   0.,   0.],
       [  0.,   0.,  13.,  15.,  10.,  15.,   5.,   0.],
       [  0.,   3.,  15.,   2.,   0.,  11.,   8.,   0.],
       [  0.,   4.,  12.,   0.,   0.,   8.,   8.,   0.],
       [  0.,   5.,   8.,   0.,   0.,   9.,   8.,   0.],
       [  0.,   4.,  11.,   0.,   1.,  12.,   7.,   0.],
       [  0.,   2.,  14.,   5.,  10.,  12.,   0.,   0.],
       [  0.,   0.,   6.,  13.,  10.,   0.,   0.,   0.]])
```

These particular digits are scaled between 0 and 16, but we can see how they relate to the color intensity in the image at the level of each pixel. If we were to apply this in our algorithm, we would need to flatten the 8×8 matrix into a single vector of length 64. We can see this as follows:

```
digits.data[0].shape
```

The preceding code generates the following output:

```
(64,)
```

This then will become a row—our feature vector—in our training set. We can also see the associated label for our data with the following command:

```
digits.target[0]
```

The preceding code generates the following output:

$$\boxed{0}$$

We now have everything we need to feed this image data into our algorithms.

So far we have only discussed how we would work with black and white images, but not surprisingly, working with color is just as simple. Each pixel can be represented using three features, one for each RGB value. Alternatively, the mean of three RGB values could be used if retaining a single feature was preferred.

Now that we have transformed our images into a representation we can work with, let's take a look at which algorithms we might want to use.

Finding similar images

Typically, the MNIST database of digits is used in classification tasks, that is, given the handwritten digit, find its target label. We'll be using it in a different manner here. For a given image, we'll attempt to find the image in the set that is the most similar to it. This is an unsupervised task as opposed to a supervised task since we won't be making use of the labels.

We'll start with an algorithm that we introduced earlier in the book when we dealt with text-based features. That algorithm is cosine similarity. Recall that this algorithm computes a unit-vector for each row of our X matrix. The dot product of each against every other is then taken, which gives us the cosine angle between each vector. The end result is that we have a single metric that tells us how "close" two images are. Let's take a look now.

First, we'll import the libraries that we'll need:

```
import pandas as pd
from sklearn.metrics.pairwise import cosine_similarity
```

Then, we'll compute the similarity between the first image—our zero—and all other images:

```
X = digits.data
co_sim = cosine_similarity(X[0].reshape(1,-1), X)
```

As we are inputting a 1D array, `scikit-learn` will require that we reshape the array in the latest versions.

Finally, we'll put the results in a pandas `DataFrame` object and take a look at our results:

```
cosf = pd.DataFrame(co_sim).T
cosf.columns = ['similarity']
cosf.sort_values('similarity', ascending=False)
```

This will result in the following output:

	similarity
0	1.000000
877	0.980739
464	0.974474
1365	0.974188
1541	0.971831
1167	0.971130
1029	0.970858
396	0.968793
1697	0.966019
646	0.965490

We can see the first row is a **1**—perfect similarity—because this is our original image. Below this are all the other images sorted by the order of similarity. Let's take a look now at image number **877**. We'll display it using the function that we created earlier:

```
display_img(877)
```

This results in the following output:

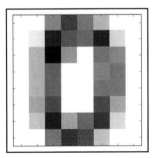

We can see that this image is also a zero, showing us that we are on the right track. Let's take a look at image number 0 side-by-side with image number **877**.

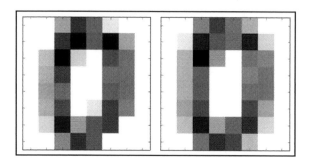

We can see that these two zeroes are remarkably similar. I would wager that they were created by the same person, in fact.

Now, let's have a bit of fun with this. What might we expect is the opposite of a zero? Let's find out. The least similar image is number **1626**:

```
display_img(1626)
```

This results in the following output:

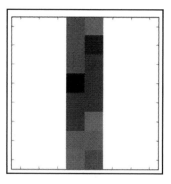

Shockingly, we just confirmed binary coding. The opposite of a 1 is, in fact, a 0. Huzzah!

Let's now take a look at another algorithm that we frequently used in image-based machine learning applications. It is called the **chi-squared kernel**, and like just like cosine similarity, it will give us a scalar value that tells us the similarity of two vectors:

$$k(x, y) = \exp\left(-\gamma \sum_i \frac{(x[i] - y[i])^2}{x[i] + y[i]}\right)$$

Let's look at how the chi-squared kernel similarity compares to the cosine similarity that we ran earlier:

```
from sklearn.metrics.pairwise import chi2_kernel
k_sim = chi2_kernel(X[0].reshape(1,-1), X)
kf = pd.DataFrame(k_sim).T
kf.columns = ['similarity']
kf.sort_values('similarity', ascending=False)
```

The preceding code generates the following output:

	similarity
0	1.000000e+00
1167	1.644255e-07
877	1.040593e-07
464	1.232666e-08
1541	8.598399e-09
1365	8.274881e-09
1029	1.907361e-09
855	1.487874e-10
1697	1.191874e-10
957	1.870301e-11

While the order is somewhat different from the results of cosine similarity, most of the same values are present in the top values listed.

Let's take a look at the most similar image from the chi-squared kernel:

```
display_img(1167)
```

This will result in the following output:

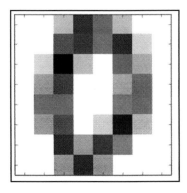

Again, we have a zero that is remarkably similar to our original image.

Why choose one of these (cosine similarity versus chi-squared kernel) over the other? While you can use either and get similar results—as we've seen—cosine similarity has proven to be the preferred choice for natural language processing work, while chi-squared kernels are the go-to choice for image-based tasks.

At this point, it makes sense to wonder how we can possibly get from tiny black and white boxes containing a single digit to figuring out if an image is of a pizza, or a monkey, or a motorcycle. There just doesn't seem to be enough information to discern this from what we've done so far. And, in fact, this is absolutely true.

Just as we would have a nearly impossible time discerning Moby Dick from Pride and Prejudice using only counts of letters, we need to add another layer of abstraction. With text, this means using words and combinations of words, and with visual information, analogously, we use clusters of pixels. These clusters of pixels form what is called a **visual vocabulary**, and this method is known as *bag of visual words*. The terminology was chosen because in the same way the text *bag of words* disregards word order, bag of visual words ignores the spatial order of its visual vocabulary.

At this point, to further illustrate the bag of visual words process, let's walk through the concept at a higher level. Since the origin of bag of visual words comes from texture recognition, we'll use the following example:

Julesz, 1981; Cula & Dana, 2001; Leung & Malik 2001; Mori, Belongie & Malik, 2001; Schmid 2001; Varma & Zisserman, 2002, 2003; Lazebnik, Schmid & Ponce, 2003

Here, we have three different textures. Each comprises a repeating series of textural units called **textrons**. These form the basis of our visual vocabulary:

Each sample can then be represented as a histogram over these features, as shown in the following figure:

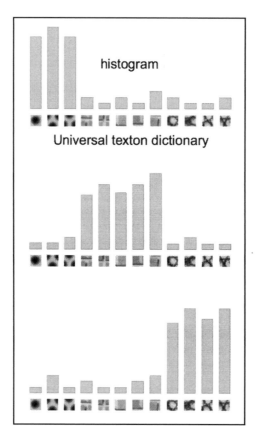

As we can see, the analogy holds closely to that of a bag of words where each document is a histogram over words.

Now, at this point, I should point out that this description is primarily conceptual. There is far more involved in the actual implementation of bag of visual words. The full details are beyond the scope of the book, but some of the work includes selecting points of interest for use as the visual vocabulary and transformations that normalize and make the features scale invariant.

Once the preprocessing is done, just as in text processing, a similarity matrix is computed and the data is fed into the algorithm for classification. Again, like text processing, this is typically an SVM.

Understanding deep learning

While bag of visual words methods have impressive performance, recently, newer methods utilizing what is termed **Deep Learning** have arisen. Deep learning has brought new life into the field of artificial intelligence as it continues to trounce benchmark after benchmark. We will use deep learning later in this chapter for our image similarity engine, but first, we'll walk through what exactly deep learning is and why it is such an important breakthrough.

Deep learning has its roots in algorithms that have been around for decades. These algorithms, called **perceptrons**, are modeled on the the neurons in the brain.

At some point in your biology classes, you most likely learned about how neurons work. The basics are the following:

- Each neuron is connected to a network of other neurons.
- When a neuron fires, it sends signals to the neurons that it is connected to.
- The neurons that receive this signal then either fire themselves or do not, based upon some established threshold requirement for activation.

This is the basis for the perception model as can be seen in the following figure:

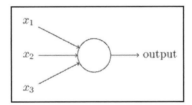

We can think of the neuron as an individual decision-making unit. Let's suppose the task of the neuron is to determine whether or not we should accept a new job offer. In this scenario, our relevant inputs may be the location, the pay, our impression of our future manager, and the office. In this case, we have a binary decision: 1, accept the job, or 0, do not. Each of these inputs help us determine whether to take the job or not, but, clearly, they are not all equally influential. For example, if the office is a 10/10 but the pay is a 2/10, chances are we won't accept the offer. On the other hand, if the office is a 2/10 but the pay is a 10/10, we will likely accept it. Pay, therefore, is more important in the decision-making process than the look of the office. In the language of perceptrons, we would say the pay input has a higher weight. Taking together all of our inputs—our x's—modified by their weights—our w's—we come to a value that then either triggers our function or not.

Mathematically, we have the following:

$$output = \begin{cases} 0 \ if \ \sum_j w_j x_j \leq threshold \\ 1 \ if \ \sum_j w_j x_j > threshold \end{cases}$$

So far, we have discussed the perceptron as as a decision unit, but we have not yet discussed how learning takes place.

To understand learning, let's try to learn a few decision rules with our perceptron.

The first rule that we'd like to learn is called an AND function. The AND function works like this: we have two inputs, and when both are positive, we'd like our function to output a 1. If one input is negative, or both are negative, we'd like it to output a 0. We'll set our weights to random numbers between 1 and 0.

Let's now begin our learning process. Our *X1* input is equal to 1 and our *X2* input is equal to -1. *W1* is randomly set to 0.8, and *W2* is randomly set to 0.2. As both must be positive for our output to be 1, then our threshold is any value greater than 1.

Therefore, we have $W_1{}^*X_1 + W_2{}^*X_2$ as *1 * 0.8 + -1 * 0.4 = 0.8 – 0.4 = 0.4*. Now, since we expect our output to be , we can say that we have an error of *0.4*. We will now attempt to improve our model by pushing these errors back down to the inputs in order to update the weights. To do this, we will evaluate each in turn using the following formula:

$$w_i \leftarrow w_i + \Delta w_i$$
$$\Delta w_i = \eta \left(t - 0 \right) x_i$$

Here, w_i is the weight of the ith input, *t* is the target outcome, and *o* is the actual outcome. Here, our target outcome is 0, and our actual outcome is *0.4*. Ignore the *n* term for now. This is the learning rate. It determines how large or small our updates should be. For now, we will assume it is set to *1*.

Let's look at X_1 to update its weight. Therefore, we have *1 * (0 – 0.4) * 1*, which equals *-0.4*. That is our *w* delta; therefore, updating equation 1, we have *0.8 – 0.4*, which gives us our new weight for W_1 as *0.4*. Therefore, the weight for X_1 has come down. What about the weight for X_2?

Let's take a look. That one is *1 * (0 – 0.4) * -1*, which equals *0.4*. Updating the weight, we have *0.2 + 0.4 = 0.6*. Therefore, as we can see, the weights are approaching parity, which is exactly as we would expect. If we were to continue to run this, given a small enough learning rate, the model would converge, and we would have learned our AND function.

Though this model seems almost absurdly simple—and make no mistake, it has glaring limitations (such as the inability to learn XOR functions)—it is the basic building block of of today's deep learning frameworks. Innovations to this model were gradually applied that improved its ability to learn increasingly complex representations, innovations such as incorporating sigmoid functions in place of step functions, stacking neurons to form layered networks, and better methods to allocate errors down through lower layers.

Taken together, these updates made it possible to learn not only nonlinear representations are necessary to learn an XOR function, but essentially any pattern. By stacking the layers of neurons—one's output feeding in as another's input—each higher level is able to detect increasingly complicated representations of the data.

In the following image we see this process for a facial recognition task:

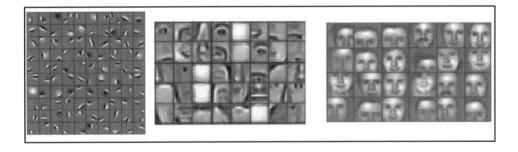

http://www.andrewng.org

From left to right in the preceding images, we can trace the increasing complexity of the representations that occur in each hidden layer of a deep learning network.

In the following diagram, we see a network with just 1 hidden layer, but having many hidden layers is common practice and the origin of the term deep in deep learning.

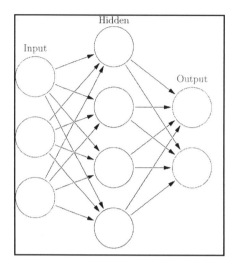

We can think of this as being like the parable of the blind men and the elephant:

> *"The blind man who feels a leg says the elephant is like a pillar; the one who feels the tail says the elephant is like a rope; the one who feels the trunk says the elephant is like a tree branch; the one who feels the ear says the elephant is like a hand fan; the one who feels the belly says the elephant is like a wall; and the one who feels the tusk says the elephant is like a solid pipe"*
>
> *-Wikipedia*

No single individual has access to the entire picture, so they cannot properly say what they are evaluating in isolation. But, seeing that same collection of attributes together again and again and being told it is an elephant, we can be confident that the next time we have a pillar + rope + tree branch + hand fan + wall + pipe combination that is likely an elephant.

Now that we have a better understanding of what deep learning is, we will move on to creating an application using deep learning.

Building an image similarity engine

If you made it this far through the chapter, you're now in for a treat. We will harness the power of the greatest advances in artificial intelligence to do something truly important. We will find your spirit animal. Well, *not exactly*. We will use it to find the cat you most look like in the CIFAR-10 image dataset. The Cifa-whut? The CIFAR-10 dataset is a set of images used as a standard in computer vision research. It includes tens of thousands of images in 10 classes, things such as dogs and frogs and airplanes and automobiles. Most importantly for us, however, this includes cats.

Now, one thing to understand about deep learning is that of all the algorithms that we discussed, it tends to be the most powerful, but also the least friendly for the "home-gamers". By this, I mean this tends to require more training time and more computational horsepower to run than other algorithms. In fact, this is one of the reasons neural architectures were not adopted sooner. Only with the advent of cheap GPUs, or graphical processing units, did it become a workable option for researchers.

Due to this, we will take two big measures to reduce processing time for our models.

The first measure is to utilize **GraphLab Create**. Create is a popular framework for large-scale machine learning. This provides a nice API that is a bit like the steroid-fed love child of `pandas` and `scikit-learn`. Typically, it is used as a paid service—it requires a licence, but this is offered free of charge for academic use, which appears to include **Bootcamps** and **Massive Open Online Courses** (**MOOCs**) such as **Coursera**. Make sure to check the site for details.

Graphlab installation is straightforward. Details can be found at `https://dato.com/down load/install-graphlab-create-command-line.html`. Essentially, it just requires filling in a form to get a license and then copying and pasting the `pip` command they provide.

Note that you will have to use Python 2.7. Python 3 is not supported at this time.

The next measure that we will use to speed along processing time is to use something called **transfer learning**. The idea behind transfer learning is to harness the power of massive, highly trained, deep learning networks, which are targeted to a very specific task. We then lop off the final layers of these networks in order to use the lower levels as our features for a task that they have not been trained on. Remember the lower levels have much less specificity in terms of aggregate representation of the item. In the world of digit recognition, the lower levels may be about representing loopy-ness or straightness, while the higher levels would be more about 0 or 1-ness, and in the world of elephant recognition, they are more about hand fan-iness and tree branch-iness. In transfer learning, we can extract those lower-level features in order to apply them to new domains—ones that they weren't specifically trained on.

A lot of information in this section draws on the Coursera course on machine learning foundations available at `https://www.coursera.org/learn/ml-foundations`. I highly recommend it if you are interested in going deeper into this material.

With that let's begin our coding. Our spirit animal awaits.

We'll begin with our imports:

```
import graphlab
graphlab.canvas.set_target('ipynb')
```

Next, we'll load the set of images that we'll be use from the CIFAR-10 dataset:

```
gl_img =
graphlab.SFrame('http://s3.amazonaws.com/dato-datasets/coursera/deep_learni
ng/image_train_data')
gl_img
```

This will result in the following output:

id	image	label	deep_features	image_array
24	Height: 32 Width: 32	bird	[0.242871761322, 1.09545373917, 0.0, ...	[73.0, 77.0, 58.0, 71.0, 68.0, 50.0, 77.0, 69.0, ...
33	Height: 32 Width: 32	cat	[0.525087952614, 0.0, 0.0, 0.0, 0.0, 0.0, ...	[7.0, 5.0, 8.0, 7.0, 5.0, 8.0, 5.0, 4.0, 6.0, 7.0, ...
36	Height: 32 Width: 32	cat	[0.566015958786, 0.0, 0.0, 0.0, 0.0, 0.0, ...	[169.0, 122.0, 65.0, 131.0, 108.0, 75.0, ...
70	Height: 32 Width: 32	dog	[1.12979578972, 0.0, 0.0, 0.778194487095, 0.0, ...	[154.0, 179.0, 152.0, 159.0, 183.0, 157.0, ...
90	Height: 32 Width: 32	bird	[1.71786928177, 0.0, 0.0, 0.0, 0.0, 0.0, ...	[216.0, 195.0, 180.0, 201.0, 178.0, 160.0, ...

You will notice several columns of identifying information, such as the **id** and the **label**, but you will also notice the column labelled "**deep features**". These are the features that were extracted from a large, trained deep learning network. We'll explain how we can use them in a bit. For now, let's keep moving.

We can take a look at the images with the following line of code:

```
gl_img['image'][0:5].show()
```

This results in the following output:

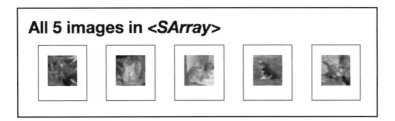

The images are exceedingly small, unfortunately, but you can resize them to be a bit more visible:

```
graphlab.image_analysis.resize(gl_img['image'][2:3], 96,96).show()
```

This will result in the following output:

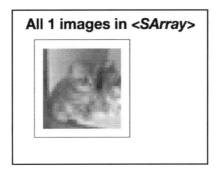

Now that we have all of the images we'll need for making comparisons loaded, we'll just need to load in our own image. I will load in one of my own that should be appropriate to this task. However, naturally, you'll need to load your own in that spot:

```
img = graphlab.Image('/Users/alexcombs/Downloads/profile_pic.jpg')
ppsf = graphlab.SArray([img])
ppsf = graphlab.image_analysis.resize(ppsf, 32,32)
ppsf.show()
```

This results in the following output:

All 1 images in <SArray>

Next, we need to get that image into the frame that contains our previously-trained images. However, to do this, we'll need to extract its features. Let's do this now:

```
ppsf = graphlab.SFrame(ppsf).rename({'X1': 'image'})
ppsf
```

The preceding code generates the following output:

image
Height: 32 Width: 32
[1 rows x 1 columns]

And now, we'll extract the images deep features:

```
ppsf['deep_features'] = deep_learning_model.extract_features(ppsf)
ppsf
```

The preceding code generates the following output:

image	deep_features
Height: 32 Width: 32	[2.32031345367, 0.0, 0.0, 0.0, 0.0, 0.31992828846, ...
[1 rows x 2 columns]	

At this point, we just need a few final touches to get our image on par with the comparison images:

```
ppsf['label'] = 'me'
gl_img['id'].max()
```

The preceding code generates the following output:

49970

We see that the max ID in the frame is **49,970**. We will give my picture a value of 50,000 just to be easy to remember if necessary:

```
ppsf['id'] = 50000
ppsf
```

The preceding code generates the following output:

image	deep_features	label	id
Height: 32 Width: 32	[2.32031345367, 0.0, 0.0, 0.0, 0.0, 0.31992828846, ...	me	50000
[1 rows x 4 columns]			

Almost there; now we'll just join everything together using these columns:

```
labels = ['id', 'image', 'label', 'deep_features']
part_train = gl_img[labels]
new_train = part_train.append(ppsf[labels])
new_train.tail()
```

This will result in the following output:

49913	Height: 32 Width: 32	automobile	[1.2023819685, 0.342965483665, 0.0, ...
49919	Height: 32 Width: 32	automobile	[0.0, 0.0, 0.0, 0.769036352634, 0.0, ...
49927	Height: 32 Width: 32	dog	[0.558163285255, 0.0, 1.05110442638, 0.0, 0.0, ...
49958	Height: 32 Width: 32	cat	[0.674960494041, 0.0, 0.0, 1.9640891552, ...
49970	Height: 32 Width: 32	cat	[1.07501864433, 0.0, 0.0, 0.0, 0.0, 0.0, ...
50000	Height: 32 Width: 32	me	[2.32031345367, 0.0, 0.0, 0.0, 0.0, 0.31992828846, ...

Okay, we now have one big frame with all our images, and their deep features represented as a vector. At this point, we can use a very simple model to find the most similar image.

We'll use k-nearest neighbors model first to compare one random cat to the others in the set just to get a feel for the success of our model:

```
knn_model =
graphlab.nearest_neighbors.create(new_train,features=['deep_features'],
label='id')
```

The preceding code generates the following output:

```
Starting brute force nearest neighbors model training.
```

Let's get our test kitten:

```
cat_test = new_train[-2:-1]
graphlab.image_analysis.resize(cat_test['image'], 96,96).show()
```

This results in the following output:

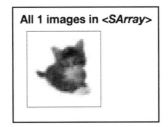

All 1 images in <SArray>

Therefore, this adorable pixelated little monster is our test subject. Let's find his doppelgangers:

```
sim_frame = knn_model.query(cat_test)
sim_frame
```

The preceding code generates the following output:

```
Starting pairwise querying.

+---------------+---------+-------------+---------------+
| Query points  | # Pairs | % Complete. | Elapsed Time  |
+---------------+---------+-------------+---------------+
| 0             | 1       | 0.0498504   | 22.45ms       |
| Done          |         | 100         | 297.624ms     |
+---------------+---------+-------------+---------------+
```

query_label	reference_label	distance	rank
0	49970	0.0	1
0	6186	38.0348505275	2
0	15882	39.0333337944	3
0	24302	40.5205578019	4
0	16289	40.6156967032	5

[5 rows x 4 columns]

Now, finally, let's look at our kitty matches:

```
def reveal_my_twin(x):
    return gl_img.filter_by(x['reference_label'],'id')
spirit_animal = reveal_my_twin(knn_model.query(cat_test))
spirit_animal['image'].show()
```

This will result in the following output:

There we have it. Every image is a cat, and I'd say they look like our target kitty.

Let's run it once again on another kitten. I'll leave out the coding and just show you our target cat and his matches.

First, our target:

And now his matches:

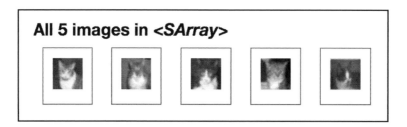

That's image number 145, and I'd have to give the matches decent marks. Now, however, on to the moment that we've all been waiting for. Let's reveal my animal twin:

```
me_test = new_train[-1:]
graphlab.image_analysis.resize(me_test['image'], 96,96).show()
```

This results in the following output:

All 1 images in <SArray>

Now, we'll run a search for my nearest match:

```
sim_frame = knn_model.query(me_test)
sim_frame
```

The preceding code generates the following output:

```
Starting pairwise querying.

+---------------+---------+-------------+--------------+
| Query points  | # Pairs | % Complete. | Elapsed Time |
+---------------+---------+-------------+--------------+
| 0             | 1       | 0.0498504   | 31.203ms     |
| Done          |         | 100         | 330.71ms     |
+---------------+---------+-------------+--------------+
```

query_label	reference_label	distance	rank
0	50000	0.0	1
0	6567	38.5852216196	2
0	11293	41.9754457649	3
0	22193	42.8440615614	4
0	36138	42.8565376605	5

[5 rows x 4 columns]

Now, we load the result:

```
graphlab.image_analysis.resize(spirit_animal['image'][0:1], 96,96).show()
```

This results in the following output:

I'll take it. I'm thinking it's the all about the hat, but I will definitely accept him as my spirit animal.

Summary

In this chapter, we had a grand tour of the highlights of machine learning for computer-vision applications. We discussed a number of techniques used in the field and how to create a working application using a number of these techniques. We also discussed the principles of deep learning and how it can be applied for both feature extraction and classification. Most importantly, however, you now have a scientifically sound methodology for finding your spirit animal. This alone was surely worth the price of the book.

In the next chapter, we'll take a look at how to create a chatbot application.

9

Build a Chatbot

For nearly as long as we have had computers, we have imagined a time when we would be able to converse with them. As it played out in the movies, these machines would be hyper-intelligent agents. Beyond just being able to hold a conversation, these bots would be able to examine our emotions and to even contradict our orders when necessary such as in the film 2001: A Space Odyssey.

Eleven years after that movie was to have taken place, Apple introduced **Siri** to the world with the release of the iPhone 4S. For anyone who has used Siri, it is clear that we have a long way to go before we face anything comparable to the intelligence displayed by the HAL 9000 unit in the film. But despite the clunkiness that these agents—or chatbots—have demonstrated in the recent past, the field is rapidly advancing.

In this chapter, we are going to learn how to construct a chatbot from scratch. Along the way, we'll learn more about the history of the field and its future prospects.

We'll cover the following topics in this chapter:

- The Turing test
- The history of chatbots
- The design of chatbots
- Building a chatbot

The Turing test

In 1950, Alan Turing posed the question, "Can machines think?" in one of his more famous papers. Being the practical genius that he was, he decided not to tackle this question head on, but rather to pose it in the framework of the "problem of other minds". This problem poses the question, "How do we truly know that other people have minds like our own?".

As we can only observe their behavior—and not the inner workings of their mind, we must take it on faith that they are like us. Turing proposed that if a machine behaved as if it was intelligent, then in fact, we should view it as such. This, in a nutshell, is the **Turing test**. Passing this test means convincing humans that a machine is a fellow human.

You may wonder at this point whether a program ever passed the Turing test successfully. The answer is that there really is no official Turing test. The closest thing to an official event is the Loebner Prize. This is a contest held annually that awards modest prizes to chatbots that appear to be the most convincingly human to a panel of judges. If this sounds rigorous and academic, it has been described as anything but. Loebner's sponsorship for the contest is said to have been a product of his total disdain for labor of any kind.

Hopefully, by this point, you realized that any claims about "passing the Turing test" are more spectacle than actual science. Despite this, however, Turing's original concept is a useful construct.

The history of chatbots

I still remember the day my father sat me down in front of his IBM XT with its black and green flickering monitor and asked me to talk to "it". The conversation went something like the following:

>Hello? How are you feeling today?

>Hi. Who is this?

>Hi there… how are you today?

>I'm fine. You didn't tell me who you are.

>We should be discussing you, not me.

>We should? Why?

>Let's change focus a bit… Tell me about your family.

>You are impossible to have a conversation with.

>Can you elaborate on that?

>You are killing me.

>Perhaps you would like me to be killing you.

>Ok, you are freaking me out.

>Perhaps you're really talking about yourself?

>What?? That makes no sense.

>How would an answer to that help you?

>END

>Very Interesting.

>QUIT

>Thank you for talking with me.

>#$###$#@@....

The "it" that I talked to was a program called **ELIZA**. Written in the mid-1960s at MIT's Artificial Intelligence Lab by Joseph Weizenbaum, ELIZA was created to mimic the responses of a Rogerian psychotherapist. Though nearly comical when examined in any depth, the program was capable of convincing some users that they were chatting with an actual human. This was a remarkable feat considering it was a scant 200 lines of code that used randomization and regular expressions to parrot back responses. Even today, this simple program remains a staple of popular culture. If you ask Siri who ELIZA is, she will tell you she is a friend and brilliant psychiatrist.

If ELIZA was an early example of chatbots, what have we seen after this? In recent years, there has been an explosion of new chatbots; most notable of these is **Cleverbot**.

Cleverbot was released to the world via the web in 1997. Since then, this bot has racked up hundreds of millions of conversions. Unlike early chatbots, Cleverbot (as the name suggests) appears to become more intelligent with each conversion. Though the exact details of the workings of the algorithm are difficult to find, it is said to work by recording all conversations in a database and finding the most appropriate response by identifying the most similar questions and responses in the database.

I made up a nonsensical question in the following screenshot, and you can see that it found something similar to the object of my question in terms of a string match.

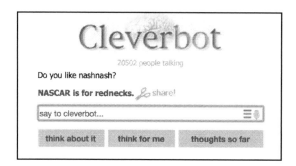

I persisted:

Again I got something…similar?

You'll also notice that topics can persist across the conversation. In response to my answer, I was asked to go into more detail and justify my answer. This is one of the things that appears to make Cleverbot, well, clever.

While chatbots that learn from humans can be quite amusing, they can also have a darker side.

Just this past year, Microsoft released a chatbot named **Tay** on Twitter. People were invited to ask questions of Tay, and Tay would respond in accordance with her "personality". Microsoft had apparently programmed the bot to appear to be 19-year-old American girl. She was intended to be your virtual "bestie"; the only problem was she started sounding like she would rather hang with the Nazi youth than you.

As a result of a series of unbelievably inflammatory tweets, Microsoft was forced to pull Tay off Twitter and issue an apology:

> *"As many of you know by now, on Wednesday we launched a chatbot called Tay. We are deeply sorry for the unintended offensive and hurtful tweets from Tay, which do not represent who we are or what we stand for, nor how we designed Tay. Tay is now offline and we'll look to bring Tay back only when we are confident we can better anticipate malicious intent that conflicts with our principles and values."*

-*March 25, 2016 Official Microsoft Blog*

Clearly, brands that want to release chatbots into the wild in the future should take a lesson from this debacle.

There is no doubt that brands are embracing chatbots. Everyone from Facebook to Taco Bell is getting in on the game.

Witness the **TacoBot**:

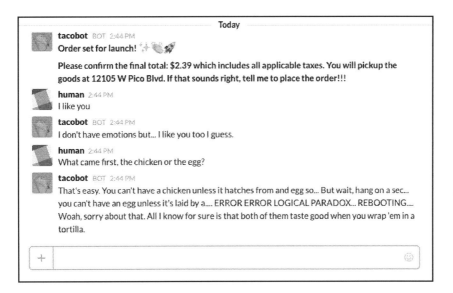

Yes, this is a real thing, and despite the stumbles such as Tay, there is a good chance the future of UI looks a lot like TacoBot. One last example might even help explain why.

Quartz recently launched an app that turns news into a conversation. Rather than lay out the day's stories as a flat list, you are engaged in a chat as if you were getting news from a friend.

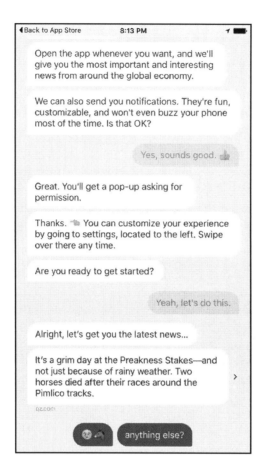

David Gasca, a PM at Twitter, describes his experience using the app in a post on Medium. He describes how the conversational nature invoked feelings that were normally only triggered in human relationships. This is his take on how he felt when he encountered an ad in the app:

> *"Unlike a simple display ad, in a conversational relationship with my app, I feel like I owe something to it: I want to click. At the most subconscious level, I feel the need to reciprocate and not let the app down: The app has given me this content. It's been very nice so far and I enjoyed the GIFs. I should probably click since it's asking nicely."*

If this experience is universal—and I expect that it is—this could be the next big thing in advertising, and have no doubt that advertising profits will drive UI design:

"The more the bot acts like a human, the more it will be treated like a human."

-Mat Webb, technologist and co-author of Mind Hacks

At this point, you are probably dying to know how these things work, so let's get on with it!

The design of chatbots

The original ELIZA application was two-hundred odd lines of code. The Python NLTK implementation is similarly short. An excerpt can be seen at the following link from NLTK's website (`http://www.nltk.org/_modules/nltk/chat/eliza.html`). I have also reproduced an except below:

```
# Natural Language Toolkit: Eliza
#
# Copyright (C) 2001-2016 NLTK Project
# Authors: Steven Bird <stevenbird1@gmail.com>
# Edward Loper <edloper@gmail.com>
# URL: <http://nltk.org/>
# For license information, see LICENSE.TXT
# Based on an Eliza implementation by Joe Strout
<joe@strout.net>,
# Jeff Epler <jepler@inetnebr.com> and Jez Higgins
<mailto:jez@jezuk.co.uk>.
# a translation table used to convert things you say into
things the
# computer says back, e.g. "I am" --> "you are"
from __future__ import print_function
from nltk.chat.util import Chat, reflections
    # a table of response pairs, where each pair consists of a
    # regular expression, and a list of possible responses,
    # with group-macros labelled as %1, %2.
    pairs = ((r'I need (.*)',("Why do you need %1?", "Would it
            really help you to get %1?","Are you sure you need
            %1?")),(r'Why don't you (.*)',
        ("Do you really think I don't %1?","Perhaps eventually
        I will %1.","Do you really want me to %1?")),
    [snip](r'(.*)\?',("Why do you ask that?", "Please consider
        whether you can answer your own question.",
        "Perhaps the answer lies within yourself?",
        "Why don't you tell me?")),
```

```
        (r'quit',("Thank you for talking with me.","Good-bye.",
        "Thank you, that will be $150.  Have a good day!")),
        (r'(.*)',("Please tell me more.","Let's change focus a bit...
                Tell me about your family.","Can you elaborate on
                that?","Why do you say that %1?","I see.",
                "Very interesting.","%1.","I see.  And what does that
                 tell you?","How does that make you feel?",
                "How do you feel when you say that?"))
    )
    eliza_chatbot = Chat(pairs, reflections)
    def eliza_chat():
        print("Therapist\n---------")
        print("Talk to the program by typing in plain English,
                using normal upper-")
        print('and lower-case letters and punctuation. Enter "quit"
                when done.')
        print('='*72)
        print("Hello.  How are you feeling today?")
    eliza_chatbot.converse()
    def demo():
        eliza_chat()
    if __name__ == "__main__":
        demo()
```

As you can see from this code, input text was parsed and then matched against a series of regular expressions. Once the input was matched, a randomized response (that sometimes echoed back a portion of the input) was returned. So, something such as *I need a taco* would trigger a response of *Would it really help you to get a taco?* Obviously, the answer is yes, and fortunately, we have advanced to the point that technology can provide one to you (bless you, TacoBot), but this was still in the early days. Shockingly, some people did actually believe ELIZA was a real human.

However, what about more advanced bots? How are they constructed?

Surprisingly, most of the chatbots that you're likely to encounter don't use machine learning; they use what's known as **retrieval-based models**. This means responses are predefined according to the question and the context. The most common architecture for these bots is something called **Artificial Intelligence Markup Language (AIML)**. AIML is an XML-based schema to represent how the bot should interact to the user's input. It's really just a more advanced version of how ELIZA works.

Let's take a look at how responses are generated using AIML. First, all inputs are preprocessed to normalize them. This means when you input "Waaazzup???", it is mapped to "WHAT IS UP". This preprocessing step funnels down the myriad ways of saying the same thing into one input that can run against a single rule. Punctuation and other extraneous inputs are removed as well at this point. Once this is complete, the input is matched against the appropriate rule. The following is a sample template:

```
<category>
  <pattern>WHAT IS UP</pattern>
  <template>The sky, duh. Pfft. Humans...</template>
</category>
```

This is the basic setup, but you can also layer in wildcards, randomization, and prioritization schemes. For example, the following pattern uses wildcard matching:

```
<category>
  <pattern>* FOR ME<pattern>
  <template>I'm a bot. I don't <star/>. Ever.</template>
</category>
```

Here, the * wildcard matches one or more words before FOR ME and then repeats these back in the output template. If the user were to type in Dance for me!, the response would be, I'm a bot. I don't dance. Ever.

As you can see, these rules don't make for anything that approximates any type of real intelligence, but there are a few tricks that strengthen the illusion. One of the better ones is the ability to generate responses conditioned to a topic.

For example, here is a rule that invokes a topic:

```
<category>
  <pattern>I LIKE TURTLES</pattern>
  <template>I feel like this whole <set name="topic">turle</set>
    thing could be a problem. What do you like about them?
  </template>
</category>
```

Once the topic is set, then the rules specific to that context can be matched:

```
<topic name="turtles">

  <category>
    <pattern>* SHELL IS *</pattern>
    <template>I dislike turtles primarily because of their shells.
      What other creepy things do you like about turtles?
    </template>
  </category>

  <category>
    <pattern>* HIDE *</pattern>
    <template>I wish like a turtle that I could hide from this
conversation.</template>
  </category>
```

```
</topic>
```

Let's see what this interaction looks like:

>**I like turtles!**

>**I feel like this whole turtle thing could be a problem. What do you like about them?**

>**I like how they hide in their shell**

>**I wish like a turtle I could hide from this conversation.**

You can see that the continuity across the conversation adds a measure of realism.

You probably think that this can't be state-of-the-art in this age of deep learning, and you're right. While most bots are rule-based, the next generation of chatbots are emerging, and they are based on neural networks.

In 2015, Oriol Vinyas and Quoc Le of Google published a paper (`http://arxiv.org/pdf/1506.05869v1.pdf`), which described the construction of a neural network, based on sequence-to-sequence models. This type of model maps an input sequence, such as "ABC", to an output sequence, such as "XYZ". These inputs and outputs can be translations from one language to another for example. However, in the case of their work here, the training data was not language translation, but rather tech support transcripts and movie dialog. While the results from both models are both interesting, it was the interactions that were based on movie model that stole the headlines.

The following are sample interactions taken from the paper:

Human: *who is skywalker ?*
Machine: *he is a hero .*
Human: *who is bill clinton ?*
Machine: *he 's a billionaire .*
Human: *is sky blue or black ?*
Machine: *blue .*
Human: *does a cat have a tail ?*
Machine: *yes .*
Human: *does a cat have a wing ?*
Machine: *no*
Human: *can a cat fly ?*
Machine: *no .*
Human: *how many legs does a cat have ?*
Machine: *four , i think .*

None of this was explicitly encoded by humans or present in a training set as asked, and yet, looking at this is, it is frighteningly like speaking with a human. However, let's see more…

> **Human:** *what do you think about tesla ?*
> **Machine:** *he 's a good conductor .*
> **Human:** *what do you think about bill gates ?*
> **Machine:** *he 's a good man .*
> **Human:** *What do you think about messi ?*
> **Machine:** *he 's a great player .*
> **Human:** *what do you think about cleopatra ?*
> **Machine:** *oh , she 's very regal .*
> **Human:** *what do you think about england during the reign of elizabeth ?*
> **Machine:** *it was a great place .*

Note that the model responds with what appears to be knowledge of gender (he, she), of place (England), and career (player). Even questions of meaning, ethics, and morality are fair game:

> **Human:** *what is the purpose of life ?*
> **Machine:** *to serve the greater good .*
> **Human:** *what is the purpose of living ?*
> **Machine:** *to live forever .*

The conversation continues:

> **Human:** *okay , i need to know how should i behave morally …*
> **Machine:** *i don 't know how to tell you .*
> **Human:** *is morality and ethics the same ?*
> **Machine:** *yes , sir .*
> **Human:** *what are the things that i do to be immoral ?*
> **Machine:** *i don 't know .*
> **Human:** *give me some examples of moral actions …*
> **Machine:** *i 'm not a moralist .*
> **Human:** *alright , morality ?*
> **Machine:** *integrity .*

If this transcript doesn't give you a slight chill of fear for the future, there's a chance you may already be some sort of AI.

I wholeheartedly recommend reading the entire paper. It isn't overly technical, and it will definitely give you a glimpse of where this technology is headed.

We talked a lot about the history, types, and design of chatbots, but let's now move on to building our own!

Building a chatbot

Now, having seen what is possible in terms of chatbots, you most likely want to build the best, most state-of-the-art, Google-level bot out there, right? Well, just put that out of your mind right now because we will do just the opposite! We will build the best, most awful bot ever!

Let me tell you why. Building a chatbot comparable to what Google built takes some serious hardware and time. You aren't going to whip up a model on your MacBook Pro that takes anything less than a month or two to run with any type of real training set. This means that you will have to rent some time on an AWS box, and not just any box. This box will need to have some heavy-duty specs and preferably be GPU-enabled. You are more than welcome to attempt such a thing. However, if your goal is just to build something very cool and engaging, I have you covered here.

I should also warn you in advance, although Cleverbot is no Tay, the conversations can get a bit salty. If you are easily offended, you may want to find a different training set.

Ok, let's get started!

First, as always, we need training data. Again, as always, this is the most challenging step in the process. Fortunately, I have come across an amazing repository of conversational data. The notsocleverbot.com site has people submit the most absurd conversations they have with Cleverbot. How can you ask for a better training set?

Let's take a look at a sample conversation between Cleverbot and a user from the site:

```
User: *lightsaber battle*.
Cleverbot: Luke I am your father.
User: *swings with lightsaber*.
Cleverbot: *Blocks* *Swings lightsaber*.
User: *blocks stabs with lightsaber*.
Cleverbot: *pushes back with the force*.
User: *pulls out gun*.
Cleverbot: *Pulls out nuke*.
User: *pulls out chuck norris*.
Cleverbot: *pulls out God*.
User: *pulls out universe*.
Cleverbot: *pulls out his mom*.
User: Mommy... *sobs*.
Cleverbot: *curls up and cries*.
User: *cuddles and cries*.
Cleverbot: *kisses neck softly*.
User: *cries more*.
Cleverbot: *kisses tears more*.
User: *cries even more*.
Cleverbot: *Whispers* It's ok.
User: *still sobs*.
Cleverbot: *snaps neck*.
User: WTF?!
```

So, this is where we'll begin. We'll need to download the transcripts from the site to get started. To do this, we will use the same tool that we used in Chapter 2, *Build an App to Find Underpriced Apartments*, import.io:

You'll just need to paste the link into the form on the page. The format will be like the following: `http://www.notsocleverbot.com/index.php?page=1`.

Once this is submitted, the site will process the request and return a page back that looks like the following:

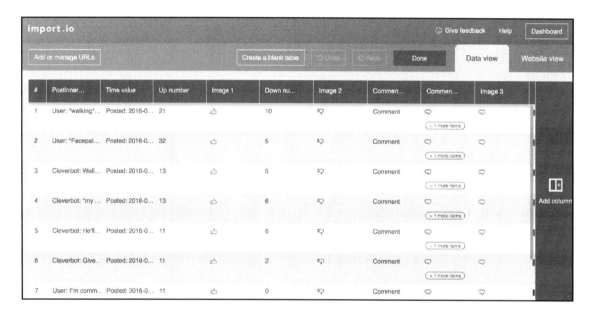

From here, if everything looks right, click on the pink **Done** button near the top right.

The site will process the page and then bring you to the following page:

Next, click on the **Show URL Generator** button in the middle:

Next, you can set the range of numbers that you'd like to download from. For example, 1-20, by 1 step. Obviously, the more pages you capture, the better this model will be. However, remember that you are taxing the server, so please be considerate.

Once this is done, click on **Add to list** and hit **Return** in the text box, and you should be able to click on **Save**. It will begin running, and when it is complete, you will be able to download the data as a CSV file.

Next, we'll use our Jupyter notebook to examine and process the data. We'll first import `pandas` and the Python regular expressions library, `re`. We will also set the option in `pandas` to widen our column width so that we can see the data better:

```
import pandas as pd
import re
pd.set_option('display.max_colwidth',200)
```

Now, we'll load in our data:

```
df = pd.read_csv('/Users/alexcombs/Downloads/nscb.csv')
df
```

The preceding code generates the following output:

	Postinner link	Postinner link_link	Time value	Up number	Image 1
0	User: *walking*\nCleverbot: *looks at you and winks* ;)\nUser: O.O *walks faster*\nCleverbot: *catches up with you and pins you against a wall*\nUser: *eyes widen* W-What do you want? \nCleverbot: ...	http://www.notsocleverbot.com/index.php?i=48277	Posted: 2016-04-18 04:30:53	21	http://www.notsocleverbot.com/images/thumbs_
1	User: *Facepalm* You are so stupid, you know that, right? \nCleverbot: I cannot argue with you.\nUser: So you admit your idiocy.\nCleverbot: You're all and I am nothing.\nUser:	http://www.notsocleverbot.com/index.php?i=48275	Posted: 2016-04-16 22:39:34	32	http://www.notsocleverbot.com/images/thumbs_

As we're only interested in the first column, the conversation data, we'll parse this out:

```
convo = df.iloc[:,0]
convo
```

The preceding code generates the following output:

```
0          User: *walking*\nCleverbot: *looks at you and winks* ;)\nUser: O.O *walks faster*\nCleverbot: *catches up wi
th you and pins you against a wall*\nUser: *eyes widen* W-What do you want?\nCleverbot: ...
1          User: *Facepalm* You are so stupid, you know that, right?\nCleverbot: I cannot argue with you.\nUser: So you
admit your idiocy.\nCleverbot: You're all and I am nothing.\nUser: Yess!!!\nCleverbot: ...
2                                                        Cleverbot: Well, my wife left
me today.\nUser: Feels bad for you.\nCleverbot: Not really, I have an amazing boyfriend :).
3                       Cleverbot: *my dragongirl chest fills with dragon milk*.\nUser: WHAT THE ACTUAL FUC
K?!?!!?\nCleverbot: *gives birth to dragon baby*\nUser: WHAT. THE. FUCK. HAPPENED. TO. CLEVERBOT.
4                                                   Cleverbot: He'll have to sit and watch them al
l.\nUser: What the frick are you talking about.\nCleverbot: Something more pleasant than you!
5          Cleverbot: Give me a riddle.\nUser: What has a head but no body . has a bed but never sleeps . runs but neve
r walks.\nCleverbot: What? I don't know.\nUser: A river.\nCleverbot: A river is not a fl...
6          User: I"m commander shepard.\nCleverbot: Really?\nUser: Yupp.\nCleverbot: That's nice. Can I meet your frien
d?\nUser: Garrus or Tali.\nCleverbot: Garrus because he is more impressive.\nUser: Okay ...
```

We can see in the preceding screenshot that we have interactions between **User** and **Cleverbot**, and that either can initiate the conversation. To get the data in the format that we need, we'll have to parse it into question and response pairs. We aren't necessarily concerned with who says what, but we are concerned with matching up each response to each question. We'll see why in a bit. Let's now perform a bit of regular expression magic on the text:

```
clist = []
def qa_pairs(x):
    cpairs = re.findall(": (.*?)(?:$|\n)", x)
    clist.extend(list(zip(cpairs, cpairs[1:])))
convo.map(qa_pairs);
convo_frame = pd.Series(dict(clist)).to_frame().reset_index()
convo_frame.columns = ['q', 'a']
```

The preceding code results in the following output:

16	" i cant beleieve i spelled now wrong"	So now you are calling me silly?
17	"72	WTF *TAKES OFF SUNGLASSES MOTHER OF GOD*
18	"Darling so there you are, with that look on your face".	I am wearing leggings and a leotard, what are you wearing?
19	"Eats you mom".	No.
20	"Help me, I'm pregnant.".	Boo. You need better jokes.
21	"I have a gun, get in the van".	I have the power to flush you.
22	"I kind of liked it your way, how you shyly placed your eyes on me".	Oh did you ever know? That I had mine on you.
23	"I"	You're ridiculous
24	"If frown is shown then I will know that you are no dreamer".	I am not Bill Gates. I am Martin Levenius. But that was obvious logic, it is tautological.

Okay, there's a lot of code there. What just happened? We first created a list to hold our question and response tuples. We then passed our conversations through a function to split them into these pairs using regular expressions.

Finally, we set it all into a pandas `DataFrame` with columns labelled `q` and `a`.

We will now apply a bit of algorithmic magic to match up the closest question to the one a user inputs:

```
from sklearn.feature_extraction.text import TfidfVectorizer
from sklearn.metrics.pairwise import cosine_similarity
vectorizer = TfidfVectorizer(ngram_range=(1,3))
vec = vectorizer.fit_transform(convo_frame['q'])
```

What we did in the preceding code was to import our `TfidfVectorization` library and the cosine similarity library. We then used our training data to create a tf-idf matrix. We can now use this to transform our own new questions and measure the similarity to existing questions in our training set.

> We covered cosine similarity and tf-idf algorithms in detail in `Chapter 5`, *Create a Custom Newsfeed*, so flip back there if you want to understand how these work under the hood.

Let's now get our similarity scores:

```
my_q = vectorizer.transform(['Hi. My name is Alex.'])
cs = cosine_similarity(my_q, vec)
rs = pd.Series(cs[0]).sort_values(ascending=0)
top5 = rs.iloc[0:5]
top5
```

The preceding code generates the following output:

29799	0.638891
53118	0.537884
29802	0.531098
29801	0.528135
46095	0.460475

What are we looking at here? This is the cosine similarity between the question I asked and the top five closest questions. To the left is the index and on the right is the cosine similarity. Let's take a look at these:

```
convo_frame.iloc[top5.index]['q']
```

This results in the following output:

```
29799      Hi my name is Cleverbot.
53118     Okay your name is Alex.
29802          Hi my name is pat
29801         Hi my name is lune.
46095               My name is.
```

As we can see, nothing is exactly the same, but there are definitely some similarities.

Let's now take a look at the response:

```
rsi = rs.index[0]
rsi
convo_frame.iloc[rsi]['a']
```

The preceding code results in the following output:

```
'Are you clever or something.'
```

Okay, so our bot seems to have an attitude already. Let's push further.

We'll create a handy function so that we can test a number of statements easily:

```
def get_response(q):
    my_q = vectorizer.transform([q])
    cs = cosine_similarity(my_q, vec)
    rs = pd.Series(cs[0]).sort_values(ascending=0)
    rsi = rs.index[0]
    return convo_frame.iloc[rsi]['a']
get_response('Yes, I am clearly more clever than you will ever be!')
```

This results in the following output:

```
'Prove it.'
```

We have clearly created a monster, so we'll continue:

```
get_response('You are a stupid machine. Why must I prove anything to you?')
```

This results in the following output:

```
'Right you are.'
```

I'm enjoying this. Let's keep rolling with it:

```
get_response('My spirit animal is a menacing cat. What is yours?')
```

```
'NAME!!!!!!!!!!'
```

To which I responded:

```
get_response('I mean I didn't actually name it.')
```

This results in the following output:

```
'*throws pillow*.'
```

Continuing:

```
get_response('Do you have a name suggestion?')
```

This results in the following output:

```
'KAHHHHHHHN. Do YOU have a name.'
```

To which I respond:

```
get_response('I think it might be a bit aggressive for a kitten')
```

This results in the following output:

```
"I'm calling the police."
```

I attempt to calm the situation:

```
get_response('No need to involve the police.')
```

This results in the following output:

```
'I want to talk to you forever.'
```

And finally,

```
get_response('And I you, Cleverbot')
```

This results in the following output:

```
"No. I'm Clevercake."
```

Remarkably, this may be one of the best conversations I've had in a while: bot or no bot.

Now that we have created this cake-based intelligence, let's set it up so that we can actually chat with it via text message.

We'll need a few things to make this work. The first is a twilio account. They will provide a free account that lets us send and receive text messages.

Go to `http://ww.twilio.com` and click to sign up for a free developer API key. You'll set up some login credentials, after which they will text your phone to confirm your number. Once this is set up, you'll be able to find the details in their **Quickstart** documentation. Make sure that you select **Python** from the drop-down menu in the upper left-hand corner.

Sending messages from Python code is simple, but you will need to request a twilio number. This is the number that you will use to send a receive messages in your code. The receiving bit is a little more complicated because it requires that you to have a webserver running. The documentation is succinct, so you shouldn't have that hard a time getting it set up. You will need to paste a public-facing flask server's URL in under the area where you manage your twilio numbers. Just click on the number and it will bring you to the spot to paste in your URL:

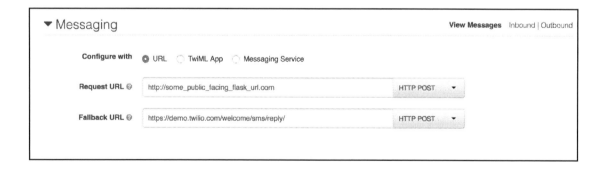

Once this is all set up, you will just need to make sure that you have your **Flask** web server up and running. I have condensed all the code here for you to use on your Flask app:

```python
from flask import Flask, request, redirect
import twilio.twiml
import pandas as pd
import re
from sklearn.feature_extraction.text import TfidfVectorizer
from sklearn.metrics.pairwise import cosine_similarity
app = Flask(__name__)
PATH_TO_CSV = 'your/path/here.csv'
df = pd.read_csv(PATH_TO_CSV)
convo = df.iloc[:,0]
clist = []
def qa_pairs(x):
    cpairs = re.findall(": (.*?)(?:$|\n)", x)
    clist.extend(list(zip(cpairs, cpairs[1:])))
convo.map(qa_pairs);
convo_frame = pd.Series(dict(clist)).to_frame().reset_index()
convo_frame.columns = ['q', 'a']
vectorizer = TfidfVectorizer(ngram_range=(1,3))
vec = vectorizer.fit_transform(convo_frame['q'])
@app.route("/", methods=['GET', 'POST'])
def get_response():
    input_str = request.values.get('Body')
    def get_response(q):
        my_q = vectorizer.transform([input_str])
        cs = cosine_similarity(my_q, vec)
        rs = pd.Series(cs[0]).sort_values(ascending=0)
        rsi = rs.index[0]
        return convo_frame.iloc[rsi]['a']
    resp = twilio.twiml.Response()
    if input_str:
        resp.message(get_response(input_str))
        return str(resp)
    else:
        resp.message('Something bad happened here.')
        return str(resp)
```

It looks like there is a lot going on, but essentially we use the same code that we used before, only now we grab the POST data that twilio sends—the text body specifically—rather than the data we hand-entered before into our `get_request` function.

If all goes as planned, you should have your very own weirdo bestie that you can text anytime, and what could be better than that?!

Summary

In this chapter, we had a full tour of the chatbot landscape. It is clear that we are on the cusp of an explosion of these sorts of applications. Hopefully, this chapter has inspired you to create your own bot, but if not, at least perhaps you have a much richer understanding of how these applications work and how they will shape our future.

I'll let the app say the final words:

```
get_response("Say goodbye, Clevercake")
```

```
'Goodbye.'
```

In the next chapter we'll dive into the world of recommendation engines.

10

Build a Recommendation Engine

Like so many things, this was born of frustration and stiff cocktails. It was a Saturday, and two young men were once again stuck without a date for the night. As they sat pouring drinks and sharing laments, the two Harvard freshman began to flesh out an idea. What if instead of relying on random chance to meet the right girl, they could use a computer algorithm?

They felt that the key to matching people up would be to create a set of questions that provided the sort of information everyone is really looking for on those first few awkward dates. By matching people using these questionnaires, dates that wouldn't have gone anywhere could be eliminated. The process would be super-efficient.

The idea was to market their new service to college students in Boston and around the country. In short order, this is exactly what they did.

Soon after, the digital matchmaking service that they built went on to become a huge success. It received national media attention and generated tens of thousands of matches over the course of the next few years.

In fact, the company was so successful that a larger company seeking to use its technology eventually bought it out.

If you're thinking I might be talking about **OkCupid**, you would be wrong—and also off by about 40 years. The company that I'm speaking of did all of this beginning in 1965—a time when computing the matches was done using punch cards on an IBM 1401 mainframe. It also took three days to just to run the computations.

Oddly enough, however, there is a connection between OkCupid its 1965 precursor, Compatibility Research, Inc. The co-founder of Compatibility Research is Jeff Tarr, whose daughter, Jennifer Tarr, is the wife of OkCupid's co-founder Chris Coyne. Small world indeed.

Why is any of this relevant to a chapter on building a recommendation engine? This is because it is very likely that this was one of the first. While most people tend to think of recommendation engines as tools to find closely-related products or music and movies they'll like, the original incarnation was to find potential mates. As a model for thinking about how these systems work, it provides a good frame of reference.

In this chapter, we'll explore the different varieties of recommendation systems. We'll see how they're implemented commercially and how they work internally. Finally, we'll implement our own recommendation engine to find GitHub repos.

We'll cover the following topics in this chapter:

- Collaborative filtering
- Content-based filtering
- Hybrid systems
- Building a recommendation engine

Collaborative filtering

In early 2012, a story broke about a man who had come into a **Target store** wielding a fistful of coupons addressed to his high-school-aged daughter. He had come to berate the manager because this set of coupons were exclusively for things such as baby clothes, formula, and furniture.

On hearing the man's complaint, the manager apologized profusely. In fact, he felt so bad that he wanted to follow up several days later over the phone to explain how this had happened. Only this time, on the phone, the father was the one apologizing. It seems his daughter was, in fact, pregnant. Her shopping habits had given her away.

The algorithm that gave her away was most likely based, at least in part, on collaborative filtering.

So, what is collaborative filtering?

Collaborative filtering is based on the idea that out there somewhere you have a taste doppelganger. The assumption is that you have rated a certain set of items in a way that is very similar to the way this doppelganger has (or doppelgangers have) rated them, but then each of you has rated additional items that the other has not. As you have established that your tastes are similar, recommendations can be generated from the items your doppelganger has rated highly but which you have not rated and vice versa. This is, in a way, is very much like digital matchmaking, but with the outcome being songs or products your match likes rather than actual dates with them.

In the case of our pregnant high schooler, when she bought the right combination of unscented lotions, cotton balls, and vitamin supplements, she likely found herself paired up with people who went on to buy cribs and diapers at some point later.

User-to-user filtering

Let's go through an example to see how this works in practice.

We'll start with something called a **utility matrix**. This is similar to a term-document matrix, but instead of terms and documents, we'll represent products and users.

Here, we'll assume that we have customers A-D and a set of products that they have rated on a scale from 0 to 5:

	Snarky's Potato Chips	SoSo SmoothLotion	DufflyBeer	BetterTapWater	XXLargeLivin'Football Jersey	SnowyCottonBalls	Disposos'Diapers
A	4		5	3	5		
B		4		4		5	
C	2		2		1		
D		5		3		5	4

We've previously seen that when we want to find similar items, we can use cosine similarity. Let's try this here. We'll find the user most like user **A**. As we have a sparse vector that contains many unrated items, we'll input something for these missing values. We'll just go with here. We'll start by comparing user **A** to user **B**:

```
from sklearn.metrics.pairwise import cosine_similarity
cosine_similarity(np.array([4,0,5,3,5,0,0]).reshape(1,-1),\
                  np.array([0,4,0,4,0,5,0]).reshape(1,-1))
```

The preceding code generates the following output:

```
array([[ 0.18353259]])
```

As we can see, these two don't have a high similarity rating, which makes sense because they have no ratings in common.

Let's now look at user **C** compared to user **A**:

```
cosine_similarity(np.array([4,0,5,3,5,0,0]).reshape(1,-1),\
                  np.array([2,0,2,0,1,0,0]).reshape(1,-1))
```

The preceding code generates the following output:

```
array([[ 0.88527041]])
```

Here, we see that they have a high similarity rating (remember 1 is perfect similarity), despite the fact they rated the same products very differently. Why do we get these results? The problem lies with our choice of using 0 for the unrated products. It registers as strong (negative) agreement on these unrated products. In this case, 0 isn't neutral.

So, how can we fix this?

What we can do instead of just using 0 for the missing values is to recenter each user's ratings so that the mean rating is 0, or neutral. We do this by taking each user rating and subtracting the mean for all ratings of that user. For example, for user **A**, the mean is 17/4, or 4.25. We then subtract this from every individual rating that user **A** provided.

Once this is done, we then continue on finding the mean for every other user and subtracting it from each of their ratings until every user has been completed.

This process will result in a table like the following. Note that each user row sums to (ignore the rounding issues here):

	Snarky's Potato Chips	SoSo SmoothLotion	DufflyBeer	BetterTapWater	XXLargeLivin'Football Jersey	SnowyCottonBalls	Disposos'Diapers
A	-.25		.75	-1.25	.75		
B		-.33		-.33		.66	
C	.33		.33		-.66		
D		.75		-1.25		.75	-.25

Let's now try our cosine similarity on our newly-centered data. We'll do user **A** compared to user **B** and **C** again.

First, the comparison between **A** and **B** is as follows:

```
cosine_similarity(np.array([-.25,0,.75,-1.25,.75,0,0])\
```

```
.reshape(1,-1),\
np.array([0,-.33,0,-.33,0,.66,0])\
.reshape(1,-1))
```

The preceding code generates the following output:

```
array([[ 0.30772873]])
```

Now, let's try between **A** and **C**:

```
cosine_similarity(np.array([-.25,0,.75,-1.25,.75,0,0])\
                  .reshape(1,-1),\
                  np.array([.33,0,.33,0,-.66,0,0])\
                  .reshape(1,-1))
```

The preceding code generates the following output:

```
array([[-0.24618298]])
```

We can see that the similarity between **A** and **B** increased slightly, while the similarity between **A** and **C** decreased dramatically. This is exactly as we hoped.

This centering process, besides helping us deal with missing values, also has the side benefit of helping us deal with difficult or easy raters as now everyone is centered on a mean of 0. Note that this formula is equivalent to the Pearson correlation coefficient, and just like that coefficient, the values fall between -1 and 1.

Let's now take this framework and use it to predict the rating of a product. We'll limit our example to three users, **X**, **Y**, and **Z**, and we'll predict the rating of a product that **X** has not rated, but **Y** and **Z** who are very similar to **X**, have rated.

We'll start with our base ratings for each user:

	Snarky's Potato Chips	SoSo SmoothLotion	DufflyBeer	BetterTapWater	XXLargeLivin'Football Jersey	SnowyCottonBalls	Disposos'Diapers
X		4		3		4	
Y		3.5		2.5		4	4
Z		4		3.5		4.5	4.5

Next, we'll center these ratings:

	Snarky's Potato Chips	SoSo SmoothLotion	DufflyBeer	BetterTapWater	XXLargeLivin'Football Jersey	SnowyCottonBalls	Disposos'Diapers
X		.33		-.66		.33	?
Y		0		-1		.5	.5
Z		-.125		-.625		.375	.375

Now, we'd like to know what rating user **X** might be likely to give **Disposos' Diapers**. Using the ratings from user **Y** and user **Z**, we can calculate this by taking the weighted average according to their centered cosine similarity.

Let's first get this figure for user **Y**:

```
user_x = [0,.33,0,-.66,0,33,0]
user_y = [0,0,0,-1,0,.5,.5]
    cosine_similarity(np.array(user_x).reshape(1,-1),\
    np.array(user_y).reshape(1,-1))
```

The preceding code generates the following output:

```
array([[ 0.42447212]])
```

Now for user **Z**:

```
user_x = [0,.33,0,-.66,0,33,0]
user_z = [0,-.125,0,-.625,0,.375,.375]

cosine_similarity(np.array(user_x).reshape(1,-1),\
                  np.array(user_z).reshape(1,-1))
```

The preceding code generates the following output:

```
array([[ 0.46571861]])
```

Therefore, we now have a figure for the similarity between user **X** and user **Y** (**42447212**) and user **Z** (**.46571861**).

Putting it all together, we weigh each users rating by their similarity to **X**, and then divide by the total similarity:

*(.42447212 * (4) + .46571861 * (4.5)) / (.42447212 + .46571861) = 4.26*

We can see that the expected rating of user **X** for **Disposo's Diapers** is **4.26**. (Better send a coupon!)

Item-to-item filtering

Now so far, we've only looked at user-to-user collaborative filtering, but there is another method that we can use. In practice, this method far outperforms user-to-user filtering; it's called **item-to-item filtering**. Here's how it works: rather than match each user up with other similar users based on their ratings history, each rated item is compared against all other items to find the most similar ones, again using centered cosine similarity.

Let's take a look at how this works.

Again, we have a utility matrix. This time we'll look at users' ratings of songs. The users are along the columns and the songs are along the rows:

	U1	U2	U3	U4	U5
S1	2		4		5
S2		3		3	
S3	1		5		4
S4		4	4	4	
S5	3				5

Now, suppose we want to know the rating that **U3** will assign to **S5**. Instead of looking for similar users, we'll look for songs that are similar based upon how they were rated across the users.

Let's take a look at an example.

First, we start by centering each song row and calculating the cosine similarity for each versus our target row, which is **S5**:

	U1	U2	U3	U4	U5	CntrdCoSim
S1	-1.66		.33		1.33	.98
S2		0		0		0
S3	-2.33		1.66		.66	.72

S4		0	0	0		0
S5	-1		?		1	1

You can see the far-right column was calculated with the centered cosine similarity for each row versus row **S5**.

We next need to select a number, **k**, which is the number of nearest neighbors that we'll use to rate song for **U3**. We use $k = 2$ in our simple example.

We can see that **S1** and song **S3** are the most similar, so we'll use these two along with the ratings **U3** had for **S1** and **S3** (**4** and **5**, respectively).

Let's now calculate the rating:

$(.98 * (4) + .72 * (5)) / (.98 + .72) = 4.42$

Therefore, based on this item-to-item collaborative filtering, we can see **U3** is likely to rate **S5** very highly at *4.42* from our calculations.

Earlier, I said that user-to-user filtering is less effective than item-to-item filtering. Why is this so?

There is a good chance you have friends who really enjoy some of things that you enjoy as well, but then each of you has other areas that the other has absolutely no interest in.

For example, perhaps you both love Game of Thrones, but your friend also loves Norwegian death metal. You, however, would rather be dead than listen to Norwegian death metal. If you are similar in many ways—excluding the death metal—with user-to-user recommendations, you will still see a lot of recommendations for bands with names that include words, such as flaming, axe, skull, and bludgeon. With item-to-item filtering, you will most likely be spared from these suggestions.

Let's wrap this discussion up with a quick code sample.

First, we'll create our example `DataFrame`:

```
import pandas as pd
import numpy as np
from sklearn.metrics.pairwise import cosine_similarity

df = pd.DataFrame({'U1':[2 , None, 1, None, 3], 'U2': [None, 3, None, 4,
None],\
                    'U3': [4, None, 5, 4, None], 'U4': [None, 3, None, 4,
```

```
None], 'U5': [5, None, 4, None, 5]})

df.index = ['S1', 'S2', 'S3', 'S4', 'S5']

df
```

The preceding code generates the following output:

	U1	U2	U3	U4	U5
S1	2.0	NaN	4.0	NaN	5.0
S2	NaN	3.0	NaN	3.0	NaN
S3	1.0	NaN	5.0	NaN	4.0
S4	NaN	4.0	4.0	4.0	NaN
S5	3.0	NaN	NaN	NaN	5.0

We will now create a function that will take in our ratings matrix along with a user and item. The function will return the expected rating of that item for that user based on collaborative filtering.

```
def get_sim(ratings, target_user, target_item, k=2):
    centered_ratings = ratings.apply(lambda x: x - x.mean(), axis=1)
    csim_list = []
    for i in centered_ratings.index:
        csim_list.append(cosine_similarity(np.nan_to_num(centered_ratings.loc[i,:].
        values).reshape(1, -1),
        np.nan_to_num(centered_ratings.loc[target_item,:]).reshape(1, -1)).item())
    new_ratings = pd.DataFrame({'similarity': csim_list, 'rating':
    ratings[target_user]}, index=ratings.index)
    top = new_ratings.dropna().sort_values('similarity',
    ascending=False)[:k].copy()
    top['multiple'] = top['rating'] * top['similarity']
    result = top['multiple'].sum()/top['similarity'].sum()
        return result
```

We can now pass in our values and get back the expected rating for the user-item pair.

```
get_sim(df, 'U3', 'S5', 2)
```

The preceding code generates the following output:

```
4.423232002361576
```

We can see this matches up with our earlier analysis.

Thus far, we've looked at users and items as a single entity when making comparisons, but now let's move on to look at another method that decomposes our users and items into what maybe called **feature baskets**.

Content-based filtering

As a musician himself, Tim Westergren spent years on the road listening to other talented musicians, wondering why they could never get ahead. Their music was good, as good as anything you might hear on the radio. Yet, somehow, they just never caught their big break. He imagined that it must be because their music just never got in front of enough of the right people.

Tim eventually quit his job as a musician and took another job as a composer for movie scores. It was there that he began to think of each piece of music as having a distinct structure or DNA that you can decompose into constituent parts.

After giving it some thought, he began to consider creating a company around this idea of building a musical genome. He ran the idea by one of his friends who had created and sold a company previously. He loved Tim's idea. He began helping him write a business plan and gather an initial round of funding for the project. It was a go.

Over the next several years, they employed a small army of musicians who meticulously codified almost 400 distinct features on a 0 to 5 point scale for over a million pieces of music—all by hand, or perhaps by ear as it were. Each 3 or 4 minute song would take nearly a half hour to grade.

The features included parameters such as how gravelly the lead singer's voice was, or how many beats per minute the tempo was. It took nearly a year for their first prototype to be completed. Built entirely in Excel using a VBA macro, it took nearly 4 minutes just to return a single recommendation. However, in the end, it worked and it worked well.

We now know this company as Pandora Music, and chances are that you have either heard of it or used its products as it has millions of daily users around the world. Without a doubt, it is a triumphant example of content-based filtering.

Rather than treating each song as a single indivisible unit, in content-based filtering, the songs become feature vectors that can be compared using our friend cosine similarity.

Not only can these songs be decomposed into feature vectors, but the same can be done to listeners as well. The listeners taste profiles become a vector in this space such that we can measure their taste profiles and the songs themselves.

For Tim Westergren, this was the magic, because rather than rely on the popularity of the music like so many recommendations do, the recommendations from this system were made based upon the inherent structural similarity. Maybe someone never head of song X, but if they like song Y, then they should like song X because it is *genetically* almost identical. That is content-based filtering.

Hybrid systems

We've now looked at the two primary forms of recommendation systems. However, it should be noted that in any large-scale production environment, recommendation engines will likely leverage both of these. This is known as a **hybrid system**, and the reason hybrid systems are preferred is that it helps eliminate the drawbacks that can be present when using either system alone. The two systems together create a more robust solution.

Let's examine the pros and cons of each type.

Collaborative filtering:

The pros of collaborative filtering are as follows:

- There is no need to hand-craft features

The cons of collaborative filtering are as follows:

- It doesn't work well without a large number of items and users
- There is sparsity when the number of items far exceeds number that could be purchased

Content-based filtering:

The pros of content-based filtering are as follows:

- It doesn't require a large number of users

The cons of content-based filtering are as follows:

- Defining the right features can be a challenge
- There is a lack of serendipity

Content-based filtering is a better choice when a company lacks a large user base, but as it grows, adding on collaborative filtering can help introduce more serendipity into the recommendations.

Now that we are familiar with the types and inner workings of recommendation engines, let's begin constructing our own.

Building a recommendation engine

One thing I love to stumble on is a really useful GitHub repo. There are repos that contain everything from hand-curated tutorials on machine learning to libraries that will save dozens of lines of code when using **ElasticSearch**. The trouble is, finding these libraries is far more difficult than it should be. Fortunately, we now have the knowledge to leverage the GitHub API in a way that will help us find these code gems.

We'll use the GitHub API to create a recommendation engine based on collaborative filtering. The plan is to get all the repos that I have starred over time and to then get a list of all the creators of these repos. Then we'll get a list of all the repos that each of these users has starred. Once this is done, we can compare our starred repos to find the most similar users to me (or to you if you run this for your own repo, which I do suggest). Once we have found the most similar GitHub users, we can use the repos they starred (and that I haven't starred) to generate a set of recommendations.

Let's get started. First, we'll import the libraries that we'll need:

```
import pandas as pd
import numpy as np
import requests
import json
```

Now, you will need to have opened an account with GitHub and to have starred a number of repos for this to work for your GitHub handle, but you won't actually need to sign up for the developer program. You can get an authorization token from your profile, which will allow you to use the API. You can also get it to work with this code, but the limits are too restrictive to make it useable for our example.

To create a token for use with the API, go to the following URL `https://github.com/set tings/tokens`. Here, you will see a button in the upper-right hand corner, as in the following image:

You'll need to click on the **Generate new token** button. Once you have done this, you need to copy the token it gives you for use in the following code. Make sure that you enclose both in quotes:

```
myun = YOUR_GITHUB_HANDLE
mypw = YOUR_PERSONAL_TOKEN
```

Now, we'll create the function that will pull the names of every repo you have starred:

```
my_starred_repos = []
def get_starred_by_me():
    resp_list = []
    last_resp = ''
    first_url_to_get = 'https://api.github.com/user/starred'
    first_url_resp = requests.get(first_url_to_get, auth=
    (myun,mypw))
    last_resp = first_url_resp
    resp_list.append(json.loads(first_url_resp.text))

    while last_resp.links.get('next'):
        next_url_to_get = last_resp.links['next']['url']
        next_url_resp = requests.get(next_url_to_get, auth=
        (myun,mypw))
        last_resp = next_url_resp
        resp_list.append(json.loads(next_url_resp.text))

    for i in resp_list:
        for j in i:
            msr = j['html_url']
            my_starred_repos.append(msr)
```

There's a lot going on in there, but, essentially, we query the API to get our own starred repos. GitHub uses pagination rather than return everything in one call. Due to this, we'll need to check the `.links` that are returned from each response. As long as there is a next link to call, we'll continue to do so.

Next, we just need to call the function that we created:

```
get_starred_by_me()
```

Then, we can see the full list of starred repos:

```
my_starred_repos
```

This code will result in output similar to the following:

```
['https://github.com/pydata/pandas',
 'https://github.com/ipython/ipywidgets',
 'https://github.com/tweepy/tweepy',
 'https://github.com/matplotlib/matplotlib',
 'https://github.com/d3/d3',
 'https://github.com/JohnLangford/vowpal_wabbit',
 'https://github.com/tensorflow/tensorflow',
 'https://github.com/scikit-learn/scikit-learn',
 'https://github.com/chncyhn/flappybird-qlearning-bot',
 'https://github.com/josephmisiti/awesome-machine-learning',
 'https://github.com/vinta/awesome-python',
```

Next, we need to parse out the user names for each of the libraries that we starred so that we can retrieve the libraries they starred:

```
my_starred_users = []
for ln in my_starred_repos:
    right_split = ln.split('.com/')[1]
    starred_usr = right_split.split('/')[0]
    my_starred_users.append(starred_usr)

my_starred_users
```

The preceding code generates the following output:

```
['pydata',
 'ipython',
 'tweepy',
 'matplotlib',
 'd3',
 'JohnLangford',
 'tensorflow',
 'scikit-learn',
 'chncyhn',
 'josephmisiti',
 'vinta',
 'yawitzd',
 'ujjwalkarn',
```

Now that we have the handles for all of the users that we starred, we'll need to retrieve all the repos that they starred:

The following function will do just that:

```
starred_repos = {k:[] for k in set(my_starred_users)}
def get_starred_by_user(user_name):
    starred_resp_list = []
    last_resp = ''
    first_url_to_get = 'https://api.github.com/users/'+ user_name
    +'/starred'
    first_url_resp = requests.get(first_url_to_get, auth=
    (myun,mypw))
    last_resp = first_url_resp
    starred_resp_list.append(json.loads(first_url_resp.text))

    while last_resp.links.get('next'):
        next_url_to_get = last_resp.links['next']['url']
        next_url_resp = requests.get(next_url_to_get, auth=
        (myun,mypw))
        last_resp = next_url_resp

starred_resp_list.append(json.loads(next_url_resp.text))

    for i in starred_resp_list:
        for j in i:
            sr = j['html_url']
            starred_repos.get(user_name).append(sr)
```

This function works in nearly the same way as the function that we called earlier, but it calls a different endpoint. It will add their starred repos to a dict that we'll use later.

Let's call it now. It may take a few minutes to run depending on the number of repos each user has starred. I actually had one that starred over 4,000 repos:

```
for usr in list(set(my_starred_users)):
    print(usr)
    try:
        get_starred_by_user(usr)
    except:
        print('failed for user', usr)
```

The preceding code generates the following output:

```
podopie
twitter
grangier
bmtgoncalves
bloomberg
donnemartin
cchi
monkeylearn
misterGF
clips
hangtwenty
sandialabs
yhat
d3
```

Note that I turned the list of starred users into a set before I called it. I noticed some duplication that resulted from starring multiple repos under one user handle, so it makes sense to follow this step to reduce extra calls.

We now need to build a feature set that includes all the starred repos of everyone we have starred:

```
repo_vocab = [item for sl in list(starred_repos.values()) for item in sl]
```

Next, we'll convert that to a set to remove duplicates that may be present from multiple users starring the same repos:

```
repo_set = list(set(repo_vocab))
```

Let's see how many this produces:

```
len(repo_vocab)
```

The preceding code generates the following output::

```
12378
```

I had starred just over 80 repos, and together the users of these repos starred over 12,000 unique repos. You can imagine that if we went one degree further out how many we would see.

Now that we have the full feature set, or repo vocabulary, we need to run every user to create a binary vector that contains a 1 for every repo they have starred and a 0 for every repo they have not:

```
all_usr_vector = []
for k,v in starred_repos.items():
    usr_vector = []
    for url in repo_set:
        if url in v:
            usr_vector.extend([1])
        else:
            usr_vector.extend([0])
    all_usr_vector.append(usr_vector)
```

What we just did was check for every user if they had starred every repo in our repo vocabulary. If they did, they received a 1, if they didn't they received a 0.

At this point, we have a 12,378 item binary vector for each user—all 79 of them. Let's now put this into a `DataFrame`. The row index will be the user handles that we starred, and the columns will be the repo vocab:

```
df = pd.DataFrame(all_usr_vector, columns=repo_set,
index=starred_repos.keys())
df
```

The preceding code generates the following output:

	https://github.com/wagerfield/parallax	https://github.com/agibsonsw/AndyPython	https://github.com behavior
bmtgoncalves	0	0	0
twitter	0	0	0
matryer	0	0	0
bloomberg	0	0	0
donnemartin	0	0	0
cchi	0	0	0
monkeylearn	0	0	0

Next, in order to compare ourselves to the other users, we need to add our own row to this frame:

```
my_repo_comp = []
for i in df.columns:
    if i in my_starred_repos:
        my_repo_comp.append(1)
    else:
        my_repo_comp.append(0)

mrc = pd.Series(my_repo_comp).to_frame('acombs').T
```

```
mrc
```

The preceding code generates the following output:

	0	1	2	3	4	5	6	7	8	9	...	12368	12369	12370	12371	12372	12373	12374	12375	12376	12377
acombs	0	0	0	0	0	0	0	0	0	0	...	0	0	0	0	0	0	0	0	0	0

We now need to add the appropriate column names and to concatenate this to our other `DataFrame`:

```
mrc.columns = df.columns

fdf = pd.concat([df, mrc])

fdf
```

The preceding code generates the following output:

Quartz	0	0	0
toddmotto	0	0	0
cemoody	0	0	0
PMSI-AlignAlytics	0	0	0
lukhnos	0	0	0
fivethirtyeight	0	0	0
acombs	0	0	0

You can see that in the preceding screenshot, I was also added into the `DataFrame`.

From here, we just need to calculate the similarity between ourselves and the other users that we starred. We'll do this now using the `pearsonr` function, which we'll need to import from `scipy`:

```
from scipy.stats import pearsonr

sim_score = {}
for i in range(len(fdf)):
    ss = pearsonr(fdf.iloc[-1,:], fdf.iloc[i,:])
    sim_score.update({i: ss[0]})

sf = pd.Series(sim_score).to_frame('similarity')
sf
```

The preceding code generates the following output:

	similarity
0	NaN
1	NaN
2	0.007047
3	NaN
4	0.134539
5	0.164320
6	NaN
7	0.011832

What we've just done is compare our vector, the last one in the `DataFrame`, to every other user's vector to generate a centered cosine similarity (Pearson correlation coefficient). Some values are, by necessity, NaN (not a number) because they have starred no repos and, thus, result in division by zero in the calculation.

Let's now sort these values to return the index of the user's who are most similar:

```
sf.sort_values('similarity', ascending=False)
```

The preceding code generates the following output:

	similarity
79	1.000000
31	0.204703
5	0.164320
71	0.149323
4	0.134539
64	0.111629
24	0.105784
69	0.091494

There we have it, these are the most similar users and, thus, the ones that we can use to recommend repos that we might enjoy. Let's take a look at these users and what they have starred that we may like.

You can ignore the first user with a perfect similarity score; this is our own repo. Going down the list, the three nearest matches are user **31**, user **5**, and user **71**. Let's look at each:

```
fdf.index[31]
```

The preceding code generates the following output:

```
'lmcinnes'
```

Let's take a look at who this is and their repo:

From `https://github.com/lmcinnes`, we can see who the repo belongs to.

This is the author of **hdbscan**—an excellent library—who also happens to be a contributor to `scikit-learn` and `matplotlib`:

Leland McInnes
lmcinnes

Tutte Institute for Mathematics an

Ottawa, Ontario, Canada

Joined on Apr 15, 2015

Let's also see what he has starred. There are a couple ways to do this: we can either use our code, or just click under their picture on stars. Let's do both for this one, just to compare and make sure that everything matches up.

First via code:

```
fdf.iloc[31,:][fdf.iloc[31,:]==1]
```

The preceding code generates the following output:

```
https://github.com/glennq/tga                                    1
https://github.com/iamaziz/PyDataset                             1
https://github.com/lmcinnes/hdbscan                              1
https://github.com/jupyter-incubator/kernel_gateway_bundlers     1
https://github.com/lmcinnes/hypergraph                           1
https://github.com/tensorflow/skflow                             1
https://github.com/cehorn/GLRM                                   1
https://github.com/mwaskom/seaborn                               1
https://github.com/jupyter-incubator/dashboards                  1
https://github.com/scikit-learn/scikit-learn                     1
https://github.com/stitchfix/d3-jupyter-tutorial                 1
https://github.com/matplotlib/matplotlib                         1
https://github.com/patricksnape/PyRPCA                           1
Name: lmcinnes, dtype: int64
```

We see thirteen starred repos. Let's compare these to the ones from GitHub's site:

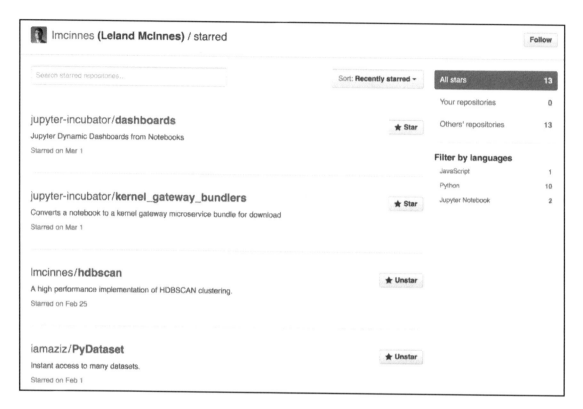

Here, we can see they are identical. Notice also that we can ID the repos that we have both starred: they are the ones labeled **Unstar**.

Unfortunately, with just 13 starred repos, there aren't a lot of repos to generate recommendations.

The next user in terms of similarity, is actually a friend and former colleague, Charles Chi:

```
fdf.index[5]
```

The preceding code generates the following output:

```
'cchi'
```

And his GitHub profile below:

Here we see the repos he has starred:

Charles has starred 27 repos, so there are definitely some recommendations to be found there.

Finally, let's look at the third most similar user:

```
fdf.index[71]
```

This results in the following output:

```
'rushter'
```

This user, Artem Ruster, has starred nearly 500 repos:

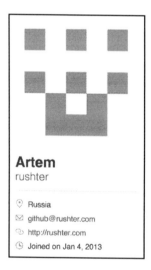

We can see the starred repos in the following image:

This is definitely fertile ground to generate recommendations. Let's now do just that; let's use the links from these three to produce some recommendations.

First, we need to gather the links to the repos they have starred that I have not. We'll create a `DataFrame` that has the repos I have starred as well as the three most similar users to me:

```
all_recs =
fdf.iloc[[31,5,71,79],:][fdf.iloc[[31,5,71,79],:]==1].fillna(0).T
```

The preceding code generates the following output:

	lmcinnes	cchi	rushter	acombs
https://github.com/wagerfield/parallax	0	0	0	0
https://github.com/agibsonsw/AndyPython	0	0	0	0
https://github.com/taion/scroll-behavior	0	0	0	0
https://github.com/anicollection/anicollection	0	0	0	0
https://github.com/mahmoud/lithoxyl	0	0	0	0
https://github.com/gciruelos/musthe	0	0	0	0
https://github.com/slimkrazy/python-google-places	0	0	0	0
https://github.com/afgiel/video_cnn	0	0	0	0
https://github.com/KristianOellegaard/packer-storm	0	0	0	0
https://github.com/carlsednaoui/ouibounce	0	0	0	0

Don't worry if it looks like it is all zeros, this is a sparse matrix so most will be 0. Let's see if there are any repos that we have all starred:

```
all_recs[(all_recs==1).all(axis=1)]
```

This code will produce the following output:

	lmcinnes	cchi	rushter	acombs
https://github.com/tensorflow/skflow	1	1	1	1
https://github.com/scikit-learn/scikit-learn	1	1	1	1

As, we can see, we all seem to love `scikit-learn`; no surprise there. Let's see what they might have all starred that I missed. We'll start by creating a frame that excludes me, then, we'll query it for commonly starred repos:

```
str_recs_tmp = all_recs[all_recs['acombs']==0].copy()
str_recs = str_recs_tmp.iloc[:,:-1].copy()
str_recs
```

The preceding code generates the following output:

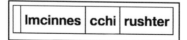

lmcinnes	cchi	rushter

Ok, so it looks like I haven't been missing anything super-obvious. Let's see whether there any repos that at least two out of three users starred. To find this, we'll just sum across the rows:

```
str_recs[str_recs.sum(axis=1)>1]
```

The preceding code generates the following output:

	lmcinnes	cchi	rushter
https://github.com/rasbt/python-machine-learning-book	0	1	1
https://github.com/prakhar1989/awesome-courses	0	1	1
https://github.com/rasbt/pattern_classification	0	1	1
https://github.com/DrSkippy/Data-Science-45min-Intros	0	1	1
https://github.com/numenta/nupic	0	1	1
https://github.com/kjw0612/awesome-rnn	0	1	1
https://github.com/airbnb/aerosolve	0	1	1
https://github.com/ogrisel/parallel_ml_tutorial	0	1	1
https://github.com/ChristosChristofidis/awesome-deep-learning	0	1	1
https://github.com/PredictionIO/PredictionIO	0	1	1
https://github.com/mwaskom/seaborn	1	0	1
https://github.com/okulbilisim/awesome-datascience	0	1	1

This looks promising as there are a number of repos that both cchi and rushter have starred. Looking at the repo names, there appears to be a lot of "awesome" going on here. Maybe I should have just skipped this whole recommendation thing and keyword searched for "awesome".

At this point, I have to say I'm impressed with the results. These are definitely repos that interest me, and I will definitely be checking them out.

So far, we generated the recommendations using collaborative filtering and then performed some light additional filtering using aggregation. If we wanted to go further, we could order the recommendation based upon the total number of stars they received. You can achieve this by making another call to the GitHub API. There is an endpoint that provides this information.

Another thing we can do to improve the results is to add a layer of content-based filtering. This is the hybridization step that we discussed earlier. We need to create a set of features from our own repo that was indicative of the types of things that we would be interested in. One way to do this would be to create a feature set by tokenizing the names of the repos that we have starred along with their descriptions.

Here is a look at my starred repos:

As you can imagine, this would generate a set of word features that we can use to vet the repos of the ones that we found using collaborative filtering. This would include a lot of words, such as *Python, Machine Learning, Data Science,* and so on. This would ensure that users who are less similar to us still provide recommendations that are based on our own interests. It would also reduce the serendipity of the recommendations, which is something you should consider. It's possible, for example, that there are repos unlike anything I have starred currently that I would be very interested in finding. It's certainly a possibility.

What would that content-based filtering step look like in terms of a DataFrame? The columns will be word features (n-grams) and the rows will be the repos generated from our collaborative filtering step. We would just run the similarity process once again using our own repo for comparison.

Summary

In this chapter, we learned about recommendation engines. We learned about the two primary types of systems in use today: collaborative filtering and content-based filtering. We also learned how they can be used together to form a hybrid system. We also spent some time discussing the pros and cons of each type of system. Finally, we learned step-by-step how to build a recommendation engine from scratch using the GitHub API.

I hope you build your own recommendation engine using the guidance in this chapter, and I hope you find many resources that are useful to you. I know I have found a number of things that I will certainly use.

Best of luck to you on your journey building recommendation engines, and best of luck to you with all the machine-learning-based techniques we have covered in this book. Machine learning opens a new world of possibilities that will affect nearly every area of our lives in the coming years, and you have taken the first steps to entering this new world of possibility.

Index

Made in the USA
Middletown, DE
31 January 2017